A CENTURY OF STRIVING FOR JUSTICE

THE MARYLAND STATE BAR ASSOCIATION 1896-1996

By James F. Schneider

THE COURTHOUSES OF MARYLAND *Photographed by Linda Johnson*

A MARYLAND COLOR PORTFOLIO *Photographed by Peter Alunans*

LANDMARKS OF MARYLAND LAW *Photographed by Coos Hamburger*

Opposite Photo: The reconstructed Maryland State House of 1676.
Photograph by Coos Hamburger.

Design by Network Publications, Inc.

Printing by Reese Press/RP Communications

To

my wife,

Susan M. Marzetta,

and to our daughters,

Laura Elaine Schneider

and

Caroline May Schneider,

I dedicate this book with love and gratitude.

J.F.S.

MARYLAND STATE
BAR ASSOCIATION

PRESIDENTIAL PHOTO CREDITS

President	Credit
Sylvan Hayes Lauchheimer	Blank and Stoller
Benjamin Rosenstock	Bradford Bachrach
J. Dudley Digges	Harris & Ewing, Washington, D.C.
Kenneth C. Proctor	Paul Jordan
Hal C. B. Clagett	Chase Ltd., Washington, D.C.
J. Michael McWilliams	Leonard L. Greif, Jr.
Jeffrey B. Smith	Guill Photo
Herbert J. Belgrad	Leonard L. Greif, Jr.
Vincent E. Ferretti, Jr.	Chase Ltd., Washington, D.C.
Herbert S. Garten	Leonard L. Greif, Jr.
Seymour B. Stern	Davis Studio
Herbert S. Garten	Elson-Alexandre, Buena Park, California
A. Hunter Boyd	Meredith Janvier

TABLE OF CONTENTS

ROBERT C. MURPHY
CHIEF JUDGE
COURT OF APPEALS OF MARYLAND
COURTS OF APPEAL BUILDING
ANNAPOLIS, MARYLAND 21401-1699

PREFACE

No association of lawyers anywhere in the country is more deserving of this rich and well-documented history of its many and varied activities over the past one hundred years than the Maryland State Bar Association.

The compiled biographies of the charter members of the Association bring into sharp focus those preeminent lawyers who gave birth to the Association and fostered its development in its early years. The photographs of the courthouses throughout Maryland, coupled with the many anecdotes featuring Association lawyers is a very special treat -- thanks to the divine inspiration of our historian, Judge James F. Schneider. A special tribute is due to Jim for what, I am sure to him, was a true labor of love.

The recognition afforded to Chief Judge James McSherry, the first president of the Association in 1896, is but one of the many highlights of this significant addition to our literature. To my way of thinking, the volume qualifies as truly worthwhile and enjoyable bedtime reading.

_____
Robert C. Murphy

ABOUT THE PHOTOGRAPHERS. . .

LINDA JOHNSON

Linda Johnson graduated from UMBC in 1983 with a major in photography and a minor in fine arts. She has been a commercial photographer for 13 years and has exhibited her artwork for 15 years. Ms. Johnson specializes in photographs of people and architecture.

Linda Johnson undertook an 18-month assignment from the law firm of Smith, Somerville & Case to photograph the courthouses of Maryland in 1987. The firm presented a framed collection of the photographs of the exteriors of the courthouses to the Circuit Court for Baltimore City, where they are on display in the second floor lobby of Courthouse East. It is with her kind permission and that of Smith, Somerville & Case that the MSBA was authorized to publish these photographs in this volume. Also included here for the first time are rare photographs taken by Ms. Johnson of the courtrooms inside the courthouses of Maryland. They were made upon the authorization of Chief Judge Robert C. Murphy and with the approval of the Judges in each locality. In addition, in May, 1995, Ms. Johnson photographed the new U.S. Courthouse in Greenbelt that was not included in the original collection.

PETER A. ALUNANS

Peter A. Alunans was born to Latvian parents in a camp for displaced persons in the English sector of Germany on March 25, 1947. Three years later, the family was sponsored by an American family and settled on a farm on the Eastern Shore of Maryland. He was educated in the public schools of Maryland and received a Bachelor of Science degree in 1970 from Towson State University, graduating with majors in biology and German. Mr. Alunans received a Fulbright Scholarship to study German literature at Georg-August University in Goettingen, West Germany. In Germany he obtained a research position in the Department of Bio-chemistry of the Max Planck Institute for Experimental Medicine, under the directorship of Dr. Heinrich Matthaei, co-discoverer of the genetic code.

Mr. Alunans is now employed as a scientist and the in-house photographer at SAFT America in Cockeysville, a company involved in the manufacture of batteries. He has been taking pictures for 35 years and has worked as a photographer/printer for the Baltimore Museum of Art, the Museum of Baltimore Legal History and the Baltimore State's Attorney's Office. His color photographs of Maryland's splendid scenery are published here for the first time.

COOS HAMBURGER

Dutch-born photographer, Coos Hamburger, has been making pictures for more than 20 years. As a self-taught freelance photojournalist, his assignments have taken him to Europe and the Middle East as well as closer to his home near Baltimore, Maryland. His photographs have appeared in a variety of publications and exhibits. A great deal of his recent work has focussed on pro bono legal services for the poor of Maryland. Mr. Hamburger currently accepts assignments through his company FOCO Photographic Services.

Mr. Hamburger received his undergraduate degree in social and behavioral sciences from the John Hopkins University. He has completed graduate work in epidemiology of disasters at the Catholic University of Louvain School of Public Health, Brussels, and at the Johns Hopkins School of Hygiene and Public Health.

His photographs in this book include not only the leaders and administrative staff of the MSBA, but also legal landmarks in every corner of the State of Maryland.

ACKNOWLEDGEMENTS

Hon. William H. Adkins, III, District Court for Talbot County
James Alfred Avirett, Esquire
E. Clinton Bamberger, Esquire
Ms. Liz Barnes, Maryland Office of Tourism
Hon. Solomon Baylor, Circuit Court for Baltimore City
George Beall, Esquire
Hon. Raymond Beck, Circuit Court for Carroll County
Mr. Joseph Bennett, Library Company of the Baltimore Bar
Mr. and Mrs. Robert D. Bittle
Hon. John Hanson Briscoe, Circuit Court for St. Mary's County
Hon. John Carroll Byrnes, Circuit Court for Baltimore City
Hon. William O. Carr, Circuit Court for Harford County
Paul V. Carlin, Esquire, Executive Director, MSBA
Mr. John A. Cerino
Mrs. Elizabeth Earle Chapman
Ms. Kai-Yun Chiu, Librarian, Library Company of the Baltimore Bar
Hal C.B. Clagett, Esquire
Hon. Marjorie Lynn McDonald Clagett, Circuit Court for Calvert County
Ernest Cornbrooks, III, Esquire
Dr. Russell Cort, District of Columbia School of Law
James J. Cromwell, Esquire
Betsy G. Cunningham, Esquire
Leonard J. Eiswert, Esquire
Ms. Janet Stidman Eveleth, MSBA
Hon. John Fader, Circuit Court for Baltimore County
Margaret Z. Ferguson, Esquire
Ms. Barbara J. Fiorino, Executive Director, Bar Association of Baltimore County
Charles O. Fisher, Esquire
Herbert S. Garten, Esquire
Mr. Arthur S. Gilbert, MSBA
Robert S. Glushakow, Esquire
Sharon E. Goldsmith, Esquire
Hon. Louis L. Goldstein, Comptroller of the State of Maryland
John B. Gontrum, Esquire
Karen L. Gooden, Esquire, Author of a biography of J. Franklyn Bourne
Alexander Gordon, IV, Esquire
Frank T. Gray, Esquire
Ms. Patricia Hargis, Fourth Circuit Librarian
Mrs. Jeanette Markell Harper
Sanford A. Harris, Esquire
Mrs. Betsy Hemmler, Camp Hill, Pennsylvania
Melvin Hoffman, Esquire, Historian of the Anne Arundel County Bar Association
Douglas M. Hofstedt, Esquire, Executive Director, Anne Arundel County Bar Association
Hon. Barbara Kerr Howe, Circuit Court for Baltimore County
Herbert Hubbard, Esquire
Hon. Frederick W. Invernizzi, District Court of Maryland
John Martin Jones, Esquire
Hon. Joseph H.H. Kaplan, Circuit Court for Baltimore City
Sharon Kazary, Inn at Walnut Bottom, Cumberland
Hon. Warren Krug, Circuit Court for Calvert County
Hon. Diane O. Leasure, Circuit Court for Howard County

Hon. Daniel M. Long, Circuit Court for Somerset County
Hon. Asa M. McCain, Jr., Mayor of Oakland
Kathleen M. McDonald, Esquire
Dr. Eileen McGuckian, Peerless Rockville
James McSherry, Esquire
Mrs. Marian McSherry
Arthur W. Machen, Jr., Esquire
Hon. Timothy F. Maloney, Former Delegate
Hon. Paul Mannes, U.S. Bankruptcy Court
Mr. and Mrs. Louis A. Marzetta
Hon. Susan M. Marzetta
Ms. Melanie J. Matesic
Hon. Peter J. Messitte, U.S. District Court
Ms. Claire Close Miller
John Philip Miller, Esquire
Ms. Beverly C. Mondin Vander-Haar
M. Peter Moser, Esquire
Thomas F. Mudd, Esquire
Hon. Robert C. Murphy
Dr. Edward Papenfuse, Maryland State Archivist
A. Eric Peltosalo, Esquire
Mrs. Dorothy Phillips
Hon. George B. Rasin, Circuit Court for Kent County
Hon. James Magruder Rea, Circuit Court for Prince George's County
Hon. Edward D.E. Rollins, Circuit Court for Cecil County
Maria Ellena Chavez Ruark, Esquire
Mr. Timothy Ryan
Ms. Katherine T. Sanzone, Executive Director, Bar Association of Baltimore City
Hon. John W. Sause, Circuit Court for Queen Anne's County
Mr. Joseph F. Schneider
Hon. J. Frederick Sharer, Circuit Court for Allegany County
Edward F. Shea, Jr., Esquire
James L. Shea, Esquire
Hon. James L. Sherbin, State's Attorney for Garrett County
General Philip Sherman
Matthew L. Silverstein, Esquire
Hon. Lloyd L. Simpkins, Circuit Court for Somerset County
Kathleen E. Smith, Esquire
William J. Smith, Esquire
Mr. John Sondheim, Enoch Pratt Free Library
Hon. Richard Sothoron, Circuit Court for Prince George's County
Mr. Carroll F. Spitzer
Ms. Jane Sween, Montgomery County Historical Society
Hon. Cornelius F. Sybert, Circuit Court for Howard County
Melvin J. Sykes, Esquire
Lisa Bittle Tancredi, Esquire
Hon. Fred A. Thayer, Circuit Court for Garrett County
Hon. Raymond G. Thieme, Circuit Court for Anne Arundel County
Hon. Alfred T. Truitt, Jr., Circuit Court for Wicomico County
Ms. Mame Warren, Maryland State Archives
Mary Ann Willis, Esquire, U. S. Supreme Court
William P. Young, Jr., Esquire

PROLOGUE

By Philip Sherman
Historian of the Maryland State Bar Association

They came from the bountiful counties of the Eastern Shore and from the mountainous counties of Western Maryland. They came from the venerable counties of Southern Maryland and from the industrial city of Baltimore. They came from every corner of Maryland; some by steamboat, some by horse and carriage, but most by steam railroad. Ninety-six lawyers and judges came to a mountain resort hotel in Pen Mar, Maryland, in answer to a call to organize a statewide bar association. It was in the summer of 1896, a century ago, that the call came; the American Bar Association and several state and metropolitan bar associations had already been organized. It was a period of reawakening of professionalism and a time of rapid industrial development. The need was apparent and the time was ripe for a bar association uniting the divergent legal communities of Maryland to their common heritage.

The handful of lawyers and judges who founded the Maryland State Bar Association at the Blue Mountain House on August 28, 1896, would scarcely recognize the 17,000-member Association of today. The MSBA now functions with 37 special and standing committees, 23 sections with specialized interests and an annual budget nearing $3 million. Today the Association monitors judicial and legislative issues, offers legal educational opportunities and promotes leadership within the legal profession. Together with the numerous public service programs designed to ensure the delivery of quality legal services to all citizens, the Association is committed to furthering the efficient administration of justice and promoting equality for all.

The account of how the Association grew from a handful of white, male, established lawyers and judges 100 years ago to an Association of over 17,000 diversified members is splendidly told here for the first time, by the Honorable James F. Schneider, United States Bankruptcy Judge for the District of Maryland. Over the past 20 years, Judge Schneider, who is the Historian and Archivist of the Circuit Court for Baltimore City, has chaired numerous bar committees dealing with legal history and has written a number of significant historical publications. Among his published works are *The Story of the Library Company of the Baltimore Bar, A Guide to the Clarence M. Mitchell, Jr. Courthouse, Historical Minutes of the First and Franklin Street Presbyterian Church,* and *A Bicentennial History of the United States District Court for the District of Maryland* (with H. H. Walker Lewis).

Judge Schneider's legal projects and activities are equally impressive. He co-founded the Museum of Baltimore Legal History in 1984, and chairs the Courthouse Portrait Committee of the Baltimore Courthouse and Law Museum Foundation. He played a leading role in planning a memorable centennial celebration of the Bar Association of Baltimore City in 1980. He chaired the Maryland State Bar Association's Special Committee for the Celebration of the Bicentennial of the United States Constitution. He edited the Bar Association of Baltimore City's publication *The Baltimore Barrister* during its formative years. In 1992 he was awarded the Baltimore Courthouse and Law Museum Foundation's Achievement Award.

For the past year, a remarkably brief period to write such a history as that of our Association, Judge Schneider has assembled over 400 photographs, visited every county seat in the State, personally interviewed numerous judges and lawyers, and extensively researched the Association's first century.

In the years to come this book will surely become a treasure for those who appreciate the proud tradition and heritage of the Maryland State Bar Association and a fountain of knowledge for future generations.

Photograph by Guill Photo.

AUTHOR'S INTRODUCTION

When I was asked to write a book celebrating the centennial of the Maryland State Bar Association, I decided to begin my search for its history in the courthouses and law offices of the State, where members of the legal profession of Maryland have labored for the past 360 years. My research was well-rewarded, with stories of people and cases that made a difference in the way we live now. I also discovered that there was plenty of unmined history at the Maryland Bar Center, the State Bar head-quarters in Baltimore, in the old *Maryland Bar Transaction* books dating back to the founding of the MSBA in 1896. The old red books not only contained the official record of proceedings at the annual and mid-year meetings, but also biographical records of the members and their contemporary views on every subject in their own words. Equally important was the discovery of our living history — the flesh and blood of the Association in the persons of our contemporaries who are the leaders of the modern bar of Maryland — Bob and Louise Gonzales, Judge Robert Bell, Jim Thompson, Toni Clarke, Herb Garten, Harry Johnson, Judge Sheila Tillerson, Cleave Miller, Bill Young, Lee Caplan, and many, many others. This book combines the official record with local stories of the Maryland legal profession.

The theme of the centennial of the Maryland State Bar Association, "A Century of Striving for Justice," was suggested by the Hon. Vincent E. Ferretti, Jr., Associate Judge of the Circuit Court for Montgomery County and former MSBA President. It could just as easily have been suggested by Moses the lawgiver, author of the *Pentateuch*. In *The Torah — A Modern Commentary* edited by W. Gunther Plaut, Deuteronomy 16:20 is translated as "Justice, justice shall you pursue, that you may thrive and occupy the land that the Lord your God is giving you." The noble profession of the law has always had as its main purpose the pursuit of justice. Since ancient times, lawyers have sworn to follow the sacred quest.

From Maryland's earliest beginnings, lawyers have been the leading members of society striving for justice. One of the first things our forebears constructed on the frontier, after their homes and places of worship, was a system of justice, symbolized by courts to enforce the law and settle controversies. They sought a sanctuary for freedom where all might live in harmony with their neighbors.

Since 1896, the MSBA has striven for justice in ways that enhance the profession of law and benefit the public by improving legal ethics and the training of lawyers; raising standards for admission to the bar; reforming the laws and our judicial system; educating people about their legal rights and responsibilities; insuring equal access to the courts and equal justice under law; and by reminding the lawyers and the citizens of Maryland of their great legal heritage as a free people.

This is the inspiring story of that quest.

Photograph by Coos Hamburger.

LEGAL MUTUAL
Liability Insurance
Society of Maryland

The Maryland State Bar Association

gratefully acknowledges

the Significant Financial Contribution

made by the

Legal Mutual Liability

Insurance Society of Maryland

toward the publication of this book

Legal Mutual is the _Only_ lawyers'
professional liability insurance company
endorsed by the Maryland State Bar Association

THE MSBA TODAY

On Saturday, September 30, 1995, 400 Maryland lawyers and their families boarded a train at Union Bridge in Carroll County for a three-hour, round-trip excursion on the Western Maryland Railroad. They followed the same route taken nearly a century earlier by some of the 100 lawyers who founded the Maryland State Bar Association at Pen Mar in Washington County, on August 28, 1896.

The modern MSBA is a distinctly different organization from that known to the founders. The Maryland State Bar Association is a voluntary professional organization that strives to include every Maryland lawyer in its membership. In 1995, out of 24,600 lawyers admitted to practice in this State, membership in the MSBA was calculated to exceed 17,000 women and men of every race, creed and ethnic background. About 7,300 of our members are women. The MSBA is geared to assist its members as they grapple with the complex, changing needs of modern law practice.

The Maryland lawyer of today has many identities: government lawyer, house counsel to a corporation, partner in a large, urban law firm or sole practitioner in a small town; private criminal defense counsel or Public Defender; collection attorney of small judgments in a State district court setting, or patent attorney trying complex cases in Federal court; family law attorney or counsel to a creditor in bankruptcy court; Legal Aid lawyer whose duties on behalf of clients may run the gamut of many different types of civil proceedings; or office attorney who concentrates on title work and real estate settlements. Regardless of the nature of their practice, the goal of all Maryland lawyers is to help people.

Now more than ever, the Maryland State Bar Association is striving to make legal services available to all and to insure that everyone has equal access to the American system of justice.

This Page: 400 Maryland lawyers and judges assembled at Union Bridge, Carroll County, about to embark on the "Centennial Express," to Pen Mar and back, September 30, 1995. Photograph by Charles L. Smith Photography, Owings Mills, Maryland.

MSBA OFFICERS, BOARD OF GOVERNORS AND CENTENNIAL COMMITTEE

Robert T. Gonzales, President.
Photograph by Guill Photo.

MSBA Past Presidents, Officers and Chairs of Centennial Committee. First row: Edward F. Shea, Jr.; Robert T. Gonzales, President; Herbert S. Garten, Chair, Centennial Committee; James McSherry, Honorary Chair; Judge Barbara Kerr Howe, President-elect; P. Dennis Belman. Second row: Cleaveland D. Miller; Vincent L. Gingerich; Judge James C. Chapin; Judge Vincent E. Ferretti, Jr.; Louise Michaux Gonzales; Jeffrey B. Smith; J. Michael McWilliams; Charles O. Fisher, Sr.

Photographs by Coos Hamburger, except where otherwise designated.

Judge Barbara Kerr Howe,
President-elect.

James L. Thompson, Secretary.
Photograph by Brooks, Bethesda,
Maryland.

Charles M. Preston, Treasurer

MSBA Baord of Governors. Seated (L-R): John C. Nason; Paul V. Carlin, Executive Director; Charles M. Preston, Treasurer; Judge Barbara Kerr Howe, President-elect; Robert T. Gonzales, President; James L. Thompson, Secretary; Kenneth L. Thompson; Judge Diane O. Leasure; P. Dennis Belman, Immediate Past President. Standing (L-R): David A. Simison; James K. Eagan, III; Philip N. Tirabassi; Timothy E. Meredith; Deborah S. Byrnes; Judge Thomas E. Marshall; Paul D. Bekman; Michael P. Whalen; Alison L. Asti; Sidney G. Leech; Gary S. Mininsohn; Lee Gordon; T. Bryan McIntire, Jr.; Carl Silverman, Parliamentarian; Julia K. Evans; John C. Monahan; Sharon Sirota Rubin; Judge Audrey J.S. Carrion; Suzanne M. Snedegar; Maureen L. Rowland; Kathleen A. Birrane; John W. Debelius, III; Rita Kaufman-Grindle. NOT PICTURED: Herbert J. Belgrad, Thomas G. Axley, W. Kennedy Boone, III, Alfred J. Brennan, Jr., Christopher R. Dunn , George E. Golomb, Jeffrey K. Gonya, William A. Hahn, Jr., Michael J. Jacobs, James L. Sherbin, George E. Simms, III, Floyd "Ron" Willis, III.

Subcommittee on the Centennial Project. Cleaveland D. Miller, Charles M. Preston, Sharon E. Goldsmith, Judge James C. Chapin, Rebecca L. N. Strandberg, Co-chair; Theodore B. Cornblatt, Co-chair; Jane Tolar Kollinger. NOT PICTURED: Lee A. Caplan, Judge Deborah K. Chasanow, Betsy G. Cunningham, Deborah C. Dopkin , Karen A. Murphy-Jensen, Eric M. Johnson, Robert S. Paye.

Subcommittee on Centennial Commemoratives. Susan M. Souder, Walter S. B. Childs, Chair; Judge James E. Kenkel, William B. Dulany, Pamila J. Brown.

Subcommittee on Centennial Events. Stephen J. Nolan, Judge Vincent E. Ferretti, Jr., James P. Nolan, Judge Richard H. Sothoron, Jr., Chair; Judge Barbara Kerr Howe; Charles M. Preston; Charles O. Fisher, Sr., Vincent L. Gingerich, Paul V. Carlin, Edward F. Shea, Jr. NOT PICTURED: Comptroller Louis L. Goldstein, Judge Irma S. Raker, Roger W. Titus.

Subcommittee on Centennial Publicity. Robert D. Anbinder, Co-chair; Janet Stidman Eveleth, John J. Kuchno, Co-chair; Thomas G. Axley. NOT PICTURED: Judge William D. Missouri, Roger W. Perkins, Seymour B. Stern.

Subcommittee on Centennial Commemorative Book. Philip Sherman and Judge James F. Schneider, Co-chairs; William P. Young, Jr.; Matthew L. Silverstein. NOT PICTURED: Judge Solomon Baylor, Judge William O. Carr, Judge Deborah K. Chasanow, M. Peter Moser, Joseph C. Reid.

MSBA SECTIONS

Administrative Law
Business Law
Correctional Reform
Criminal Law Practice
Delivery of Legal Services
Elder Law
Environmental Law
Estate and Trust Law
Family and Juvenile Law
General Practice Law
Health Law
International Commercial Law
Judicial Administration
Labor Law
Law Practice Management
Legal Education & Admission to the Bar
Litigation
Negligence, Insurance and Worker's Compensation
Real Property, Planning and Zoning
Senior Lawyers
State and Local Government Law
Taxation
Young Lawyers

MSBA STANDING COMMITTEES

Alternative Methods of Settling Disputes
Budget & Finance
Client Protection
Continuing Legal Education
Ethics
Gender Equality
Judicial Appointments
Law Practice Quality
Laws
Lawyer Counseling
Local and Specialty Bar Liaison
Membership
Pattern Jury Instructions
Planning
Professionalism
Program
Public Awareness
Resolution Fee Disputes

SPECIAL COMMITTEES

Alcoholism and Drug Problems
Centennial of the MSBA
Defense of Legal Services
Editorial Advisory
Governance
Hispanic-Latino Lawyers
1996 Host Committee (1996 ABA Mid-Year Meeting)
Korean Bar
Law Links
Law-Related Education
Lawyer Dispute Resolution
Committee on Minorities
Paralegals
Pro Bono Legal Services
Professional Conduct
Sexual Harassment Prevention
Solo and Small Firm Practitioners
Technology
Joint Committee on Travel

THE PROFESSIONAL STAFF
OF THE
MARYLAND STATE BAR ASSOCIATION

The members of the Maryland State Bar Association and the public at large are well served by the dedicated people who direct the operations and carry out the mandates of the Association at its headquarters in the Maryland Bar Center.

PAUL V. CARLIN
Executive Director

Paul V. Carlin has been Executive Director of the MSBA since March, 1985. Looking back over his ten years in that position, he recently enumerated some of the most important programs he worked on, including the creation of Legal Mutual Liability Insurance Society of Maryland, the People's Pro Bono Campaign and Action Center, the Professionalism Course, the Doctor/Lawyer Partnership Against Drug Abuse, Law Links Student Internship Project and the Law Office Management Program. He is particularly proud of the restructuring and retooling of the whole office administration undertaken after his arrival in 1985, the centerpiece of which was the hiring of a top notch team of professional directors. The new staff brought a sense of urgency and action to their daily work at Bar Headquarters. Their enduring challenge is to provide service to our members. Paul recently confided: "My greatest satisfaction, and indeed challenge, has been to work with such talented, intelligent and dedicated bar leaders, all with their own individual personalities, to accomplish so many projects that benefit our members and the public."

He was born in McKeesport, Pennsylvania on November 11, 1945, and graduated with high honors from McKeesport Senior High School in 1963. He graduated with honors from Grove City College, Grove City, Pennsylvania (A.B. 1967) and from the Dickinson School of Law, Carlisle, Pennsylvania (J.D. 1970). He served in the U.S. Army Reserves from 1968-74. During the 1972 Olympics in Munich, West Germany, he was personal assistant to the late Howard Cosell.

He speaks fluent German and is moderately fluent in Swedish. He is married to Hildegard R. Waltl of West Germany. They are the parents of two daughters, Anna Katarina and Kristana Andrea.

Before he came to occupy his present position with the MSBA, Paul Carlin was the Executive Director of the Connecticut Bar Association during 1984-85; Executive Director of the Bar Association of Baltimore City from 1981-84; Director of the Lawyer Referral and Information Service of the District of Columbia Bar from 1977-81; and Director of Legal Services of the Philadelphia Bar Association from 1975-77. He was President of the National Association of Bar Executives in 1993-94.

JANET STIDMAN EVELETH
Director of Communications and Editor of the
Maryland Bar Journal

In 1987 Janet Stidman Eveleth joined the MSBA as Director of Communications. She is responsible for the Association's internal and external communications, public relations and media relations. She is the Editor of the *Maryland Bar Journal* and the *MSBA Annual Report,* and writes for and oversees the production of the *Bar Bulletin,* MSBA's monthly newsletter. She also directs the Association's public awareness projects and special public service programs.

Janet attended the Baltimore City public schools before graduating from Washington College in Chestertown, Maryland (A.B. 1972) and Johns Hopkins University (M.S. 1973). In 1984 she completed the Communications Certificate Program of the American Society of Association Executives. Before joining the MSBA, she worked as a lobbyist and public affairs director for the Mid-Atlantic Food Dealers Association, headed the Communication/Membership/Events Department for the Home Builders Association of Maryland, and began her association career as the Communications Specialist for the Medical and Chirurgical Society of Maryland.

Janet Stidman Eveleth is the Immediate Past Chair of the National Association of Bar Executives' Communications and Public Relations Section and served as President of the Maryland Society of Association Executives in 1992-93.

ARTHUR S. GILBERT
Director of Administration

Arthur S. Gilbert has been the Director of Administration for the MSBA since December, 1985. He is responsible for the day-to-day operations of Bar Headquarters and has direct

9

Paul V. Carlin

Janet Stidman Eveleth

Arthur S. Gilbert

Wanda A. Claiborne

Albert ("Buz") Winchester

Richard B. Vincent

Sharon E. Goldsmith

line responsibility for the Maryland Bar Foundation, Women's Bar Association, Young Lawyers' Section, and the Committee on Resolution of Fee Disputes. He supervises the accounting, membership, computer and daily meeting functions. He is also the Editor of the *Maryland Lawyers' Manual* and Co-Editor of the *Bar Foundation Newsletter*.

Mr. Gilbert graduated from Pace University (A.B. 1967) and Columbia University (M.S. 1969). In 1981 he earned an M.B.A. degree in finance from Loyola College. Mr. Gilbert was previously employed as CEO of a primary health care organization and for an organization providing long and short term health care facilities. He was also Executive Vice President of Finance in two telecommunications corporations.

WANDA A. CLAIBORNE
Director of Meetings and Bar Liaison

Wanda A. Claiborne serves as MSBA Director of Meetings and Bar Liaison. As the first African-American Director at the Maryland State Bar Association, her duties include planning and coordinating the Association's Annual and Midyear meetings, the Local and Specialty Bar Presidents' Conference, New Admittees Luncheons, Professionalism Course required of all new attorneys, as well as serving as the liaison between the MSBA and local and specialty bar associations throughout Maryland. She also serves as Co-Chairperson of the Minorities Involvement Committee of the National Association of Bar Executives, Vice Chairperson of the Board of Directors for the National Association of Sickle Cell Disease, as well as holding National, Regional and State offices with Zeta Phi Beta Sorority, Inc.

Ms. Claiborne was born and raised in Baltimore and received her education in the Baltimore City public schools. She was graduated from Morgan State University in 1985 with a bachelor's degree in telecommunications. Ms. Claiborne joined the MSBA in April, 1986, as an office clerk, was promoted to Communications Assistant the following July, and after a year was appointed Meetings Manager in July, 1987.

ALBERT ("BUZ") WINCHESTER, III
Director of Legislative Relations

As Director of Legislative Relations since 1987, Mr. Winchester is the staff liaison between the MSBA and all state legislative and regulatory agencies. In this capacity he represents the MSBA before governmental bodies and supervises the implementation of the Association's legislative program.

Albert Winchester has been an association executive with National, Regional, State and Local organizations since 1974. He presently serves as a member of the Maryland Affordable Housing Trust and was recently appointed Staff Director of the Commission on the Future of Maryland Courts.

He is a graduate of Towson State University (B.S. 1969) and the University of Rhode Island (A.M. 1971).

RICHARD B. VINCENT
Director of Lawyer Counseling

In 1981 Richard B. Vincent joined the MSBA as Director of the Standing Committee on Lawyer Counseling, which is a confidential helping resource for Maryland attorneys and judges who are experiencing difficulties in their lives and practices due to drug and alcohol dependency or abuse.

Mr. Vincent attended Dundalk High School and graduated from various colleges throughout Maryland. He is a Certified Alcohol and Chemical Dependency Counselor (CCDC) and a Certified Employee Assistance Professional. He has been qualified by the courts of Maryland as an expert in substance abuse.

SHARON E. GOLDSMITH
Executive Director of People's Pro Bono Action Center, Inc.

Sharon E. Goldsmith has been the Executive Director of People's Pro Bono Action Center, Inc., since it was incorporated on January 16, 1990. She graduated with honors from the University of Maryland at College Park in 1981 and from the National Law Center at George Washington University in 1985. Ms. Goldsmith was a law clerk to Judge John Carroll Byrnes of the Circuit Court for Baltimore City from 1985-87 and was admitted to the Maryland bar in 1986. From 1987-89 she was a litigation associate with the law firm of Whiteford, Taylor & Preston. She is a member of the MSBA, the Women's Law Center and the Women's Bar Association of Maryland. As Executive Director, Sharon Goldsmith plans and coordinates the activities of the People's Pro Bono Action Center to encourage Maryland attorneys to voluntarily assist needy clients who are otherwise unable to obtain legal representation. The Center sponsors training programs for attorneys on various legal topics and matches attorneys with potential clients.

MSBA Administrative Staff. First row (L-R): Albert ("Buz") Winchester; Arthur Gilbert; Janet Stidman Eveleth; Paul V. Carlin; Wanda Claiborne; and Richard Vincent. Second row: Tina Emerson; Sharon E. Goldsmith; Theresa L. Mooring; Rozanne M. Batton; Hilda Jungclaus; Erin Sartoris; Kelley McDonald; Barbara Minnick; Ann Byrd; Beth Snyder Henre; Tammy Posluszny; Gregory Derwart; Stephen Scopp; Lee Ann Brazelton; Patricia Yevics; Annette Primeaux; Bernadette Simmons. Photograph by Coos Hamburger.

PUBLIC SERVICE PROJECTS OF THE MARYLAND STATE BAR ASSOCIATION

People's Pro Bono Action Center: In 1990, MSBA launched an intensive campaign to recruit every Maryland lawyer for *pro bono publico* service. The campaign, which attracted nationwide attention, led to the creation of the People's Pro Bono Action Center as a permanent program of the MSBA.

Speakers' Bureau: MSBA offers an active Speakers' Bureau composed of outstanding MSBA volunteer experts to speak to community groups and civic organizations on a variety of legal topics.

Law Links: In the summer of 1994, MSBA introduced LAW LINKS, a summer internship program that employed students from 47 Baltimore high schools at 47 local law firms and agencies. The law firms volunteered to pay the interns for eight hours of work, and allow them time off to partici-

The first Arthur W. Machen, Jr. Award of the Maryland Legal Services Corporation is presented to former U.S. Attorney General Benjamin R. Civiletti (R) by Mr. Machen (L) on May 20, 1985. (L-R): U.S. Senator Paul S. Sarbanes, Mr. Machen, U.S. District Judge Joseph H. Young, and Mr. Civiletti. Photograph by Guill Photo.

pate in an educational component of the program known as the Law Leadership Institute.

Law Day, U.S.A.: The first Law Day, U.S.A. was observed on May 1, 1958 as an occasion to celebrate the American legal system. Each year on this date, the MSBA has sponsored various activities and programs to remind our citizens of their rights and responsibilities under the law. One such program was "Ask A Lawyer," offering free legal advice dispensed over a phone bank by volunteer attorneys.

People's Law School: Every year in celebration of Law Day, the MSBA Public Awareness Committee, in conjunction with the Young Lawyers Section, sponsors an adult education program in which the public is invited to attend classes taught by volunteer lawyers. The curriculum features basic legal information on current legal issues.

Trial By Jury: Every two years, MSBA presents "Trial By Jury: The Lawyer's Craft," a series of five, dramatic mock trials at the Maryland State Fair in Timonium. Volunteer judges and lawyers participate for the dual purposes of entertaining and educating the public about the workings of our legal system.

Public Awareness Brochures: MSBA's Public Awareness Committee publishes a series of 23 informative brochures to provide the public with basic legal knowledge related to subjects of major importance. These brochures are available at the Maryland Bar Center and in most courthouses.

Legal-Line: For ten years, the MSBA has sponsored Legal-Line, an audiotaped series of messages offering legal information to the public over the telephone.

Courthouse Day: Every winter, the MSBA through its Public Awareness Committee invites middle school students to come to their district and circuit courts to tour the buildings, meet the judges and lawyers, and observe the trial of cases.

Annual High School Education Seminar: Every spring, the MSBA through its Public Awareness Committee invites high

Winners of 1995 pro bono awards, Ocean City, Maryland, June 10, 1995. (L-R): Marielsa A. Bernard, Karen Siler, Judge Thomas E. Marshall, Thomas J. Mulrenin, Leonard R. Goldstein, David V. Diggs, Winifred Borden, Mary Beth Beattie, Lee A. Caplan, Sharon E. Goldsmith, Augustus F. Brown, IV. Photograph by Coos Hamburger.

school students across the state to attend a seminar on topics including school violence, journalism and protecting the environment.

Court User-Friendly Project: In 1994, in conjunction with WBAL-AM Radio, MSBA launched the Court User-Friendly project to solicit public opinion on ways to make Maryland Courts more user-friendly.

Literacy Black, White & Read Ball: In 1991, MSBA sponsored the first black tie literacy ball to draw attention to the problem of literacy in Maryland and to raise money for a literacy project.

Middle Income Legal Needs Survey: In 1994, MSBA launched the first middle class income needs assessment to determine the legal needs of this segment of the population, then devise new technology to match these needs with unemployed or under-employed Maryland attorneys.

Doctor/Lawyer/Teacher Partnership Against Drugs: In 1990, MSBA introduced the Doctor/Lawyer/ Teacher Partnership Against Drugs, sending teams of doctors and lawyers into middle school classrooms across the state to acquaint students with the legal and medical consequences of drug and alcohol use and abuse. The program won an award from the ABA in 1991.

Gender Bias Study: In partnership with the Special Committee on Gender Equality, MSBA conducted a comprehensive study of gender bias in the courts and offered corrective recommendations.

Settlement Week: In 1988, to encourage expansion of alternative dispute resolution (ADR), various Maryland subdivisions under the auspices of MSBA declared specific Settlement Days and Settlement Weeks, when volunteer judges and lawyers met to settle old civil cases and clear them from overcrowded court dockets.

Lawyer Advertising Study: As a result of a comprehensive study of lawyer advertising in 1990, MSBA has proposed changes to the Rules of Professional Conduct that have been adopted by the Rules Committee of the Maryland Court of Appeals.

Citizenship Law-Related Education Committee Projects: MSBA's Citizenship Law-Related Education Program in Maryland Schools sponsors an array of law-related programs, including Mock Trials, Peer Mediation and Mentorship.

Lawyer Referral Service: For many years, MSBA sponsored a Lawyer Referral Service for the purpose of matching members of the public with attorneys of their choice to handle specific legal problems. This function has now been taken over by local bar associations.

ABOVE LEFT: Volunteer Lawyers help documented residents at the Citizenship Workshop held at Towson State University. Photograph by Coos Hamburger.

BOTTOM LEFT: Kathleen Kelly Howard and Pamela Bresnahan welcome attorneys to a benefit auction for the Maryland Volunteer Lawyers Services, Inc., October 29, 1986. Photograph by Guill Photo.

ABOVE RIGHT: People's Pro Bono Action Center presents All-Star Volunteer Recognition Night at Oriole Park at Camden Yards, September 29, 1993. (L-R): Christopher Lambert (and son Jack), James Gorney, Catherine Cronin, Joann Asparagus, Orioles' Marketing Manager David Cope, Paul V. Carlin, Executive Director, Edward F. Shea, Jr., MSBA President; Sharon E. Goldsmith, Peoples Pro Bono Action Center Director, and the Oriole Bird. Photograph by Coos Hamburger.

BOTTOM RIGHT: Prince George's County Circuit Judge G. R. Hovey Johnson with high school participants in MSBA mock trial competition, Court of Appeals, May 2, 1985. Photograph by Guill Photo.

TOP LEFT: Volunteer lawyer Joel Simon, counsels child in need of assistance (CINA) client before court proceeding. Photograph by Coos Hamburger.

BOTTOM LEFT: Michael A. Milleman receives the H. Vernon Eney Fund Award of the Maryland Bar Foundation, Inc.,"for selfless dedication to the better administration of justice and the improvement of government in the State of Maryland and the City of Baltimore," June 13, 1985. The presenters (L-R) are George D. Solter, Maryland Attorney General Stephen H. Sachs and Vincent L. Gingerich. Photograph by Guill Photo.

TOP RIGHT: Pro Bono Attorney Andrew Gendron assists Homeless Persons Representation client at Christopher's Place, a men's shelter in Baltimore City. Photograph by Coos Hamburger.

BOTTOM RIGHT: Shirley L. Bigley (L) receives the MSBA/Young Lawyers' Distinguished Service Award from Louise Michaux Gonzales (R), June 14, 1985. Photograph by Guill Photo.

THE FOUNDING OF THE MARYLAND STATE BAR ASSOCIATION

" The most important event to the bar of Maryland, from the adoption of the constitution of 1867 to the close of the century, was the formation of the Maryland State Bar Association." So stated Conway W. Sams and Elihu S. Riley in their *Bench and Bar of Maryland* (1901). Indeed, there was no Maryland bench and bar in any formal sense until a statewide bar association was founded that created a *Maryland* bar by establishing formal admission requirements to practice before the bar of the Court of Appeals. Before that, each county had its own fraternity of lawyers whose offices were clustered around the county courthouse, each lawyer having been admitted to practice by a local judge upon oral examination.

When the Maryland State Bar Association was founded in 1896, the practice of law was far different than it is today. There were few government lawyers before the advent of social legislation and little emphasis placed upon the right of public access to the courts: no Legal Aid, Public Defenders, or right to counsel for the indigent. Except when the poor transgressed the criminal law or were injured by the machines of industry, the courts were the exclusive domain of paying clients who could afford to litigate their disputes. Banks, railroads, and trust companies were high on the list of the lawyer's clientele.

1896! It seemed to be the Age of Miracles — the Age of Edison and his electric light and phonograph. Steamships crossed the Atlantic in six days. An audience in New York City witnessed the first public showing of a motion picture in history. Samuel Pierpont Langley successfully tested an unmanned flying machine over the Potomac River in Charles County, Maryland. Seven more years would pass until the Wright brothers became the first to fly a manned aircraft at Kitty Hawk in 1903.

The Census of 1890 had declared that the West had been won, that the American frontier was no more, and that the legendary era of the cowboy was over. The wealth

LEFT: The Blue Mountain House, Pen Mar, Washington County, Maryland. The hotel was built in 1883, burned to the ground in August, 1913, and was never rebuilt. Color postcard courtesy of Victor E. Arentz.

Mark Twain was America's favorite author and humorist during the "Gilded Age."

William Jennings Bryan.

William McKinley.

of the nation was concentrated in the hands of a few, while huge numbers of the population lived in poverty and slums. The "Gay '90s" were rapidly drawing to a close and the world was on the brink of a new century. The Age of the Horse and Buggy was coming to a close as well — Henry Ford produced his first automobile in 1896.

The Civil War had been history for 30 years, but the challenges posed by the abolition of slavery continued. The edict of the Supreme Court that year in *Plessy v. Ferguson* institutionalized the doctrine of "separate but equal" over a telling dissent of Justice John Marshall Harlan who reminded his colleagues that "Our Constitution is color-blind." Frederick Douglass, the foremost African-American spokesman in the nation, died in 1895. His successor, Booker T. Washington, summarized his ideas on race relations in a speech in Atlanta: "In all things that are purely social we can be as separate as the fingers, yet one as the hand in all things essential to mutual progress."

Horatio Alger was filling boys' heads with stories of financial success through "pluck and luck." Mark Twain, Oscar Wilde and Sherlock Holmes were household names in 1896. H.G. Wells imagined the conquest of the Fourth Dimension in *The Time Machine*.

You can still hear much of the music of 1896 — a barbershop quartet singing *Sweet Adeline*, a band blaring out *A Hot Time in the Old Town Tonight* at a political convention, or Sousa's *El Capitan* march in a Fourth of July parade. It was the year that saw the premiere of Puccini's *La Bohème* (a success) and Gilbert & Sullivan's last operetta, *The Grand Duke* (a flop). Richard Strauss, well ahead of his time, composed *Also sprach Zarathustra*, later to become known as the futuristic theme of the film *2001*.

In England, Queen Victoria was nearing the end of her reign, while in Russia, her granddaughter Alexandra's husband, Czar Nicholas II, was just beginning his. Over here, Democrat Grover Cleveland was in the White House, but would not be renominated by his party. The Republicans had gained control of Congress in 1894 and captured the Maryland State House and Baltimore City Hall in the elections of 1895. America's economic woes fore-shadowed a change of administrations in 1896. In the last Presidential election of the old century, Republican William McKinley emerged as the victorious candidate in a well-oiled, big-money campaign. The Democrats nominated a 36-year-old populist lawyer named William Jennings Bryan on a promise to take the country off the gold standard and give aid to labor and the farmers. He took his message to the people in the first whistlestop campaign, an 18,000-mile national tour by train that lasted three months and brought him within a half million votes of winning the White House.

Author F. Scott Fitzgerald, named for Maryland attorney

18

Company, Easton Ice Company, Hotel Avon Company, and director of Easton National Bank; Associate Judge, Second Judicial Circuit, 1906-19; Associate Judge, Court of Appeals of Maryland, 1919-34; died October 11, 1950.

James M[urray] AMBLER (1854-1934)
BALTIMORE

Born August 21, 1854, Winchester, Virginia; Education: William and Mary and University of Virginia, left without graduating in 1874; taught school for several years; studied law, came to Baltimore 1881; entered the law office of Barton & Wilmer, Major Barton being his kinsman; Democrat; chairman of the Public Service Commission of Maryland, 1910-1912; Associate Judge, Supreme Bench of Baltimore City, 1912-24; returned to the practice of law with firm known as Barton, Wilmer, Ambler & Barton; died April 8, 1934.

Rufus W. APPLEGARTH (1844-1921)
BALTIMORE

In 1896, he was a Republican member of the Maryland House of Delegates from Baltimore City.

Born August 2, 1844, Baltimore, Maryland; educated in public schools, and taught in the public schools before he became a lawyer; read law in the offices of Brown & Brune in Baltimore; Republican; elected to Maryland House of Delegates for two terms, died June 17, 1921, Baltimore, Maryland.

William Hughlett Adkins
From Cordell, *The University of Maryland* (1907).

Thomas S. Baer
From *Baltimore-American Illustrated Edition, The State of Maryland* (1896).

Alexander ARMSTRONG, Sr. (1847-1905)
HAGERSTOWN

In 1896, he was a "Gold Democrat," a delegate to the convention of the National Democratic Party that nominated a rival slate to the official Democratic Party nominee, William Jennings Bryan.

Born December 5, 1847, Hagerstown, Maryland; Education: Hagerstown Academy, Princeton, A.B. 1868, M.A. 1871; admitted to the bar, November, 1871; elected Maryland House of Delegates 1885; Democrat active in 1895 reform movement; married Elizabeth Key Scott, daughter of Dr. Norman B. Scott, whose mother was cousin of Francis Scott Key; died October 26, 1905, Hagerstown, Maryland. His son, Alexander Armstrong (1877-1939), was President of the Maryland State Bar Association, 1926-27.

Thomas S[argent] BAER (1843-1906)
BALTIMORE

Born March 16, 1843, Baltimore, Maryland; Education: graduated Baltimore City College, 1859; taught school; studied law in the office of William S. Waters; admitted to the bar May 18, 1865; specialized in equity and real estate matters; Democrat identified with independent movements; elected Maryland House of Delegates, 1894; Baltimore City School Board, 1884-88, 1900-03; lectured on real property, titles and copyrights at the University of Maryland School of Law; Master in Chancery, 1894 until his election to the Supreme Bench as an associate judge on November 3, 1903, filling the vacancy caused by the death of Judge Albert Ritchie; died July 18, 1906, Baltimore, Maryland.

Adial P[arker] BARNES (1848-1913)
SNOW HILL

In 1896 he was a member of the Maryland Republican Committee.

Born September 10, 1848, Worcester County, Maryland; Education: Law School of the University of Virginia; University of Maryland School of Law, LL.B. 1873; admitted to the bar at Snow Hill; bar examiner appointed by the Circuit Court for Worcester County for 14 years; Republican; Referee in Bankruptcy for Worcester, Wicomico and Somerset Counties; published *The Worcester Advocate* newspaper; indicted and convicted of criminal libel in 1897 for publishing an article highly critical of the Democratic Mayor of Snow Hill, John P. Moore; the conviction was reversed on appeal, *Barnes v. State*, 88 Md. 347, 41 A. 781 (1898); died December 23, 1913.

Adial Parker Barnes
From Cordell, *The University of Maryland* (1907).

John S. Biddison
From *Distinguished Men of Baltimore and Maryland, Baltimore American* (1914).

Hope H[orsey] BARROLL (1860-1925)
CHESTERTOWN

In 1896, he was a Democratic regular who pledged to support the free silver ticket headed by William Jennings Bryan.

Born August 6, 1860, Chestertown, Maryland; admitted to the bar, 1883; Education: Washington College and University of Virginia; read law in the office of his father, J. Leeds Barroll, who was a fifth generation lawyer in his family; president of the Citizens Bank of Chestertown; died September 22, 1925.

J[oseph] Franklin BATEMAN (1852-1899)
EASTON

Born February 27, 1852, Easton, Maryland; law partner of Ex-Governor Philip Francis Thomas, until the latter's death in 1890; succeeded Charles H. Gibson as Talbot County State's Attorney for one term; counsel in important equity cases and specialized in real estate law; died July 7, 1899, in his office in the "Moreland Block," Easton, Maryland.

William W[alker] BECK (1870-1923)
CHESTERTOWN

Born February 15, 1870, near Chestertown, Kent County, Maryland; Education: Washington College, U.S. Naval Academy; University of Maryland Law School; admitted to the bar, July, 1892; large criminal practice in Chestertown; elected State's Attorney for Kent County, 1903;

reelected 1907; Democrat; elected Maryland Senate, 1911; reelected, 1913; defeated, 1915; State Tax Commission, 1918; died April 5, 1923.

Alfred D[uncan] BERNARD (1868-1916)
BALTIMORE

Born March 25, 1868, Baltimore, Maryland; son of Richard Bernard, attorney; Education: parochial schools, Loyola Prep., Baltimore City College; University of Maryland School of Law, LL.B. 1889; admitted June 3, 1889 to practice before the Supreme Bench of Baltimore City; special assessor for the Appeal Tax Court; author of treatise on taxation; died April 19, 1916, Baltimore, Maryland.

Richard BERNARD (1840?-1916)
BALTIMORE

Born 1840? County Cork, Ireland; came to America at age 17 and settled in Washington, D.C.; came to Baltimore and took up the study of law; admitted November 9, 1877 to practice before the Supreme Bench of Baltimore City; in practice with his son, Alfred D. Bernard; member of the Baltimore City Water Board; Democrat; Presbyterian; elder of Brown Memorial Presbyterian Church; founder and counsel of Loyola Perpetual Building Association; died November 20, 1916, Baltimore, Maryland.

John S. BIDDISON (1873-1921)
TOWSON

Born February 18, 1873, Gardenville, Baltimore, Maryland, on the place where his ancestors had lived since colonial days; studied law at University of Maryland and in the law office of John F. Gontrum, later his senior partner; elected to Maryland Senate, reelected 1908; leader of Democrats in the Annex (that part of Baltimore County annexed by Baltimore City in 1919); counsel to the county commissioners with James L. Lindsay; director of Towson National Bank and Hamilton Bank, 1910; and founded the Overlea Bank, 1916; died July 9, 1921. His grandson, Thomas N. Biddison, Jr., practices law in Baltimore City.

D[avis] J[ames] BLACKISTON (1846-1915)
CUMBERLAND

Born February 23, 1846, Kent County, Education: public schools of Kent County; Chestertown College, graduated 1864; studied law in the offices of Judge Joseph A. Wickes of Chestertown and Judge Richard B. Carmichael of Queen Anne's County; admitted to the bar at Chestertown, October, 1866; admitted to the Cumberland Bar, 1867; Democrat; Mayor of Cumberland, 1890; died January 17, 1915.

R[obert] R[aphael] BOARMAN (1836-1915)
TOWSON

Born April, 1836, near Bryantown, Charles County; Education: Belair Academy, Harford County; studied under Rev. John O'Neal, a Roman Catholic priest; read law with his uncle, Otho Scott; admitted to bar several months before his 21st birthday; practiced law for a few years in Bel Air, later moved to Towson; one of the first practitioners at Towsontown; his practice began immediately upon the completion of the courthouse and his presence was noted almost continuously at the trial of cases in that building until the time of his retirement; his Towson home and office were located on Chesapeake Avenue on the present site of the U.S. Post Office; died March 30, 1915, Hyattsville, Maryland.

James A[lexander] C[hesley] BOND (1844-1930)
WESTMINSTER

In 1896 he was a delegate to the convention of the National Democratic Party that nominated a rival slate to run against the regular Democratic candidate, William Jennings Bryan.

Born September 3, 1844, Calvert County, Maryland; Education: Charlotte Hall School, 1863; entered sophomore class Princeton, A.B. 1866; read law under James T. Briscoe and William Meade Allison; admitted to the bar of Baltimore City, 1867; came to Westminster 1868; Associate Judge of the fifth Judicial Circuit May 1, 1890; served until 1891, defeated for renomination by Charles B. Roberts; Chief

Judge of Fifth Judicial Circuit, defeated by I. Thomas Jones; President of the Maryland State Bar Association, 1904; counsel to the Baltimore & Ohio Railroad until his death; died August 17, 1930.

Nicholas P. BOND (1855-1915)
BALTIMORE

Born September 27, 1855; son of Judge Hugh Lennox Bond; Education: private tutors, Phillips Academy at Exeter, Harvard University 1878; studied law in office of George H. Chandler; admitted to the bar, April 15, 1880; he was a modern business lawyer, with knowledge of business and business conditions; died June 21, 1915, at summer home, Blue Ridge Summit.

M[adison] B[rown] BORDLEY (1873-1937)
CENTREVILLE

Born January 9, 1873, Centreville, Maryland; Education: Lehigh University; Trinity College, Hartford, Connecticut; University of Maryland Law School, LL.B. 1885; began to practice law in Centreville, 1886; director, Centreville National Bank; associate editor, *Centreville Record;* supervisor of assessments for Queen Anne's County; deputy county treasurer, 1904-08; clerk of county commissioners, 1908-12; operated three farms that were in his family for years; died 1937.

A[ndrew] Hunter BOYD (1849-1925)
CUMBERLAND

In 1896, he was Chief Judge of the Fourth Judicial

D. J. Blackiston
From *Baltimore-American Illustrated Edition, The State of Maryland* (1896).

Robert R. Boarman
From *Baltimore-American Illustrated Edition, The State of Maryland* (1896).

Judge James A. C. Bond
From *Baltimore-American Illustrated Edition, The State of Maryland* (1896).

Nicholas P. Bond
From *Distinguished Men of Baltimore and Maryland, Baltimore American* (1914).

William T. Brantly
From Cordell, *The University of Maryland* (1907).

D. L. Brinton
From *Baltimore-American Illustrated Edition, The State of Maryland* (1896).

Circuit (Allegany, Washington and Garrett Counties) and Associate Judge of the Court of Appeals of Maryland.

Born July 15, 1849, Winchester, Virginia; Chief Judge, Fourth Judicial Circuit, 1893-1924; Associate Judge, Court of Appeals of Maryland, 1893-1907; Chief Judge, Court of Appeals of Maryland, 1907-24; Democrat; died August 2, 1925.

William T[heophilus] BRANTLY, III (1852-1945)
BALTIMORE

In 1896 he was Reporter for the Court of Appeals of Maryland.

Born November 17, 1852, Richmond County, Georgia; Education: Mercer University, Georgia, A.B. 1871, A.M. 1874; University of Maryland, 1874, LL.B.; studied for a year at Leipzig; admitted to the bar at Baltimore, June 10, 1874; practiced law there until 1914; professor at the University of Maryland Law School (personal property, bailments, contracts, sales and suretyship), 1885 for a quarter century; at death of Severn Teackle Wallis (1894) he served briefly as Provost; author of *Law of Personal Property, The English in Maryland,* and *Notes on the Law of Contracts*; former Secretary of State of Maryland (1893); died April 21,1945, Washington, D.C.

Daniel L. BRINTON (1858-1906)
BALTIMORE

Born June 14, 1858, Cecil County, Maryland; Education: public schools of the city, one of the first students at Johns Hopkins University; LL.B. 1881, University of Maryland School of Law, 1883; served in the office of Phelps & Findlay

as law clerk while in law school; admitted May 30, 1883, to practice before the Supreme Bench of Baltimore City; real estate lawyer and negotiable instruments; elected to the U.S. Congress, 1888; President of the League of Republican Clubs of Maryland, 1889-90; appointed bankruptcy referee 1898; Republican; died May 28, 1906.

John P[arran] BRISCOE (1853-1925)
Prince Frederick

In 1896, he was Chief Judge of the Seventh Judicial Circuit (Prince George's, Charles, Calvert and St. Mary's Counties), and Associate Judge of the Court of Appeals.

Born August 24, 1853, Calvert County; admitted to the bar of Calvert County, 1875; 1879, 1883, 1887, elected State's Attorney; appointed February, 1890, Chief Judge of Seventh Judicial Circuit by Governor Jackson to succeed Chief Judge Frederick Stone of Charles County; served for 34 years; retired January, 1924, practiced law after retirement with his son, Philander B. Briscoe, with offices in Baltimore City; President of the Maryland State Bar Association in 1906; died April 14, 1925, Washington, D.C.

Arthur George BROWN (1842-1925)
BALTIMORE

Born September 26, 1842; son of George William Brown, who founded the law firm of Brown and Brune, and was Mayor of Baltimore (1860-62) and Chief Judge of the Supreme Bench of Baltimore City (1873-1888); admitted to practice before the Supreme Bench of Baltimore City, December 20, 1867; one of the first three members of the Board of Law Examiners in Maryland; died June 2, 1925.

F[rederick] W[illiam] BRUNE, Jr. (1854-1899)
BALTIMORE

Born 1854; Education: Harvard Law School; University of Maryland School of Law, LL.B. 1876; admitted May 27, 1876, to practice before the Supreme Bench of Baltimore City; member of the firm of Brown and Brune; died February 27, 1899. His son was Frederick W. Brune (1894-1972), Chief Judge of the Court of Appeals of Maryland and President of the Maryland State Bar Association in 1947-48.

W[illiam] H[enry] BRUNE, Jr. (1857-1924)
BALTIMORE

Born July 15, 1857, Baltimore, Maryland; Education: St. Paul's School, Concord, New Hampshire; Harvard University, A.B. 1878; University of Maryland School of Law, LL.B. 1880; admitted to practice before the Supreme Bench of Baltimore City, May 31, 1880; Judge of the Appeal Tax Court, 1903; died December 30, 1924, Baltimore, Maryland.

Emil BUDNITZ (1862-1944)
BALTIMORE

Born July 28, 1862, Baltimore, Maryland; Education: graduated University of Maryland School of Law, 1881 at age 19, had to wait two years to practice; admitted to practice before the Supreme Bench of Baltimore City, September 10, 1883; associated with Peter J. Campbell, one-time president of the Maryland Senate; Republican active in state and city politics; died January 13, 1944.

J. Briscoe BUNTING (1862-1940)
PRINCE FREDERICK

Born 1862; Education: University of Maryland School of Law, LL.B. 1886; counsel to the Board of County Commissioners of Calvert County; lifelong Democrat; Episcopalian; president of the Calvert County School Board; before that County Superintendent of Schools; owner and editor of the *Calvert Journal,* a weekly newspaper; died Prince Frederick, May 8, 1940.

Peter J[oseph] CAMPBELL (1860-1919)
BALTIMORE

Born April 13, 1860, Baltimore, Maryland; attended lectures at the University of the City of New York; private student of Woodrow Wilson, who was then living in Baltimore; attended University of Maryland School of Law, LL.B. 1885; admitted May 30, 1885, to practice before the Supreme Bench of Baltimore City; partner with Emil

Budnitz; he enjoyed a large general practice in real property, equity and decedents' estates; served in the House of Delegates and State Senate; elected President of the Senate 1916, 1917, 1918 and 1919; director of the Patapsco Title Company and the Baltimore Enamel Company; died December 20, 1919.

Francis King CAREY (1858-1944)
BALTIMORE

Born July 1, 1858, Baltimore, Maryland; Education: Haverford College, A.B. 1878, A.M. 1881; University of Maryland Law School, 1880; admitted May 31, 1890, to practice before the Supreme Bench of Baltimore City; senior member of Steele, Semmes & Carey, which dissolved December 31, 1904; later formed Carey, Piper & Hall (with James Piper and J. Bannister Hall, Jr.); industrialist; Democrat; author of *Law of Husband and Wife, Municipal Ownership of Natural Monopolies, Carey's Forms & Precedents;* died October 3, 1944, Baltimore, Maryland.

Edward C[odrington] CARRINGTON, Jr. (1872-1938)
BALTIMORE

Born 1872, Washington, D.C.; admitted to Harford and Baltimore County bars, 1892, after his family moved to Maryland; admitted March 8, 1894, to practice before the Supreme Bench of Baltimore City; Republican; widely addressed as Colonel after his appointment by Governor Phillips Lee Goldsborough in 1912; owned 1300 acre farm in

Arthur George Brown
From *The Baltimore City Courthouse* (1900).

Senator Peter J. Campbell, Attorney-At-Law, Club Men of Maryland In Caricature, Drawings by Ray O. Evans and Associates, Baltimore, Maryland 1915.

Francis King Carey
From Cordell, *The University of Maryland* (1907).

E. C. Carrington
From *Baltimore-American Illustrated Edition, The State of Maryland* (1896).

Eben J. D. Cross
From *The Baltimore Courthouse*
(1900).

W. C. Devecmon
From *Baltimore-American Illustrated
Edition, The State of Maryland*
(1896).

William H. Deweese, Jr.
Photograph from *Eastern Shore of
Maryland.*

Baltimore County; Maryland manager for Theodore Roosevelt's Bullmoose party, 1912; unsuccessful Republican candidate for U.S. Senate, 1914; moved to New York, 1916; retired and returned to Maryland, 1933; died December 30, 1938.

A[rthur] Bernard CHANCELLOR (? - 1931)
BALTIMORE

Born Middleburg, Loudoun County, Virginia; Education: Pantops Academy, Virginia; Roanoke College, B.S. 1885; attended University of Virginia Law School but withdrew after one year because of eye trouble; University of Maryland School of Law, LL.B.; admitted April 30, 1890, to practice before the Supreme Bench of Baltimore City; associated with Shriver, Bartlett & Company for a year, then practiced alone for the rest of his life; Episcopalian; Democrat; held no public office; died September 14, 1931, Baltimore, Maryland.

Philemon H. CHEW (1865-1915)
UPPER MARLBORO

Extensive research failed to produce any information regarding Mr. Chew, except that he was born May 26, 1865, and died May 4, 1915.

Jacob I. COHEN (1841-1920)
BALTIMORE

Born Baltimore, Maryland, November 6, 1841; Education: private schools, University of Maryland Law School; admitted December 9, 1867, to practice before the Supreme Bench of Baltimore City; practiced as an associate

of Severn Teackle Wallis before opening his own office; believed to have been the first Jewish attorney to practice in Maryland; specialized in corporation law; died January 22, 1920.

Oliver D. COLLINS
SNOW HILL

Extensive research failed to produce any information regarding Mr. Collins, except that he served as Clerk of the Circuit Court for Worcester County, 1907-25.

Eben J[ackson] D[ickey] CROSS (1838-1906)
BALTIMORE

Born December 28, 1838, Baltimore, Maryland; Education: Princeton, A.B. 1860; read law at the firm of Brown & Brune in the office of Mayor George William Brown; admitted to practice, 1863; partnership first with Louis Fischer, later with John K. Cowen; counsel to the Baltimore & Ohio Railroad; President of the Bar Association of Baltimore City, 1901-02; died May 2, 1906.

Richard K. CROSS (1846-1909)
BALTIMORE

Born May 22, 1842, Baltimore, Maryland; brother of E.J.D. Cross; Education: private school of George C. Carey of Baltimore; Princeton, 1863; University of Maryland Law School, LL.B. 1876; admitted to practice before the Supreme Bench of Baltimore City, May 27, 1876; confined himself to office practice; died August, 1909, at summer home, Wianno, Massachusetts.

W[illiam] Irvine CROSS (1852-1932)
BALTIMORE

Born February 20, 1852, Oxford, Pennsylvania; Education: Princeton, A.B. 1873; taught at George Carey's school while he studied law; University of Maryland Law School, LL.B. 1876; admitted May 27, 1876, to practice before the Supreme Bench of Baltimore City; associated with the law firm of John K. Cowen and Eben J.D. Cross, his first cousin; later became a member of the Law Department of the Baltimore & Ohio Railroad; student of English literature; enjoyed hunting, rowing and horseback riding; died December 18, 1932.

Walter I[reland] DAWKINS (1858-1936)
BALTIMORE

Born October 21, 1858, Leonardtown, St. Mary's County, Maryland; Education: St. John's College, A.B. 1880; University of Virginia Law School; admitted to practice at Leonardtown, 1883; practiced in Chattanooga, Tennessee for several years, then came to Baltimore; appointed Associate Judge of the Supreme Bench of Baltimore City, 1911; served until 1934 past the mandatory retirement age of 70 by legislative dispensation; Democrat; President of the Maryland State Bar Association, 1913-14; died February 10, 1936.

W[illiam] H[ammond] DAWSON (1842-1923)
BALTIMORE

Born December 10, 1842, Baltimore, Maryland; Education: primary school and Loyola College; read law in the office of George Hawkins Williams; admitted to the bar at Baltimore, July, 1866; general practitioner; Democrat; died November 24, 1923.

Adam DENMEAD (1854-1898)
BALTIMORE

Born 1854, Baltimore, Maryland, the son of Talbott Denmead, a member of the bar; Education: engineering course at Pennsylvania Military Academy, 1875; University of Maryland School of Law, 1877; admitted to practice before the Supreme Bench of Baltimore City, June 3, 1878; associated with his brother-in-law, Frank Gosnell; died July 29, 1898, Baltimore, Maryland.

William C[oombs] DEVECMON (1861-1939)
CUMBERLAND

Born June 2, 1861, Cumberland, Maryland; Education: Allegany County Academy; St. John's College, 1881; taught Latin and Greek at St. John's for three years; read law with S. Thomas McCulloh of the Annapolis bar; admitted to practice, 1884; settled in Cumberland, 1885; Shakespearean

scholar; Democrat; President, Maryland State Bar Association, 1908-09; moved to Baltimore, 1916; associated with Senator George Arnold Frick in the practice of law at Baltimore; died May 22, 1939, Baltimore, Maryland.

W[illiam] H. DEWEESE, Jr. (1870-1907)
DENTON

In 1896, he was State's Attorney for Caroline County.

Born May 9, 1870, Caroline County, Maryland; Education: Camp Grove District School and Denton Academy; West Chester Normal School, graduated Dickinson Law School,1893; admitted to the bar of Caroline County and began practicing law there, April, 1893; elected State's Attorney for Caroline County, 1895; Democrat; president and founder of Caroline County Bank at Greensboro; identified with other enterprises, including the Law Building, Peoples National Bank and the Citizens Light and Fuel Company; greatest interest outside of his profession was agriculture; died February 6, 1907, Laurel, Maryland. His nephew, Judge J. Deweese Carter (1904-1977), was President of the MSBA in 1964-65.

William T. DICKERSON
SNOW HILL

Extensive research has failed to produce any information regarding Mr. Dickerson.

John J[enkins] DOBLER (1852-1923)
BALTIMORE

In 1896, he was an Associate Judge of the Supreme Bench of Baltimore City.

Born Baltimore, Maryland, June 6, 1852; Education: Graduated Baltimore City College, 1868; University of Maryland School of Law, LL.B. 1873 (first in his class); admitted June 9, 1873, to practice before the Supreme Bench of Baltimore City; associate in the office of Henry Stockbridge; elected Associate Judge of the Supreme Bench of Baltimore City, 1894; Republican; served until retirement, June 2, 1922; died July 12, 1923.

John J[ohnston] DONALDSON (1850-1916)
Baltimore

Born 1850 near Elkridge, Howard County, Maryland; son of Thomas N. Donaldson (1815-1877), an eminent attorney; Education: University of Maryland School of Law, LL.B. 1876; President of the Bar Association of Baltimore City, 1891-92; lectured at the University of Maryland Law School; trustee of the Peabody Institute, 1883; died November 19, 1916, near Relay, Maryland.

Albert A. Doub, Sr.
From *The Book of Maryland*
(1920).

E. C. Eichelberger
From *Baltimore-American*
Illustrated Edition, The State of
Maryland (1896).

Edward S. Eichelberger

Albert A[lvin] DOUB, Sr. (1865-1946)
CUMBERLAND

Born April 11, 1865, Beaver Creek, Washington County; Education: attended University of Kentucky, A.B. Johns Hopkins University, 1886; elected Treasurer of Allegany County, 1893; admitted to the bar, 1894; city attorney to both Frostburg and Cumberland; Republican; elevated to the bench, 1921; retired from bench, 1935; President, Allegany County Bar Association; Director of Fidelity Savings Bank in Frostburg and the Commercial Savings Bank in Cumberland; founded the Cumberland Free Public Library and served as its president for more than 22 years; two sons and one daughter became members of the legal profession; died November 14, 1946.

Daniel W. DOUB (1858-1944)
HAGERSTOWN

Born December 21, 1858, Beaver Creek, Washington County, Maryland; brother of Judge Albert A. Doub of Cumberland; Education: Hagerstown High School and Mercersburg Academy; studied law in the office of U.S. Senator Louis E. McComas; admitted to the bar of Washington County, 1884; President, Washington County Bar Association; appointed court auditor of Circuit Court for Washington County, 1893-1900; died August 16, 1944.

Edward DUFFY, Jr. (1867-1956)
BALTIMORE

Born February 11, 1867, Baltimore, Maryland; son of Judge Edward Duffy and the brother of Judge Henry Duffy, both Associate Judges of the Supreme Bench of Baltimore City; Education: public schools of Baltimore City; Johns Hopkins University, A.B. 1887; University of Maryland School of Law, LL.B. 1889; admitted June 3, 1889, to practice before the Supreme Bench of Baltimore City; associated in practice with Cowen, Cross & Bond; when he became partner in 1905, the firm became known as Bond, Robinson & Duffy; trial lawyer; died February 20, 1956, Baltimore, Maryland.

Edward C[ary] EICHELBERGER (1850-1906)
BALTIMORE

Born November 1, 1850, Winchester, Virginia; Education: studied medicine; after a year read law in the office of Abraham Sharp; admitted January 21, 1874, to practice before the Supreme Bench of Baltimore City; admitted to the Maryland Court of Appeals in May, 1876, and to the U.S. Supreme Court in 1881; member of the committee to examine candidates for admission to the bar, when such examinations were conducted in open court in the presence of the Supreme Bench; died January 2, 1906, at "Hilton," his residence in Walbrook, Baltimore City.

Edward S. EICHELBERGER (1856-1914)
FREDERICK

Born June 16, 1856, Frederick, Maryland; born in the same house in which he resided all his life on Court Square, Frederick; eldest living son of Grayson Eichelberger, one of the leading members of the Frederick legal profession; Education: Frederick Academy, Princeton, 1875; studied law in Frederick in office of Milton G. Urner; admitted to the bar, 1878; Republican; died July 25, 1914.

Charles E[dward] FINK (1852-1919)
WESTMINSTER

In 1896 he was State's Attorney for Carroll County.

Born May 21, 1852, Adams County, Pennsylvania; Education: Gettysburg High School; Gettysburg College, 1867 to 1869; St. Charles College, Ellicott City, graduated 1872; assistant professor of Languages at St. Charles College, 1873; admitted to practice in Ellicott City, September, 1878, went to Gettysburg where he practiced for a short time; admitted to the Carroll County Bar, May 12, 1879; practiced in Westminster until his death; formed partnership with Charles T. Reifsnider under the name Reifsnider & Fink; elected State's Attorney for Carroll County in 1891; Democrat; counsel to Westminster and the County Commissioners for a number of years; died January 16, 1919, Baltimore, Maryland. He was the great-grandfather of Louise Michaux Gonzales, who became the first woman President of the MSBA in 1991.

D[avid] K[irkpatrick] Este FISHER (1860-1953)
BALTIMORE

Born February 16, 1860, Cincinnati, Ohio; son of William A. Fisher, Judge of the Supreme Bench of Baltimore City; his maternal grandfather was Judge D.K. Este of Cincinnati; Education: George G. Carey School of Baltimore; Episcopal High School of Alexandria, Virginia; St. Paul's School, Concord, N.H.; Princeton University, A.B., 1883; A.M. 1886; University of Maryland Law School, LL.B. 1885; admitted May 30, 1885, to practice before the Supreme Bench of Baltimore City; clerk for two years in Colonel Charles Marshall's law office; joined firm of Fisher, Bruce & Fisher, 1887; Democrat; died April 2, 1953, Ruxton, Maryland.

T. Pliny FISHER (1859-1931)
DENTON

Born May 13, 1859; President, Caroline County Bar Association; superintendent of the Sunday School of the Methodist Protestant Church, Denton, May 23, 1897; died April 22, 1931, Baltimore, Maryland.

George FORBES (1873-1941)
ANNAPOLIS

Born June 25, 1873, Annapolis, Maryland; Education: St. John's College; studied law in the office of James M. Monroe in Annapolis; associated with the firm of Blackstone & Blackstone, Baltimore; practiced mainly in the Federal courts, specializing in admiralty; member of Rules Committee of the U.S. District Court for the District of Maryland, 1909, 1933; one of the nation's outstanding admiralty lawyers; died March 8, 1941, Elkridge, Maryland.

David FOWLER (1836-1911)
TOWSON

Born 1836, Washington County, Maryland; Education: St. James' College, 1858; read law in the office of Brown & Brune, Baltimore; admitted to the bar, 1862; early in his career had close professional relationship with Reverdy Johnson; Associate Judge of the Third Judicial Circuit, 1882-89; Chief Judge, 1889-1905; formed partnership after retirement with George Whitelock, John B. Deming and W. Thomas Kemp under the name Whitelock & Fowler; died February 5, 1911, Baltimore, Maryland.

Joseph C[halmers] FRANCE (1862-1938)
BALTIMORE

Born October 11, 1862, York, Pennsylvania; Education: Baltimore City College; Johns Hopkins University; Baltimore University Law School, 1883 (merged with University of Maryland in 1913); began practice in the office of John P. Poe; later formed the firm of Willis, Homer, France & Smith; general counsel to the United Railways and Electric Company; taught elementary law, pleading and corporations at the University of Maryland; a poll taken among Baltimore lawyers named him as the city's leading lawyer; died July 26, 1938.

Edgar H[ilary] GANS (1856-1914)
BALTIMORE

Born November 24, 1856, Harrisburg, Pennsylvania; Education: public schools of Norristown, Pennsylvania; Baltimore City College, 1875, with honors; University of Maryland School of Law, 1877; admitted November 23, 1877, to practice before the Supreme Bench of Baltimore City; first associated with the law office of John P. Poe; Deputy State's Attorney for Baltimore City, 1879-87; sponsored admission of Everett J. Waring, first African-American attorney admitted to practice in the Maryland State courts, 1885; Professor of Criminal Law, University of Maryland, 1882-1901; mentioned as possible appointee to the U.S. Supreme Court, 1911; died September 20, 1914.

Edward Guest GIBSON (1872-1932)
BALTIMORE

Born April 17, 1872, Baltimore, Maryland; Education: Marston's School and University of Maryland Law School;

Charles E. Fink
From *Baltimore-American Illustrated Edition, The State of Maryland* (1896).

Edgar H. Gans
From Cordell, *The University of Maryland* (1907).

Edward Guest Gibson, Lawyer, Club Men of Maryland In Caricature, Drawings by Ray O. Evans and Associates, Baltimore, Maryland 1915.

Robert P. Graham
From Hall, *Baltimore, Its History and Its People* (1912)

admitted to practice before the Supreme Bench of Baltimore City, May 29, 1893; auditor to the Supreme Bench, 1899 until death; Treasurer of the Bar Association of Baltimore City, 1916 until his death; died October 4, 1932.

John F. GONTRUM (1857-1909)
TOWSON

Born February 16, 1857, Gardenville, Baltimore County; Education: Baltimore County schools, including the German-Lutheran Parochial School; while yet a boy, he had poems published in leading magazines of the country; Bethel Military Academy, Virginia; St. John's College, A.B. 1878; studied law; admitted to the bar at Towson, 1880; died December 27, 1909. His great-grandson, John B. Gontrum, practices law in Baltimore County.

Robert H. GORDON (1852-1910)
CUMBERLAND

Born March 6, 1852, Cumberland, Maryland; son of Josiah Gordon, prominent member of the bar and Associate Judge of the Fourth Circuit; Education: Allegany County Academy, Roanoke College and Princeton; left Princeton without graduating in 1874; admitted to the bar, 1875; in partnership with his father until latter's death in 1887, appeared in many cases in Circuit Court and Court of Appeals; died May 10, 1910, Cumberland, Maryland.

James P[olk] GORTER (1858-1939)
BALTIMORE

In 1896, he was City Attorney of Baltimore.

Born August 27, 1858, Baltimore, Maryland; State Senator 1892-94; Associate Judge, Supreme Bench of Baltimore City, 1907-21; Chief Judge, 1921-28; died November 10, 1939.

Frank GOSNELL (1854-1927)
BALTIMORE

Born December 13, 1854, Baltimore County, Maryland; Education: Loyola College; read law in the office of Thomas W. Lanahan; University of Maryland, LL.B. 1876; admitted May 27, 1876, to practice before the Supreme Bench of Baltimore City; associated with Mr. Lanahan; founded the firm of Marbury & Gosnell with William L. Marbury, 1903, in which he practiced until his death; Republican; died February 19, 1927.

Robert P[atterson] GRAHAM (1868-1921)
SALISBURY

In 1896, he was Republican Comptroller of the State of Maryland. He was also a delegate to the Republican National Convention that nominated William McKinley for the Presidency at St. Louis, June, 1896.

Born April 7, 1868, Salisbury, Maryland; Education: private tutors; Johns Hopkins University, with honors; University of Maryland Law School, LL.B. 1888; admitted to practice at Salisbury; Republican candidate for Mayor of Salisbury, 1893; elected Comptroller of the State of

General in the first Cleveland Administration, 1885-89; his law office in the Calvert Building was destroyed in the 1904 Baltimore fire; lectured at the Baltimore University School of Law, (which was later merged into the University of Maryland) 1900; became Dean, 1905; died April 18, 1918, Baltimore, Maryland.

J. Clarence LANE (1850-1914)
HAGERSTOWN

Born March 13, 1850, Frederick County, Maryland; Education: Princeton, A.B. 1872; University of Maryland Law School, LL.B., 1874; studied in the office of Bernard Carter; admitted to the bar of Washington County, July, 1874; practiced alone until 1884 when represented Baltimore & Ohio Railroad, Cumberland Valley Railroad, and the Blue Mountain House; Democrat; State Senate, 1883, 1885; died May 6, 1914.

Clarence P. LANKFORD (1864- ?)
CRISFIELD

Born February 8, 1864, Baltimore, Maryland; Education: Washington Academy, Princess Anne; Washington College, A.B. 1882; vice principal of the public schools in Crisfield; Deputy Clerk at the Somerset County Court House, 1884-91; admitted to the bar, April, 1891; defeated for State's Attorney, 1891; Republican; Presbyterian; moved to Crisfield, 1892; counsel to the New York, Philadelphia & Norfolk Railroad.

J.M.T. LAWRENCE
TOWSON

Extensive research has failed to produce any information regarding Mr. Lawrence.

Richard Laws LEE (1866-1938)
BALTIMORE

Born December 19, 1866, Baltimore, Maryland; Education: Baltimore City College, University of Maryland, LL.B. 1889; admitted to the Baltimore bar on June 3, 1889; business lawyer seldom seen at the trial table; died Baltimore, May 21, 1938.

J[ohn] H[enry] C[linton] LEGG (1868-1937)
CENTREVILLE

Born June 2, 1868, Kent Island, Queen Anne's County; Education: Baltimore City College; Charlotte Hall College, A.B. 1887; University of Maryland Law School, 1889; practiced at Baltimore, later at Centreville, 1890; elected to the Maryland Senate, 1914, 1918; City Counselor to Centreville for 12 years; identified with American Bar Association and the Commercial Law League; died March 10, 1937.

Martin LEHMAYER (1861-1936)
BALTIMORE

Born July 17, 1861, Baltimore, Maryland; Education: Friends School; University of Maryland School of Law, LL.B. 1882; studied in the law office of Isidor Rayner; admitted to practice September, 1882, before the Supreme Bench of

Martin L. Keedy
From Steiner, *Men of Mark in Maryland* (1907).

A. Leo Knott
From *Baltimore-American Illustrated Edition, The State of Maryland* (1896).

Richard Laws Lee
From *Distinguished Men of Baltimore and Maryland,* Baltimore American (1914).

Martin Lehmayer
From Cordell, *The University of Maryland* (1907).

Baltimore City; engaged in the practice of law with Mr. Rayner until 1886; House of Delegates, 1900-08; appointed Associate Judge of the Supreme Bench of Baltimore City, Maryland's first Jewish Circuit Court Judge, September, 1909; defeated for election, November, 1909; resumed the practice of law; died September 5, 1936. His grandson, M. Peter Moser, was President of the Maryland State Bar Association, 1979-80.

Henry R. LEWIS (1850-1939)
DENTON

In 1896 he was a delegate to the Democratic National Convention that nominated William Jennings Bryan for the Presidency, and took an active part in the Bryan campaign.

Born December 15, 1850, Kent County, Delaware; Education: Farmington Academy; studied law in the office of John B. Pennington, of Dover, the Attorney General of Delaware; came to Denton two years later and established his practice; elected State's Attorney for Caroline County, 1887; elected to the Legislature, 1893, reelected 1895; Democrat; died June 11, 1939.

James J. LINDSAY (1859-1924)
TOWSON

Born August 31, 1859, Baltimore, Maryland; Education: studied law in Towson in law office of Judge N. Charles Burke who was then engaged in practice; admitted to practice in Towson, 1884; elected House of Delegates, 1884, 1886; Democrat; elected to Maryland Senate at age 28; after leaving the Senate devoted time to practice of law; entered into partnership with R.R. Boarman, 1900, under the firm name of Boarman & Lindsay; counsel to Board of County Commissioners; died November 26, 1924, Towson, Maryland.

C[harles] A. LITTLE (1854-1920)
HAGERSTOWN

Born January 23, 1854, Fairfield, Adams County, Pennsylvania; Education: Franklin & Marshall, 1878; read law in the office of Henry Kyd Douglas; admitted to the Washington County bar, November, 1883; elected House of Delegates, 1883; State's Attorney for Washington County, 1891-95; Brigadier General, Maryland National Guard; skilled trial lawyer; died November 29, 1920, Hagerstown, Maryland.

Henry LLOYD (1852-1920)
CAMBRIDGE

In 1896 he was Associate Judge of the First Judicial Circuit (Worcester, Wicomico, Dorchester and Somerset).

Born February 21, 1852, Dorchester County, Maryland; grandfather was Edward Lloyd, Governor of Maryland,

1809-11; maternal grandfather was John Henry, first U.S. Senator from Eastern Shore; Education: public schools and Cambridge Academy; was not a college graduate; read law in the offices of his uncle, Daniel Henry and his uncle by marriage, Charles F. Goldsborough; admitted to the bar in 1875; Maryland Senate, 1881, 1884; elected President of the Senate; succeeded to Governorship when President Cleveland appointed Governor McLane Ambassador to France; elected Governor in 1886 to fill out McLane's term; returned to Dorchester County at end of term to practice law; appointed to fill out term of his uncle, Judge Charles F. Goldsborough, 1892; elected Associate Judge, First Judicial Circuit, 1893; President, Dorchester National Bank; died December 30, 1920, Cambridge, Maryland.

George E. LOWEREE (1844-1903)
LAUREL

Born 1844, Flushing, Long Island, New York; served in the Union Army during the Civil War; afterwards served in the Pension Office in Washington; worked in the Custom House, Baltimore, until 1887; appointed Deputy Clerk of Circuit Court No. 2 of Baltimore City, 1887; admitted to the bar of the District of Columbia; admitted to the bar of Baltimore City, October 1, 1883; selected by Governor Lowndes to be Assistant Secretary of State, 1896-1900; lived last few years of his life in Washington, D.C., where he worked in the office of the U.S. Marshal of the District of Columbia; died April 4, 1903.

John A. LYNCH (1825-1904)
FREDERICK

Born October 3, 1825, Frederick County, Maryland; both grandfathers were Revolutionary War soldiers; Education: country schools near his home and at Pennsylvania College, Gettysburg, but did not graduate; returned to Frederick and studied law in office of Montjoy B. Luckett; admitted to the bar, November, 1851; commenced the practice of law in Frederick; elected State's Attorney for Frederick County, 1855, 1859; Associate Judge of the Sixth Judicial Circuit for thirty years, first elected 1867; President of the Frederick County Historical Society; died January 31, 1904, Frederick, Maryland.

G[eorge] Norbury MACKENZIE (1851-?)
BALTIMORE

Born May 4, 1851, Baltimore, Maryland; Education: private schools in Baltimore, Pembroke School; University of Maryland School of Law, LL.B. 1890; admitted May 3, 1890, to practice before the Supreme Bench of Baltimore

City; helped found the American Bonding and Trust Company, 1895; editor and publisher of *The Colonial Families of the United States of America*; Republican.

Frederick F. McCOMAS (1849-1897)
HAGERSTOWN

Born February 9, 1849, near Williamsport, Washington County, Maryland; Education: Dickinson College, Carlisle, Pennsylvania, A.B. 1872; admitted to the bar, 1874; equity practice; died March 27, 1897, Hagerstown, Maryland. "He lived in the present, loved to talk of the past, its traditions, its legends and stories, rather than of its history, and to the future he gave little concern. He was a kind husband and a fond father. He was as brave as a lion and as tender as a child, a strange combination of strength and weakness, of contrasts and contradictions, such a man as you rarely meet, and such as every man would love to meet again." 1903 *Maryland Bar Transactions* 30.

James A. McHENRY (1825-1906?)
CUMBERLAND

Born March, 1825 in Vermont; Education: St. Mary's Seminary in Baltimore; moved to Cumberland, 1845; Chief Deputy County Clerk, 1852-65; admitted to the bar of Allegany County, 1865, having studied under Josiah H. Gordon; associated in practice for 30 years with his son, James A. McHenry, Jr.; Democrat.

Judge John A. Lynch
Photograph from Portrait and Bio-graphical Record of the Sixth Congressional District of Maryland (1898).

George Norbury MacKenzie
From Cordell, *The University of Maryland* (1907).

J[ames] Roger McSHERRY (1867-1938)
FREDERICK

In 1896 he was Secretary of the Maryland State Senate.

Born July 27, 1867, Frederick, Maryland; eldest son of Chief Judge James McSherry; Education: Frederick College; Georgetown University (did not graduate); read law in the office of his father; admitted to the bar of Frederick County, June, 1889; married to Cornelia Ringgold Ross, daughter of Charles W. Ross, October 29, 1890; elected to Maryland General Assembly, 1891; Secretary of the Maryland Senate, 1894, 1896; Democrat; divorced, left Frederick, moved to Chicago, 1907; admitted to practice before the Supreme Court of Illinois, April, 1907; counsel to Chicago & Eastern Illinois Railroad; moved to Leesburg, Virginia; died February 7, 1938.

Richard M[eredith] McSHERRY (1842-1898)
BALTIMORE

Born November 13, 1842, Martinsburg, West Virginia, (then Virginia); Education: Loyola and Georgetown Colleges; went to Argentina, 1865, where he engaged in commercial pursuits; studied law at University of Virginia, graduated University of Maryland; admitted June 6, 1877, to practice before the Supreme Bench of Baltimore City; Democrat; King of Italy made him Knight of the Royal Order of the Crown of Italy for exposing and punishing the padrone system under which men, women and children were brought to the United States as virtual slaves, 1886; died June 28, 1898, Baltimore, Maryland.

William L[uke] MARBURY, Sr. (1858-1935)
BALTIMORE

Born December 26, 1858, Prince George's County, Maryland; Education: special course at Johns Hopkins University; read law with Colonel Charles Marshall; University of Maryland School of Law, LL.B. 1882; admitted May 30, 1882, to practice before the Supreme Bench of Baltimore City; U.S. Attorney for Maryland, 1894-97; Democrat; President of the Maryland State Bar Association, 1910-11; died October 26, 1935, Baltimore, Maryland. His son, William L. Marbury, Jr., was President of the Maryland State Bar Association in 1965-66. His grandson, Luke Marbury, is a partner in the firm of Venable, Baetjer & Howard.

William R[ichardson] MARTIN (1854-1906)
EASTON

Born May 27, 1854, Worcester County, Maryland; Education: Delaware College, A.B. 1874; came to Easton, September, 1875, as teacher at Easton Academy; read law under Judge John R. Franklin; admitted to the bar, November 20, 1876; practiced law with Isaac C.W. Powell of

William L. Marbury, Sr.
From Cordell, *The University of Maryland* (1907).

John T. Mason R.
From *Baltimore-American Illustrated Edition, The State of Maryland* (1896).

Alonzo L. Miles
From Hall, *Baltimore, Its History and Its People* (1912).

Joshua W. Miles
From *The Book of Maryland* (1920).

Talbot County under firm name of Powell & Martin until 1883; Associate Judge of the Second Judicial Circuit, 1895, died September 5, 1906.

John T. MASON, R. (1844-1901)
BALTIMORE

Born March 9, 1844, Detroit, Michigan; son of Major Isaac S. Rowland; after father's death, his name was changed by act of the Virginia Legislature to that of his mother's family, with the "R" to symbolize his father's name; at the outbreak of the Civil War he enlisted at age 16 in the Confederate Army and later served as a midshipman in the Confederate Navy; studied law at University of Virginia; admitted to the Baltimore bar, 1871; died June 21, 1901.

William P[inkney] MAULSBY, Jr. (1843-1911)
FREDERICK

Born February 21, 1843, Westminster, Maryland; son of Judge William Pinkney Maulsby; his father served on the Court of Appeals as Chief Judge of the Sixth Judicial Circuit; Education: St. James College, Washington County, 1861; enlisted in the Union Army; fought in the battles of Harpers Ferry, Charlestown, Martinsburg, Monocacy and Gettysburg; left the service as First Lieutenant, Autumn, 1864; began the study of law in his father's office, admitted to Frederick bar, 1866; Democrat; died November 14, 1911.

Alonzo L[ee] MILES (1864-1917)
CAMBRIDGE

Born February 3, 1864, Somerset County, Maryland;

Education: Western Maryland College, A.B. 1883; attended University of Maryland Law School, 1884; read law in the office of Judge Henry Page at Princess Anne; admitted to the bar, 1885 at Princess Anne; appointed Collector of the Port of Crisfield by President Cleveland; moved to Cambridge; represented Dorchester County in the Legislature and was Presidential elector for Cleveland, 1892; moved to Baltimore and formed partnership with Arthur Pue Gorman, Jr., 1898-1906; counsel to Baltimore City Police Department, 1900-12; delegate to National Democratic Convention in Baltimore, 1912; lived in Baltimore for 20 years, moved to Salisbury, where he resided for four years until his death in November, 1917. His son, Clarence W. Miles, served as the 60th President of the Maryland State Bar Association in 1953-54.

Joshua W[eldon] MILES (1858-1929)
PRINCESS ANNE

Born December 9, 1858, Somerset County, Maryland; Education: Western Maryland College, A.B., 1878; University of Maryland Law School; studied in the offices of Judge Charles B. Roberts in Westminster and Dennis & Brattan in Princess Anne; admitted to the bar at Princess Anne, July, 1880; elected State's Attorney for Somerset County, November, 1883; partner of Henry Page, 1888-92; Democrat; elected to Congress, 1894; senior partner of Miles & Stanford; died March 4, 1929, Baltimore, Maryland.

John C[olumbus] MOTTER (1844-1915)
FREDERICK

Born December 4, 1844, Emmitsburg, Frederick County, Maryland; Education: Dickinson Seminary, Williamsport, Pennsylvania; studied law at Frederick in the office of Grayson Eichelberger; established a law practice in Frederick, 1868; specialized in criminal cases; elected State's Attorney for Frederick County, 1879; Republican; elected Associate Judge, 1897, served 15 years as Sixth Judicial Circuit Judge in Montgomery and Frederick Counties; after retirement he returned to the practice of law; President of the Emmitsburg Railroad Co.; Director of the Citizen's National Bank; died June 12, 1915, Frederick, Maryland.

Alexander NEILL (1844-1910)
HAGERSTOWN

Born August 5, 1844, Hagerstown, Maryland; Education: St. James College, Washington County, 1863; studied law under his father and Judge William Motter; admitted to the bar of Washington County, June, 1865; President of Washington County Bar Association; represented Washington County in the Maryland General Assembly, 1870; President of Maryland Bankers Association; died July 14, 1910, at summer home, Blue Ridge Summit.

Frank C. NORWOOD (1855-1934)
FREDERICK

In 1896 he was a Republican State Senator from Frederick County.

Born September 12, 1855, Frederick County, Maryland; Education: Maryland Agricultural College, 1874; University of Maryland Law School, LL.B. 1879; admitted to the bar in Frederick; Republican; elected State's Attorney for Frederick County, 1883; elected to House of Delegates, 1889; elected to State Senate, 1895; President, First National Bank of Frederick, 1896-1909; died January 5, 1934.

William J. O'BRIEN, Jr. (1863-1931)
BALTIMORE

Born July 7, 1863, Baltimore, Maryland; Education: Loyola College, A.B.; University of Maryland Law School, did not graduate; admitted to practice, 1888; in partnership with his father, William J. O'Brien, Sr.; M.A., Loyola College, 1908; died May 31, 1931, Miami Beach, Florida.

Frederick R. OWENS (1862-1947)
DENTON

Extensive research failed to disclose any information regarding Mr. Owens, other than his dates of birth and death.

Joseph PACKARD, Jr. (1842-1923)
BALTIMORE

In 1896 he was President of the Baltimore Reform League (1894-1900).

Born April 10, 1842, Fairfax County, Virginia; cousin of Robert E. Lee, and a descendant of Richard Henry Lee, a signer of the Declaration of Independence; Education: Episcopal High School, Kenyon College, Ohio, 1860; during the Civil War he was a lieutenant in the famous Rockbridge

John C. Motter
From *Baltimore-American Illustrated Edition, The State of Maryland* (1896).

F. C. Norwood
From *Baltimore-American Illustrated Edition, The State of Maryland* (1896).

William J. O'Brien, Jr.
From Cordell, *The University of Maryland* (1907).

Henry Page
Photograph of his portrait in the Somerset County Courthouse.

Battery, part of the Stonewall Brigade; graduated from University of Virginia Law School, came to Baltimore; admitted to practice before the Supreme Bench of Baltimore City, September 22, 1868; founder of the firm of Venable & Packard with Richard M. Venable, 1871-1892; Democrat; President of the Bar Association of Baltimore City, 1892-93; died November 24, 1923.

Henry PAGE (1841-1913)
PRINCESS ANNE

Born June 28, 1841, Princess Anne, Maryland; name changed from John Woodland Crisfield, Jr., to Henry Page, by act of the Legislature, 1843 (after his mother's death he was raised in the home of his maternal grandmother who named him after his maternal grandfather); Education: University of Virginia, Charlottesville; studied law in the office of his father, John Woodland Crisfield (1808-1897); admitted to the bar at Princess Anne, 1864; member, Maryland Constitutional Convention, 1867; State's Attorney for Somerset County, 1870-84; Democrat; U.S. Congressman, 1891-92; Associate Judge, Court of Appeals of Maryland, 1892-1908; died January 7, 1913, Princess Anne, Maryland.

Charles E[dward] PHELPS (1833-1908)
BALTIMORE

In 1896 he was an Associate Judge of the Supreme Bench of Baltimore City.

Born May 1, 1833; Guilford, Vermont; his mother was Almira Hart Phelps, a noted educator; Education: Princeton University, 1852; Harvard Law School; also studied law in the office of Robert J. Brent; admitted to the bar in 1855; Union veteran of the Civil War, colonel with the Seventh Maryland Regiment (U.S.A.); winner of the Congressional Medal of Honor for distinguished gallantry at the Battle of Spotsylvania Court House, 1864; retired with the rank of brigadier general; U.S. Congress, 1865-69; elected Associate Judge of the Supreme Bench of Baltimore City, 1882; died December 27, 1908.

Clayton PURNELL (1857-1933)
FROSTBURG

Born October 12, 1857, near Berlin, Worcester County, Maryland; Education: private tutors; taught school in Dorchester County at age 17; studied law under S.T. Milbourne of Cambridge during summer of 1878; admitted to the bar at Cambridge, November 15, 1881; vice-principal at Beall High School in Frostburg, 1882; resigned and dedicated himself to practice, 1891; one of organizers of Western Maryland Telephone Co., of which he was a director; Frostburg City Attorney; Democrat; President of the Allegany County Bar Association, 1893; active in the organi-

zation of the Maryland State Bar Association, 1896; Judge of the Peoples Court of Frostburg, 1930; died April 11, 1933.

Clayton J[ones] PURNELL (1856-1908)
SNOW HILL

Born January 22, 1856; Deputy Clerk of Worcester County; founder of First National Bank of Snow Hill, Pocomoke City National Bank and the Pocomoke Electric Light and Power Company; president of numerous banks; died February 10, 1908.

George W[ashington] PURNELL (1841-1899)
SNOW HILL

Born April 14, 1841, Snow Hill, Maryland; Education: Snow Hill Academy; Princeton University (did not graduate); joined the First Maryland Cavalry (Confederate Army); taken prisoner and held for 18 months at Johnson's Island, Lake Erie, until July, 1865; read law in the office John R. Franklin; University of Virginia Law School, LL.B.; admitted to the bar at Snow Hill, 1868; one of the founders of The Atlantic Hotel, Ocean City, Maryland, 1875; died May 9, 1899.

Jackson H. RALSTON
HYATTSVILLE

Extensive research has failed to disclose any information regarding Mr. Ralston.

D[avid] Meredith REESE, Sr. (1845-1918)
BALTIMORE

Born April 12, 1845; admitted September 28, 1868, to practice before the Supreme Bench of Baltimore City; died December 27, 1918.

Benjamin F. REICH (1861-1943)
FREDERICK

Extensive research failed to produce any information regarding Mr. Reich, except that he was born June 18, 1861, and died June 17, 1943.

Charles T[rimble] REIFSNIDER, Sr. (1840?-1903)
WESTMINSTER

Born 1840? Westminster, Maryland; Education: Franklin & Marshall College, Pennsylvania; Gettysburg College; studied law with William Ross of the Frederick bar; admitted to the bar, 1862; served for several months as First Lieutenant, Union Army; opened law office in Westminster; partnership with Elijah F. Crout; State's Attorney for Carroll County, 1867-71; Democratic Conservative, later Republican; Associate Judge, Fifth Judicial Circuit, 1899-1901; died October 11, 1903, Westminster, Maryland.

Jay WILLIAMS (1859-1933)
SALISBURY

Born June 28, 1859, near Salisbury; Education: St. Johns College, Annapolis, 1880; postgraduate work at Wesleyan University; read law in office of State Senator Thomas Humphreys at Salisbury; admitted to the Wicomico County bar, July, 1884; died February 26, 1933.

John F[letcher] WILLIAMS (1849-1913)
BALTIMORE

Born February 8, 1849, Anne Arundel County, Maryland; Education: early education at West River Classical Institute and Cumberland Valley Institute were interrupted by the Civil War; at end of war entered Dickinson College, graduating in 1870; admitted to the Snow Hill bar, July 1873; came to Baltimore, 1873, admitted November 1, 1873, to practice before the Supreme Bench of Baltimore City; son Raymond S. Williams was his law partner; Democrat; elected to the House of Delegates from Anne Arundel County, 1880; represented Baltimore in the House of Delegates, 1884; died May 11, 1913, Baltimore, Maryland.

Stevenson A[rcher] WILLIAMS (1851-1932]
BEL AIR

Born May 6, 1851, Brooklyn Navy Yard Hospital, Brooklyn, New York; Education: Princeton, A.B. and A.M.; University of Maryland, LL.B.; practiced law at Bel Air, 1873 until his death; Republican; elected to the Maryland Senate, 1898-1902; President, Maryland State Bar Association, 1900-01; unsuccessful candidate for Governor, 1903; at his death he was the dean of the Harford County bar; died February 20, 1932. His great-granddaughter, Clare Close Miller, is married to Baltimore attorney John Philip Miller.

L[emuel] Allison WILMER (1849-1932)
LaPLATA

In 1896 he was Adjutant General of Maryland.
Born September 17, 1849, Charles County, Maryland; Education: St. John's College, A.B. 1871; studied law; appointed Adjutant General of Maryland, February 19, 1896; died Newark, New Jersey, March 19, 1932.

Skipwith WILMER (1843-1901)
BALTIMORE

In 1896, he was Judge Advocate General of Maryland.
Born February 22, 1843, Northampton County, Virginia; Education: College of St. James; University of Pennsylvania; fought in the Civil War; studied law at University of Louisiana; came to Baltimore to practice, 1867; served two terms in the Baltimore City Council, 1881; Presidential elector, 1884;

President, Second Branch of the Baltimore City Council, 1889; Trustee, Johns Hopkins Hospital and Greenmount Cemetery; director of railroads and steamship lines; first secretary of the Bar Association of Baltimore City, 1880 and later President; died July 12, 1901, Nahant, Massachusetts.

George W. ("Sunny") WILSON (1874-1908)
EASTON

Born February 11, 1874, Caroline County, Maryland; Education: Easton High School, law office of William R. Martin, attended lectures at the University of Maryland Law School; after election of William R. Martin as judge in 1897, formed partnership with Joseph B. Seth, under the name Seth & Wilson; director of banks in Easton; commercial lawyer; died January 5, 1908.

William S[ydney] WILSON (1853-1897)
SNOW HILL

Extensive research has failed to disclose any information regarding Mr. Wilson, other than his date of birth of November 18, 1853, that he was the son of Senator Ephraim K. Wilson, and that he died on November 14, 1897.

William J[ohn] WITZENBACKER (1861-1916)
HAGERSTOWN

Born December 1, 1861, Hagerstown, Maryland; father was immigrant from Odenwald, Hesse Darmstadt, Germany; Education: Hagerstown High School, 1880; Johns Hopkins University, A.B. 1883; studied law in the office of Alexander Neill; admitted to the Washington County Bar, November, 1886; Democrat; appointed City Attorney for Hagerstown, 1890-95; appointed Judge of the Circuit Court, 1902; defeated by Judge M.L. Keedy, 1904; active in establishing the Bar Library in the Washington County Courthouse; died February 11, 1916.

Glenn H. WORTHINGTON (1858-1934)
FREDERICK

Born 1858 near Frederick; as a small boy he witnessed the Battle of the Monocacy, 1864; in his

Glenn H. Worthington
Photograph from Williams and McKinsey, *History of Frederick County, Maryland* (1910).

retirement he wrote about the battle in a book entitled *Fighting For Time,* dealing with the invasion of Maryland in July, 1864, by a Confederate force under General Jubal A. Early; State's Attorney and Superintendent of Schools of Frederick County; for 15 years Associate Judge of the Third Circuit; he was appointed Chief Judge in 1907, but was defeated by Judge Hammond Urner two years later; Associate Judge of the Maryland Court of Appeals; prominent in Frederick Democratic politics; died August 7, 1934.

Daniel G[iraud] WRIGHT (1840-1922)
BALTIMORE

Born June 1, 1840, Rio de Janeiro, Brazil; son of Robert Clinton Wright, an American coffee merchant and member of the firm of Maxwell, Wright & Co.; Education: left the University of Virginia in 1861, and joined the Confederate Army; served under Generals Robert E. Lee, Stonewall Jackson and John Singleton Mosby as one of "Mosby's Rangers;" captured and imprisoned for the balance of the war; admitted November 25, 1867, to practice before the Supreme Bench of Baltimore City; served for 15 years as an examiner for the Supreme Bench of Baltimore City, taking in longhand all the testimony in equity cases; Associate Judge of the Supreme Bench of Baltimore City, 1888-1910; died February 19, 1922, Baltimore, Maryland. •

John S. YOUNG (1856?-1939)
BEL AIR

Born 1856?; his father was William Young (1828-1892), a Harford County attorney, whose portrait is in the Courthouse at Bel Air; Democrat; delegate to the 1912 Democratic National Convention in Baltimore; died February 17, 1939, Baltimore, Maryland.

(L-R): Governor Edwin Warfield and William Jennings Bryan, at the Governor's Mansion, Annapolis, 1905. Courtesy of the Maryland State Archives, Merrick Collection, MSA SC 1477-610.

ADDRESS OF CHIEF JUDGE JAMES McSHERRY,

FIRST PRESIDENT OF THE MARYLAND STATE BAR ASSOCIATION

THE ATLANTIC HOTEL, OCEAN CITY, MARYLAND

JULY 28, 1897

Gentlemen of the Maryland State Bar Association:

It is a little singular, if not indeed paradoxical, that a learned and venerable profession, which for centuries has numbered and enrolled among its members the most enlightened and accomplished leaders of thought, has never yet been supplied with a satisfactory or an adequate definition of the very subject to which that profession pertains - *Law*. Whether Hobbes or Blackstone, Austin or Markby be followed, or the more flexible and perhaps more accurate description of Professor Holland be approved, "law, as the lawyer has to deal with it," says Judge Dillon in his admirable lectures on the Laws and Jurisprudence of England and America, "is concerned only with legal rights." "Coercion by the State," he continues, "is the essential quality of law, distinguishing it from morality or ethics." Adopting, as he does with some misgiving, the definition of Holland in the latter's "Elements of Jurisprudence," Judge Dillon states "law may be defined as a general rule of civil conduct or of external human action enforced, or at all events purporting to be enforced, by a sovereign political authority." This, I venture with great diffidence to suggest, is subject to some qualification. There may be a rule of civil conduct enforced by the State, and thus answering the definition, but still so repugnant to reason or revelation that, as Blackstone tells us, it would possess no binding authority as law. An enactment that is hostile to natural justice—an arbitrary one, the *"hoc volo, sic Jubio, sit pro ratione voluntas"* of Juvenal, that is antagonistic to divine law—is no law at all though clothed in all its outward trappings and its garb. Dr. Whewell has remarked "the adjective right belongs to the domain of *morality;* the substantive right to the domain of law." Be this as it may and however you define that great overmastering system called the law; and though coercion by a dominant superior power be the method of its ultimate manifestation in dealing with concrete rights; its sources - numerous and diversified - give efficacy and shape to its practical administration; and what is more important still, in its loftiest conception, its foundations lie deeply embedded in the moral code. Whilst, perhaps, strictly and technically speaking it may have

no immediate or necessary concern with mere ethics in the abstract, yet we all know and intuitively feel that it takes deepest hold of humanity and is most elevating in its influences when closest akin to the decalogue. Of course I have no reference in this remark to the comparatively unimportant instances where rules of civil conduct that are in themselves or inherently indifferent, are prescribed. Such enactments not affecting in any way either natural rights or revealed law are merely the emanations of the law-maker's will. I allude to the broader view epitomized by Justinian; *"Juris praecepta sunt hac; honeste vivere, alterum non ladere, suum cuiqui tribuere."* ["These are the precepts of the law: To live honorably; to hurt nobody; to render to every one his due."] It was no doubt that conception of the law—its potency and at least one fountain of its origin—that induced Bishop Hooker to exclaim: "I bow with reverence before the majesty of the law. Her seat is the bosom of God; her voice the harmony of the world. All things in heaven and on earth do her homage; the very least, as feeling her protection; the greatest, as not above her power."

Though you distinguish the ethical from the physical coercive concept, there can be no total obscuration of the former in the daily multiform applications of the latter. A legal right, in some way or other, always involves a correlative duty, and in the multitudinous transactions of life, the clashing of those rights and duties may and frequently does evoke in their ultimate adjustment, an essentially moral principle. And so, however we may regard the science itself—whatever formula of words we may employ to give expression to our notion of it—in the last analysis, the lawyer's work, the practical adaptation of the law and its underlying principles to the varying affairs of men, is to a greater or less degree, an interweaving or blending of ethical precepts and conventional commands. It follows of course, that those who aid in the administration of a system thus complexly composed as regards its origin, and diversified as respects its functions, should possess, to fit them for the delicate and difficult task, intellectual and moral attainments commensurate with the magnitude of the obligation which their responsible position inexorably imposes. And, hence, the members of the Bar—

the most important functionaries who assist in the dispensation of jural justice—ought to be men of wisdom, enlighten-
ment and integrity.

Lord Chancellor Westbury, more than forty years ago,
declared that lawyers "from the beginning to the end of their
lives, ought to regard themselves as students of the most
exalted branch of knowledge, moral philosophy embodied and
applied in the laws and institutions of a great people. There
is no other class or order in a community," he went on to say,
"on whom so much human happiness depends, or whose
pursuits and studies are to intimately connected with the
progress and well-being of mankind." Sneered at by the
cynical and derided by the ignorant this may be, but its truth
is attested most conclusively. That the American lawyer has
always been the leader of thought in this country; and that
his influence has been most cogent in moulding and executing
beneficent legislation, will, in a measure, appear if I may
venture to briefly state a few facts with which probably many
even of our own calling have not had either opportunity or
occasion to become familiar. Mr. I.H. Benton, Jr. of the Boston
Bar, in an interesting paper on the "Influence of the Bar in
State and Federal Government," read by him in February,
1894, before the Southern New Hampshire Bar Association,
presents some valuable and striking facts bearing on this
subject. He shows that of the fifty-six signers of the
Declaration of Independence, twenty-five were lawyers, as
were thirty out of the fifty-five members of the Convention
which framed the Federal Constitution. Out of three thousand one hundred and twenty-two United States Senators,
since 1787, two thousand and sixty-eight were lawyers; and of
the eleven thousand eight hundred and eighty-nine
Representatives, five thousand eight hundred and thirty-two
were lawyers; of the twenty-five Presidents of the Republic
twenty have been lawyers; whilst of the one thousand one
hundred and fifty-seven Governors of all the States, five
hundred and seventy-eight out of nine hundred and seventy-
eight whose occupations he was able to ascertain, have been
members of the Bar. These figures become even more significant when it is remembered that the lawyers make up but a
small percentage of the whole population. In fine, to quote
from the exhaustive report of the Committee on Legal
Education, submitted to the America Bar Association at
Saratoga, in August, 1892: "The mind of the lawyer is the
essential part of the machinery of justice; no progress or
reforms can be made until the lawyers are ready. Their influence at the Bar, be made until the lawyers are ready. Their
influence at the Bar, on the bench and in legislation is practically omnipotent. The progress of the law means the
progress of the lawyer, not of a few talented men who are on
the out-posts of legal thought, but the great army of the

common place who constitute the majority in every occupa-
tion. What the lawyers do not understand or what they
pronounce visionary and impracticable, will not be accepted
by the legislatures or courts of the country."

But his vast influence in giving shape to legislation, his
conceded power in directing government and in moulding
public opinion are not the exclusive spheres of the lawyer's
usefulness. In the less glittering but not less important
routine of duty he is called upon to confront vice, to denounce
crime, to unmask fraud, to expose its disguises, to explore the
hidden and secret ways of the crafty, the cunning and the
dishonest. Innocence commits its vindication to his skill; and
the weak, the helpless and the oppressed invoke his generous
aid. The property and the reputations of the living, the estates
of the dead and the inheritance of the orphan may all be the
subjects of his watchful vigilance and anxious solicitude. Vast
pecuniary interests and the most delicate social and domestic
relations, when dragged into litigation, demand his ceaseless
attention. He becomes of necessity identified with the strifes
of others and as a consequence is often visited with the
unmerited criticism which the bitter feelings engendered by
an angry law-suit frequently provoke. His is, many times, the
guiding hand that steers, unseen, mighty financial and
commercial undertakings; and in the seclusion of his office,
with none of the pomp and circumstance of the forum to win
the plaudits of the multitude, his judgment and his counsel
give shape to enterprises of great pith and moment.

If what I have thus far said with respect to the position of
the lawyer and his relation to the administration of the law in
its broadest sense, be true—and it is demonstrable if need
be—then it results as a necessary and an obvious consequence that the practitioner of today, whose duties and
responsibilities and whose position in the community place
him in such pre-eminence of power and influence and leadership, owes to his calling to himself and to his country an
inflexible obligation to maintain, unimpaired, the intellectual
and moral ascendancy of the legal profession. In the precise
ratio that he falls short in either respect will the deterioration
of his and his brethrens' usefulness be measured. Crowding
the ranks with incompetent men will inevitably lower the
intellectual average of the bar; whilst the venality and the
unscrupulous conduct of a few unworthy practitioners will, by
the verdict of public opinion which is seldom discriminating
on such a subject, affix the stigma of obloquy and contempt
upon the whole body of the profession.

Losing sight of, or not knowing the traditional integrity
of the true lawyer has been instrumental in developing the
modern commercialism pervading a noble pursuit, and this,
with an insatiate greed for questionable gains, must eventu-
ate in a transformation from the exalted to the vicious, alike

Maryland State Bar Association, July 1899.
Atlantic Hotel, Ocean City, Md.

Earliest known photograph of the Maryland State Bar Association, the Fourth Annual Meeting on the front porch of the Atlantic Hotel, Ocean City, Maryland, July, 1899. (Gift of Arthur W. Machen, Jr.)

FIRST ROW (L-R): Adial P. Barnes, Peter J. Campbell, A. Hunter Boyd, W. Burns Trundle, Conway W. Sams, John Parran Briscoe, Frank Turner, Unknown, James McSherry, John Prentiss Poe, Samuel D. Schmucker.

SECOND ROW (L-R): A. Morris Tyson, Alonzo L. Miles, Unknown, William C. Devecmon, Unknown, Thomas W. Simmons, Walter I. Dawkins, Unknown, George M. Sharp, J. Upshur Dennis, John S. Wirt, Thomas Hall Robinson, Henry Page, Unknown, Unknown, Benjamin A. Richmond, John Hinkley, T. Foley Hisky, James Alfred Pearce, Richard Bernard, Charles E. Fink, James A. C. Bond, David G. McIntosh, William J. O'Brien, Robert R. Henderson, Joseph C. France, Robert P. Graham.

Several men in the front row have umbrellas. There is an unidentified boy in the second row.

R. Bennett Darnall (1875-1957).

JULY 26-28, 1910 The only joint meeting of the Virginia and Maryland State Bar Associations convenes at the Homestead, Hot Springs, Virginia. MSBA membership totals 425. The treasury contains $834.25.

JULY 1, 1911 "What is accounted to have been the most successful annual meeting of the MSBA comes to a close at Cape May, New Jersey, at a banquet featuring toasts by eminent legal lights. Nearly every incoming train since the session began has added to the number of lawyers in attendance, and tonight they fairly overran the place. Many of them came with wives or other members of their families and practically all attend the banquet held in the Hotel Cape May and furnished the occasion for uncorking much eloquence in addition to more material things. Speaker of the House Champ Clark is the guest of honor with Mrs. Clark. He arrived on a train that left Washington at noon and got in here at about seven o'clock. The ballroom of the Cape May Hotel, where the association meets, is the place of the feast, the room being decorated in white and gold, and presenting a beautiful appearance was a head table for the speakers, and three long tables at right angles for the others.

"An elaborate menu is served, the card being decorated with pictures of the terrapin, lobster and crab, and quotations from Shakespeare. This is what the members of the association had for dinner:

Caviar sur canape   Cocktails

Clam cocktail

Clear green turtle

Salted nuts, radishes, olives

Soft shell crabs

Sauce tartare   Sauternes

Sweetbreads a la King

Cape May Farmstead chicken a la Maryland

New asparagus

G.H. Mumm & Co. Extra Dry

Sorbet a la Blackstone

Roasted plover on toast

Lettuce and tomato salad   Mayonnaise dressing

Apollinaria

Ice in fancy forms

Cakes

Cheese with toasted crackers   Coffee

Liqueurs   Cigars   Cigarettes"

—Baltimore *Sun*, July 2, 1911

JUNE 23, 1917 At its annual meeting in Atlantic City, New Jersey, MSBA sends a message of loyal support to President Woodrow Wilson in his conduct of World War I.

JUNE 27, 1918 The Committee on Legal Education reports its success in having the General Assembly enact Chapters 270 and 475, Acts of 1918, by which prospective lawyers are required to be graduates of an approved high school or college, or must submit to an examination to show that their education is substantially equivalent to a high school education in Maryland.

JUNE 24, 1920 Chief Judge Morris A. Soper calls for the modernization of the Maryland judiciary in his address as MSBA President. His proposals for reform are not adopted until the State Constitution is amended in 1944.

The membership of the Association is 528. The treasury contains $3,508.52.

JULY 1, 1922 MSBA adopts Canons of Ethics drafted by the American Bar Association, including a revised oath of admission for attorneys.

FEBRUARY 23, 1923 The American Law Institute is founded at a meeting in Washington, D.C., to which MSBA sends a delegation composed of Judges Bond, Boyd,

1917 Annual Meeting at the Marlborough-Blenheim Hotel in Atlantic City, New Jersey. Among those standing are Eldridge Hood Young (far left), George Dobbin Penniman (fifth from left), Chief Judge Henry D. Harlan, Chief Judge Morris A. Soper. Fourth from the right is James W. Chapman, Jr. In front of Mr. Chapman are his son, S. Vannort Chapman, Mrs. Chapman, and their daughter, Mary Clare.

Briscoe, Stockbridge, Offutt; Attorney General Alexander Armstrong; Henry D. Harlan, Charles F. Harley, John Hinkley, Charles McHenry Howard, W. Thomas Kemp, Sylvan Hayes Lauchheimer, Alfred S. Niles and Edgar Allen Poe. The meeting is called by the American Association of Law Schools "to promote the clarification and simplification of the law and its better adaptation to social needs, etc." The result is the publication of digests of judicial decisions on various branches of law, the Restatements of the Law.

JUNE 26, 1930   Membership in the MSBA totals 664. The treasury contains a balance of $11,187.85.

AUGUST 29, 1930   MSBA welcomes to Maryland a visiting delegation of 150 attorneys and judges from England, France, Scotland, and the Irish Free State. They are greeted by Governor Ritchie at a reception at the State House in Annapolis and given a tour of the city. At the Naval Academy they board the steamship City of Richmond for a cruise to Baltimore.

DECEMBER, 1936   Publication of the first issue of the *Maryland Law Review*. For many years, this effort of the students and faculty of the University of Maryland School of Law is underwritten by MSBA, which provides copies to its member attorneys.

MAY 12, 1937   MSBA Special Committee on Preservation of the Independence of the Supreme Court organizes a mass meeting in Washington, D.C., to lobby Maryland Senators and representatives to oppose President Franklin D. Roosevelt's plan to "pack" the Supreme Court. Approximately 500 citizens from all parts of the State attended. The President's plan is defeated in the Congress.

JANUARY 20, 1940   The first Midwinter Meeting of the MSBA convenes at the Belvedere Hotel in Baltimore, attended by 244 members.

JUNE 27, 1940   Membership in the Association numbers 711. The treasury contains a cash balance of $8,262.48.

The lobby of the Courts of Appeal Building, Annapolis, Maryland. The MSBA memorial to Maryland lawyers killed in World War I is on the right. The memorial was dedicated on January 11, 1921, in memory of Major German H.H. Emory, Captain Frederick C. Colston, Lieutenant Stanley L. Cochrane, Lieutenant William Earl Fraley, Lieutenant George Rogers Page, Lieutenant Merrill Rosenfeld and Ensign John Ganster. Photograph by Linda Johnson.

1931 Annual Meeting at the Ambassador Hotel, Atlantic City, New Jersey. Among those standing are Walter L. Clark (far left), T. Foley Hisky (ninth from left), S. Vannort Chapman (twelfth from the left), Chief Judge Carroll T. Bond, Albert Blum, and Mary Clare Chapman Gieske. Mrs. James W. Chapman is next to Mrs. Gieske and the gentleman in the front wearing white trousers is President James W. Chapman, Jr. Attorney General (later Governor) William Preston Lane, Jr., is third from the right.

JANUARY 11, 1941   At the 1941 Midwinter Meeting of the MSBA, Attorney General William C. Walsh proposes restructuring the Maryland judiciary. A commission is later appointed under the direction of Chief Judge Carroll T. Bond that proposes that Judges of the Court of Appeals no longer serve a dual function in the counties as trial judges of the Circuit Courts. The Bond Plan is supported by the Association.

SEPTEMBER 1, 1941   The first Maryland Rules of Procedure promulgated by the Court of Appeals become effective. They are the result of the first study of Maryland civil procedure undertaken in 70 years. MSBA and the Bar Association of Baltimore City urged the passage of legislation by the General Assembly (Chapter 719, Acts of 1939) that conferred rule-making authority upon the Court of Appeals.

JULY 1, 1944   MSBA is awarded recognition by the Secretary of War and the Secretary of the Navy for participating in a plan sponsored by the ABA to provide legal assistance to military personnel and their dependents during World War II.

NOVEMBER 7, 1944   By a vote of 130,478 to 72,773, the voters of Maryland approve the Bond Amendment to the State Constitution that reorganizes the Court of Appeals of Maryland and limits its members to strictly appellate functions.

JUNE 29, 1945   President Frederick W.C. Webb of Salisbury proposes that the MSBA include in its membership every practicing lawyer in the State of Maryland.

MSBA creates the Committee on Refresher Courses for Veterans. Working with the University of Maryland School of Law, the committee organizes 20 lectures designed to bring returning veterans up to date on developments in the law. Prior to these refresher courses, the Association's only attempt to offer continuing legal education consisted of occasional panel discussions or the reading of scholarly papers at the annual meetings.

Hotel Chelsea, Atlantic City, New Jersey. The MSBA held its annual conventions there in 1918, 1919, 1920, 1924, 1925 and 1926. Photograph courtesy of the Atlantic County Historical Society.

FEBRUARY-MARCH, 1946   Twenty lectures, aggregating 36 hours, are given by a faculty of distinguished judges and lawyers during a five-week period at the University of Maryland School of Law at Baltimore, attended by 179 returning veterans. The course is designed to bring veterans up to date on developments in the law since 1941. At the conclusion of the course, a mock trial is held in Courtroom 400 of the Baltimore City Courthouse, Judge Emory H. Niles presiding, with William D. Macmillan and Eben J.D. Cross appearing as counsel.

OCTOBER, 1946   Admission of Rose S. Zetzer as the first woman member of the MSBA, reported by the Executive Council at the Midwinter Meeting on February 1, 1947.

JUNE 21, 1947   S. Vannort ["Norty"] Chapman is elected Secretary of the MSBA, continuing a family tradition begun by his father, James W. Chapman, Jr., who served as Secretary from 1908 until his death in 1943, except for 1930-31 when he served as President. Norty will serve 18 years as Secretary, until 1965. Thereafter, in 1969, he will be appointed Historian.

JUNE 24, 1948   The MSBA Committee on Legal Education, Bridgewater M. Arnold, chairman, proposes the creation of a special committee to consider the advisability of having courses for the continuing legal education of the bar, and to plan and organize such programs, in possible conjunction with the American Law Institute.

JANUARY 29, 1949   The Continuing Legal Education Committee, R. Carleton Sharretts, Jr., chairman, reports at the Midwinter Meeting that it held its first educational program the preceding week at the Belvedere Hotel in Baltimore, attended by 380 people. The subject of the program was pretrial rules, rules of practice and procedure, and summary judgment. The participants in a mock trial were John Marshall Butler, Roszel C. Thomsen, John Henry Lewin, Constance K. Putzel, Wilson K. Barnes, William D. Macmillan, Jr., F. Edward Wheeler, Paul L. Cordish, William B. Somerville, and Charles P. Coady, Jr. The program was chaired by Judge Emory H. Niles and H. Vernon Eney.

JUNE 29, 1950   Membership in the MSBA totals 1,120. The treasury contains $11,206.24.

Ocean view of the Hotel Traymore, Atlantic City, New Jersey. The MSBA held its annual conventions there in 1922, 1923, 1927, 1942, 1947-60, and 1962-63. Photograph courtesy of the Atlantic County Historical Society.

JUNE 20, 1958   Announcement of the creation of The Maryland Conference of Local Bar Presidents, to distribute data, program materials and publications to local bar groups, especially in rural areas that lack full-scale bar libraries.

JUNE 21, 1958   Vivian V. Simpson of Rockville, elected as the Vice President of the MSBA from the Sixth Circuit, becomes the first woman officer elected by the Association.

OCTOBER 22, 1958   The MSBA Committee to Study the Caseload of the Court of Appeals chaired by H. Vernon Eney submits its final report in which it recommends the creation of an intermediate appellate court to be known as The Court of Special Appeals of Maryland. Frederick W. Invernizzi, director of the Administrative Office of the Courts, acts as secretary to the committee. [A referendum of the members in the Autumn of 1959 indicates that two-thirds disapprove of the recommendation, favoring instead increasing the membership of the Court of Appeals from five to seven members.]

MAY 2, 1959   The organizational meeting of the Conference of Local Bar Associations is held in Baltimore. President John B. Gray, Jr., tells the assembled bar presidents that although the MSBA is anxious to lend its aid to local associations through the Conference, the local bar associations will retain their autonomy. The President forecasts the need for coordinated programs of continuing legal education and public relations,

JUNE 19, 1959   President John B. Gray, Jr., advocates greater efforts by the MSBA to promote continuing legal education. He reports on the Arden House Conference of December, 1958, attended by the Presidents of every state bar association and a number of law school deans. The conference recommended that the bar associations shoulder the responsibility for continuing legal education. A local conference is convened thereafter that proposes a statewide program of continuing legal education with a part-time paid director.

JUNE 20, 1959   Jeffrey B. Smith proposes a resolution that the MSBA create a standing Committee on Continuing

At the 54th Annual Convention of the MSBA, held at the Traymore Hotel, Atlantic City, New Jersey, July, 1949. (L-R): S. Vannort Chapman, Secretary; William C. Walsh, outgoing President; Frank B. Ober, President; and Robertson Griswold, Treasurer.

Education of the Bar, and that in conjunction with the Bar Association of Baltimore City and the Junior Bar Association of Baltimore City, a statewide program of continuing legal education be developed. The resolution is approved.

JANUARY 23, 1960 MSBA membership totals 1,458. Of that number, 794 are from Baltimore City. The treasury contains total assets of $29,323.66.

JUNE 23, 1960 A new Committee to Study the Caseload of the Court of Appeals reports that the General Assembly has enacted its recommendation that the Court of Appeals be increased from five to seven judges, and that an amendment to the State Constitution will come before the voters of Maryland on Election Day [November 8, 1960].

JUNE 24, 1960 The Maryland State Bar Association admits Linwood G. Koger, Sr., and John Raymond Hargrove, its first African-American members, after a spirited debate. Speaking in favor of admission are James McSherry of Frederick, William Taft Feldman, Louis Samuels, and Francis D. Murnaghan, Jr., of Baltimore. Arguing against admission is George Washington Williams, of Baltimore.

JUNE 25, 1960 In the only contested election for President in the history of the MSBA, Judge William J. McWilliams of Annapolis, the nominee of the Nominations

Committee, defeats Michael Paul Smith of Towson, 194-138. In a graceful gesture, Mr. Smith moves the election of Judge McWilliams be made unanimous.

JULY 1, 1960 William P. Cunningham, Esquire, Professor of Law of the University of Maryland, takes office as part-time Executive Director and Assistant Secretary of the MSBA, at an annual salary of $2500 and clerical expenses up to $2500, it being understood that he will also serve as Director of the program of the Committee on Continuing Education of the Bar. He was Dean of the University of Maryland School of Law from 1962-75.

1962-63 Alexander Gordon, III, Esquire (1909-1963), serves as first full-time Executive Director of the MSBA, until his untimely death on July 11, 1963.

JUNE 23, 1962 In a landmark address as outgoing President of MSBA, Judge Emory H. Niles proposes the "Niles Plan" for removing the selection of Judges from politics. Under his proposal, Judges would be chosen by the Governor from a list of qualified candidates compiled by a nominating commission. At the next general election, the Judges' names would be placed before the electorate, who either approve or reject them. The plan is later adopted in Maryland for district and appellate courts, but not the circuit courts.

At the 53rd annual MSBA Convention in Atlantic City, New Jersey. (L-R): S. Vannort Chapman, Abby Griswold, G.C.A. ("Andy") Anderson, Libby Chapman and Robertson Griswold, June 26, 1948. Photograph by Fred Hess & Son.

William P. Cunningham

Alexander Gordon, III.

Paul R. Schlitz

Senior U.S. District Judge John R. Hargrove was one of the first two African-American members of the MSBA.

JULY 1963   Professor John W. Ester of the University of Maryland School of Law becomes MSBA Director of Continuing Legal Education. During the next 13 years, he personally supervises the many courses taught under the auspices of the Association and prepares most of the printed materials. The State Bar's continuing legal education function is assumed by the Maryland Institute of Continuing Professional Education of Lawyers (MICPEL) in July, 1976.

JULY 10, 1964   The appointment of Paul R. Schlitz, Esquire, as second full-time Executive Director of the MSBA, at an annual salary of $8,000-10,000, is announced at the annual meeting in Atlantic City, New Jersey. He is a Maryland lawyer, former Chief Attorney of the Legal Aid Bureau. (Mr. Schlitz later served as Clerk of the U.S. District Court for the District of Maryland.)

MARCH 9, 1965   Incorporation of the Maryland State Bar Association, Inc. The incorporators are Judge J. Deweese Carter, H. Vernon Eney, and William L. Marbury. The resident agent is S. Vannort Chapman, whose office address is 1012 Mercantile Trust Building, Baltimore and Calvert Streets, Baltimore, Maryland.

MARCH 19, 1965   Incorporation of the Maryland Bar Foundation, Inc., is approved by the Midwinter Meeting of the Maryland State Bar Association on January 16, 1965. Among the Foundation's stated purposes are the advancement and improvement of the study of law, the practice of

law and the administration of justice and an increase in public respect for and understanding of the law through educational, scientific, literary and charitable means. The first board of directors is composed of the Hon. J. Deweese Carter, President; S. Vannort Chapman, Secretary-Treasurer; Hal C.B. Clagett; William L. Marbury; and Benjamin B. Rosenstock. Mr. Chapman served as Secretary-Treasurer from 1965-74.

JUNE 1, 1965   Effective date of Chapter 779, Acts 1965, enacted by the Maryland General Assembly, authorizing the Court of Appeals of Maryland to establish "The Clients' Security Trust Fund of the Bar of Maryland" for the protection of clients of erring lawyers.

MARCH, 1966   The Maryland Court of Appeals promulgates rules for the operation of the Clients' Security Trust Fund of the Bar of Maryland and appoints seven trustees to oversee its operation. Marvin H. Smith, first chairman of the trustees, devotes untold hours to the initiation of the Fund. Upon his appointment as Associate Judge of the Court of Appeals, he is succeeded by E. Dale Adkins, Jr., then President-elect of the MSBA. By 1970, more than 6,500 lawyers and judges are contributing to the Fund.

NOVEMBER 8, 1966   The Court of Special Appeals, Maryland's intermediate appellate court, is created by ratification of an amendment to the State Constitution (Art. IV, Section 14A) by the voters of Maryland. MSBA supported the passage of legislation to create the Court by

Cover of 1946 Annual Meeting program.

Manley E. Davis, MSBA Executive Director, 1967-76.

Robert R. Bair, Secretary of the MSBA, 1965-71.

William J. Smith, MSBA Executive Director, 1977-84.
Photograph by Guill Photo.

constitutional amendment (Chapters 10, 11,and 12, Acts of 1966) to alleviate the substantial backlog of cases pending in the Court of Appeals.

JANUARY 12, 1968   Publication of the first Maryland Lawyers' Manual by the MSBA. The first edition, copy No. 1, is inscribed: "To Herbert S. Garten, Without whose vision, ingenuity, enthusiasm, tact, perseverance and great

ability this significant publication never would have been possible. Rignal W. Baldwin, President. January 11, 1968."

MARCH 14, 1968   House Bill No. 1 sponsored by MSBA providing for a unified bar is defeated on the floor of the Maryland House of Delegates, by a vote of 72-60. Similar legislation is defeated in the 1969 session.

MSBA Annual Convention in Atlantic City, circa 1952. (L-R): Thomas N. Biddison, City Solicitor of Baltimore; Robin Biddison; Herman Moser, Associate Judge, Supreme Bench of Baltimore City; and Henrietta Moser. Photograph by Fred Hess & Son.

MSBA, Annual Convention in Atlantic City, June, 1960. (L-R): Chief Judge Emory H. Niles, Anne Whitridge Niles, S. Vannort Chapman, Libby Chapman and Hal C. B. Clagett. Photograph by Fred Hess & Son.

MAY 14, 1968   A proposed new State Constitution is overwhelmingly rejected by the voters of Maryland at a special election, 367,101 to 284,033. The MSBA, which took the lead in drafting and promoting the document, advocates the salvage of key features, many of which are later incorporated piecemeal into the existing State Constitution.

JULY 11, 1968   MSBA adopts the recommendations of the Special Committee on the Democratization of the Bar chaired by Norman P. Ramsay for opening up MSBA to all who wish to join. New By-Laws provide for a revised organizational structure featuring sections rather than committees, enhanced authority to be exercised by the Executive Director and the election of the Board of Governors by the membership.

AUGUST, 1968   MSBA wins ABA Award of Merit for its publication of the *Maryland Lawyers' Manual*, implementation of the Clients Security Trust Fund, a vigorous membership drive that increased the size of the Association by over 25%, steps toward ABA accreditation of all Maryland law schools and other progressive programs.

OCTOBER, 1968   The first issue of *The Maryland Bar Journal* is published and sent to all 5,600 practicing lawyers in Maryland. The first editor (1968-74) is Charles T. LeViness, who writes: "Gone is the familiar old *Red Book [Maryland Bar Transactions]* as well as the more recent Newsletter. The Journal will print items of interest on a statewide basis and also reports from the various Bar sections." Volume I, No. 1 lists the new address and telephone number of the MSBA:

905 Keyser Building, Calvert & Redwood Streets, Baltimore, Maryland 21202, Telephone: 685-7878

DECEMBER 18, 1968   Adoption of By-Laws of The Fellows of the Maryland Bar Foundation, an ancillary organization the purpose of which is to fund and otherwise aid the Foundation in accomplishing its purposes. Membership in The Fellows is a professional honor restricted to persons whose professional, public and private careers have demonstrated their outstanding dedication to the welfare of the community and who have particularly distinguished themselves in matters of the law and in the administration of justice. In May, 1969, the first 60 Fellows had accepted invitations to membership.

MARCH 15-22, 1969   MSBA holds its "Convention at Sea" in the form of a Caribbean cruise aboard the S.S. ARGENTINA of the Moore-McCormick Lines, visiting San Juan, Puerto Rico and St. Thomas, Virgin Islands. In addition to the regular business of the Association, an extensive continuing legal education program is presented. The "Convention at Sea" is in addition to the regular winter meeting in Baltimore and the summer meeting at Atlantic City.

Past Presidents of the MSBA were honored by the Association at the Presidents' Ball on April 5, 1986. (L-R): Wilbur D. Preston, Jr., Judge John B. Gray, Jr., William L. Marbury, Jr., and Hal C. B. Clagett. Photograph by Guill Photo.

Luncheon for new admittees to the bar sponsored by MSBA Young Lawyers Section. (L-R): Eli Frank, Jr., President; J. Richard O'Connell, Section Chair; Chief Judge W. Hall Hammond; and Attorney General Francis B. Burch, December 19, 1969. Photograph by Guill Photo.

SEPTEMBER 5-6, 1969   Robert L. Weinberg presides at the first "Citizens' Conference on Court Improvement," which convenes at the State House in Annapolis, jointly sponsored by MSBA and the American Judicature Society. The purpose of the Conference is to inform the public regarding efforts to modernize the judicial system of the State and what the MSBA is doing to improve the courts and to assure equal justice for all. Former Supreme Court Justice Tom Clark is the principal speaker. The Conference issues a call for a statewide, unified system of district courts staffed by full-time professional judges.

JANUARY, 1970   Vivian V. Simpson, Esquire, of Montgomery County, writes in *The Maryland Bar Journal*: "A recent communication from the Maryland State Bar Association reveals that out of its 4,006 members, 108 are women. Girls, we have arrived — but we are really only on the threshold!"

APRIL 16, 1970   Governor Marvin Mandel signs into law a bill supported by MSBA to enlarge the membership of the Court of Special Appeals from five to nine judges and to enlarge its jurisdiction. (The size of the Court is later increased to its present complement of 13 judges.)

JULY 9, 1970   MSBA adopts the Code of Professional Responsibility as approved by the American Bar Association in its final draft dated July 1, 1969, as the new minimum standard for members of the bar of the State of Maryland and members of the Association. Wilbur D. Preston proposes the action by resolution.

JULY 11, 1970   In the only contested election for President-elect of MSBA, Judge Roszel C. Thomsen of Baltimore is declared the winner over Robert S. Bourbon of Silver Spring by a vote of 224 to 104.

MSBA membership as of May 31, 1970, is stated at 4,224. The Treasurer reports total assets of $64,125.54.

JUNE 14, 1971   MSBA presents oil portraits of Maryland Justices Samuel Chase and Gabriel Duvall to Chief Justice Warren E. Burger at special ceremonies at the Supreme Court. The portraits, painted by artist Larry Dodd Wheeler. are presented by President E. Dale Adkins, Jr., President-elect Roszel C. Thomsen, and immediate Past President Eli Frank, Jr. In attendance, in addition to the artist and officers of the Association, are former Chief Justice Earl Warren and Justice Potter Stewart.

JUNE 17-19, 1971   MSBA holds its first convention in Ocean City, Maryland, since it last met there in 1907. A record 682 Maryland lawyers attend. The return to Ocean City was made possible by the construction of the new Convention Hall.

JUNE 18, 1971   The Long Range Planning Committee recommends the abolition of the Committee on Legal Biography, one of the original committees established at the founding of the MSBA in 1896. Biographies of deceased members are published for the last time in Volume 72, *Maryland Bar Transactions* (1967).

JULY 5, 1971   Pursuant to constitutional amendment supported by MSBA, the District Court of Maryland comes into formal existence as a court of record, replacing the old Magistrates Courts and Justices of the Peace. The court has uniform jurisdiction throughout the State, except that in Montgomery County it also has juvenile jurisdiction.

JANUARY 9, 1973   MSBA presents a new lectern to the Court of Appeals of Maryland at the rededication of the courtroom in the new Courts of Appeals Building on Rowe Boulevard in Annapolis. President David E. Betts makes the presentation and credits former President H. Vernon Eney for the idea. The lectern contains a short wave radio system that transmits statements of Court and counsel to a recording device. President Betts addresses the Court as "My Lords," by reason of their attire in red judicial robes.

JANUARY 31, 1974   The Committee on Public Awareness of the Judicial System holds its organizational meeting, chaired by Herbert Morrison, and launches a program of

1976 Annual Conference of Local Bar Presidents. (L-R): William J. Smith, MSBA Executive Director and James H. Cook, MSBA President, October 23, 1976. Photograph by Guill Photo.

education and information. The committee is the product of the Second Citizens' Conference on Modernization of the Courts held in Annapolis in September, 1973, which issued the following statement:

> It is the responsibility of the Bar and the Judiciary and other public officials to establish lines of communication so that informed public opinion can be created.

MAY 2, 1974   The Court of Appeals of Maryland hands down a landmark decision in *Maryland State Bar*

Association v. Agnew, 271 Md. 543, 318 A.2d. 811 (1974), the only disbarment of a former Vice President of the United States.

JULY 1, 1975   A statewide system for attorney discipline goes into effect with the creation of the Attorney Grievance Commission of Maryland by new Maryland Rules of Procedure BV1-BV11 promulgated by the MSBA Special Committee on Uniform Grievance Procedures chaired by Wilbur D. Preston and adopted by the Court of Appeals of Maryland.

MARCH 12, 1976   The Maryland Institute for the Continuing Professional Education of Lawyers [MICPEL] is incorporated for the purpose of centralizing the continuing legal education programs of the MSBA, the University of Maryland and University of Baltimore Schools of Law. The incorporators are Wilbur D. Preston, Jr., MSBA President; James H. Cook; Hal C.B. Clagett; Marvin J. Garbis; Michael Kelly, Dean of the University of Maryland School of Law; and Joseph Curtis, Dean of the University of Baltimore School of Law. Laurence M. Katz, (later Dean of the University of Baltimore Law School), is the first executive director. Robert H. Dyer has been the executive director since 1978.

JULY, 1976   MSBA celebrates the bicentennial of American independence by publishing H.H. Walker Lewis' *The Maryland Constitution of 1776,* and *The U.S. District Court of Maryland,* the following year.

DECEMBER 30, 1976   MSBA submits an *amicus curiae* brief prepared by Alfred L. Scanlan and George W. Liebmann against lawyer advertising in the case of *Bates v. State Bar of Arizona* pending before the U.S. Supreme Court.

CHIEF JUDGE ROBERT F. SWEENEY

When Robert F. Sweeney retires as Chief Judge of the District Court of Maryland in 1996, the court will lose the only Chief Judge it has ever known since it began operating in July, 1971. Chief Judge Sweeney is credited with organizing the court, establishing its reputation for competence and fairness, and guiding its successful operation from the beginning. The District Court of Maryland touches the lives of more Marylanders than any other court in the State, exercising both civil and criminal jurisdiction in every Maryland subdivision.

Photo: Chief Judge Robert F. Sweeney

MARCH, 1977   MSBA joins the Bar Associations Insurance Trust as a sponsoring association to negotiate life and disability insurance benefits for its members.

JUNE 27, 1977   *Bates v. State Bar of Arizona*, 433 U.S. 350, 97 S.Ct. 2691, 53 L. Ed.2d. 810(1977) decided by the U.S. Supreme Court, holds that blanket suppression of lawyer advertising violates the Free Speech Clause of the First Amendment. The decision results in the legalization of lawyer advertising.

SEPTEMBER 2, 1978   MSBA President Vincent L. Gingerich announces the establishment of a statewide lawyer referral service, effective September 5, 1978.

JANUARY 12, 1979   The Public Awareness Committee, chaired by John Sandbower, III, unveils plans for a media campaign to improve the public image of the legal profession in Maryland. The focus of the campaign, entitled "The Lawyers of Maryland Want You to Know," is to educate the public regarding its rights and responsibilities and available bar association services.

JUNE 30, 1980   MSBA membership totals 7,394. The Treasurer reports total assets of $169,316.

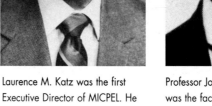

Laurence M. Katz was the first Executive Director of MICPEL. He later served as Dean of the University of Baltimore School of Law.

Professor John Sentman Strahorn was the faculty advisor to the Maryland Law Review when it began publication in 1936.

MARCH 24, 1981   Maryland Volunteer Legal Services, Inc., a statewide organization to provide pro bono legal services, is incorporated by Charles H. Dorsey, Jr., Gerald R. Walsh, Nevett Steele, Jr. and Frank T. Gray. The MSBA Board of Governors approves funding from the State Bar Association, which also appoints half of the MVLS board. From 1981 to 1995, the MSBA and the Maryland Bar Foundation provide over $150,000 to MVLS, which has been housed at Bar Headquarters and receives in-kind services.

JUNE 11, 1981   MSBA approves a new statewide system for the arbitration of fee disputes between Maryland attorneys and their clients. Under the plan, a client who objects to a legal bill may file a complaint, which after review, is submitted to arbitration.

JUNE 1, 1982   In response to MSBA initiatives, the Maryland General Assembly enacts a voluntary Interest on Lawyer Trust Account (IOLTA) program for the purpose of funding legal services to the poor and establishes Maryland Legal Services Corporation (MLSC) to supervise the distribution of revenues.

DECEMBER 20-21, 1985   MSBA takes possession of its new headquarters, the Maryland Bar Center, 520 West Fayette Street, formerly the Edgar Allan Poe School, which has been extensively renovated after a successful endowment campaign.

The receiving line at the President's Reception at the 1978 Annual Convention of the MSBA. President and Mrs. Vincent L. Gingerich greet William J. Smith, MSBA Executive Director, June 8, 1978. Photograph by Guill Photo.

JULY 1, 1986   The Legal Mutual Liability Society of Maryland, the only malpractice insurance company endorsed by MSBA to write professional liability insurance for attorneys, is incorporated. Enabling legislation proposed by MSBA, enacted in the preceding session by the Maryland General Assembly, imposed a $150 tax upon every practicing lawyer in the State. After a $2 million fund is accumulated, the Society issues its first legal malpractice insurance policies in 1988. Herbert J. Belgrad is the first Chairman, succeeded by the current Chairman, Cleaveland D. Miller. By 1995, Legal Mutual's gross premium sales exceed $5 million.

DECEMBER 6, 1986   MSBA and the League of Women Voters jointly sponsor a "Jefferson Meeting" of public debate on a variety of current issues in celebration of the bicentennial of the Constitution of the United States. The town meeting convenes in Annapolis attended by hundreds of citizens chaired by Judge John P. Corderman.

DECEMBER 17, 1987   Action Plan for Legal Services to Maryland's Poor is promulgated by the Advisory Council of the Maryland Legal Services Corporation, based upon a perception that available resources are insufficient for its purposes. The 30-member Council includes MSBA Presidents as well as judges, legislators, law professors and others. One of its proposals, that mandatory pro bono legal services be required of every Maryland lawyer, sparks debate.

Fifty years at the Maryland Bar - First row (L-R): Benjamin Swogell, Milton R. Rothstein, W. Page Dame, Jr. Second row (L-R): George V. Parkhurst, Norwood Orrick and Bernard G. Peter, April 11, 1983. Photograph by Guill Photo.

The Maryland Bar Center at 520 West Fayette Street, at the northeast corner of West Fayette and North Greene Streets, has been the first permanent headquarters of the MSBA since 1985. Designed by Francis E. Davis, it was built by the City of Baltimore in 1880 as the Male Grammar and Primary School No. 1.

OCTOBER 2, 1988 MSBA Board of Governors adopts recommendations of Special Committee on Pro Bono Services that voluntary pro bono service by all Maryland lawyers be encouraged.

JUNE 11, 1989 Herbert S. Garten, incoming MSBA President, makes voluntary pro bono legal services the highest priority of his administration. He appoints an expanded Special Committee on Pro Bono Services under the chairmanship of Stephen J. Nolan.

OCTOBER 16-20, 1989 Designated "People's Pro Bono Week in Maryland" by Governor William Donald Schaefer as part of the MSBA publicity campaign to encourage attorneys to render voluntary pro bono services.

NOVEMBER 21, 1989 People's Pro Bono Action Center, Inc., is unanimously approved by the Board of Governors as a nonprofit agency to be funded by the Maryland State Bar Association.

JANUARY 16, 1990 Articles of incorporation for the People's Pro Bono Action Center, Inc., are filed by directors Herbert S. Garten, Louise Michaux Gonzales, Stephen J. Nolan and Paul V. Carlin. Among the Action Center's purposes are to support and benefit charitable and educational activities of the MSBA and to act as statewide coordinator and clearinghouse for voluntary legal services for

Bob and Louise Gonzales, September 26, 1987. In 1991, she became the first woman elected to the Presidency of MSBA. Bob became President in 1995. Photograph by Guill Photo.

Maryland's poor. Sharon E. Goldsmith is named Executive Director of the Action Center.

JUNE 30, 1990 MSBA membership totals 13,985. The Treasurer reports total assets of $889,583.

AUGUST 4, 1990 The Harrison Tweed Award of the Standing Committee on Legal Aid and Indigent Defendants of the American Bar Association and the National Legal Aid

May 10, 1985 - First statewide long range planning conference of the MSBA convenes at the Columbia Inn. Photograph by Guill Photo.

Presentation to the MSBA of the ABA's Harrison Tweed Award for pro bono service , Chicago, August 4, 1990. (L-R): Herbert S. Garten, MSBA President; Paul V. Carlin, Executive Director; Joanne M. Garvey, Chair, ABA Standing Committee on Legal Aid and Indigent Defendants, and Clinton Lyons, Executive Director of the National Legal Aid and Defender Association.

and Defender Association is awarded to the MSBA "in recognition of the outstanding leadership and support given in developing and implementing the Maryland People's Pro Bono Campaign, an outstanding and innovative program to recruit volunteer lawyers."

JUNE 8, 1991   The first People's Pro Bono Awards are presented by the People's Pro Bono Action Center and the MSBA Special Committee on Pro Bono Legal Services at the MSBA Annual Meeting in Ocean City. The awards ceremony becomes an annual event during the business meeting of each successive convention.

1992   MSBA institutes a Professionalism Course required to be taken by new lawyers admitted to the bar of Maryland, pursuant to Bar Admission Rule 11.

APRIL 15-17, 1993   Maryland hosts the 1993 American Bar Association's Pro Bono Conference at the Omni Hotel in Baltimore, the largest in history, with over 600 participants.

SPRING 1994   The MSBA Young Lawyers Section initiates a mentorship program at Largo High School in Prince George's County, a one-on-one program between lawyers and tenth and eleventh grade students. Entitled "Each One Reach One," the program's purpose is to encourage atten-

dance in school, improve grades, and increase the student's chances to excel in careers and life. By 1995, the program expands into Montgomery County and Baltimore City.

MARCH 21, 1995   The Board of Governors of the MSBA votes to recommend to the Court of Appeals that it require that attorneys practicing in Maryland complete 30 hours of continuing legal education every two years. The proposal came from a special committee headed by former MSBA President Cleaveland D. Miller and endorsed by President P. Dennis Belman.

MARCH 31-APRIL 1, 1995   The MSBA convenes "Vision 2000," the first statewide long range planning conference in a decade at the Columbia Inn, Columbia, Maryland. The focus is on strategic planning to chart the course of the MSBA into the 21st Century. Attended by 100 bar leaders from across the State, the program features intensive day and evening working sessions, discussion groups, and speakers.

APRIL 1995   In the last five minutes of the 1995 session of the Maryland General Assembly, the Commission on the Future of Maryland's Courts, the legislative initiative of the MSBA, is enacted into law. Sponsored by Delegate Mary Louise Preis and 22 other delegates, the 31-member commission will study the Maryland judicial system and recommend long and short-range changes. Credit for the passage of the bill is given to Albert ("Buz") Winchester, MSBA Director of Legislative Relations.

JUNE 10, 1995   At the 100th annual convention of the MSBA, held in Ocean City, Maryland, Robert T. Gonzales is inducted as the 102nd President. MSBA approves changes in governance districts to reflect demographic shifts. The size of the Board of Governors (42 members) is retained, but the 12 districts from which they are elected is changed. The election of a President from Baltimore on alternating years is discontinued, to commence with the nominations for the 1996-97 President-elect.

MSBA EXECUTIVE DIRECTORS	
William P. Cunningham	1961-62
Alexander Gordon, III	1962-63
Paul R. Schlitz	1964-67
Manley E. Davis	1967-76
Arthur L. Mullen, Jr.	1976-77
William J. Smith, Jr.	1977-84
Paul V. Carlin	1985-

ADDRESS OF ROBERT T. GONZALES,
102nd PRESIDENT OF THE MARYLAND STATE BAR ASSOCIATION
SHERATON CONFERENCE CENTER, OCEAN CITY, MARYLAND
JUNE 10, 1995

"The Secretary of this Association tells me, although I knew it already, that the unbroken custom is for the President of the Association to make an address. It is called an annual address, although only made once. As a conservative man, I am going to follow the unbroken custom. It is also true that invariably in the past the President's address has been much too long. I shall also follow that precedent."

In 1920, at the MSBA's Twenty-Fifth Annual Meeting, then MSBA President Morris A. Soper opened his address with the words I just spoke to you. In those days it already was the custom for the President to address the members of the Association, and that address usually took two hours or more. I offer a compromise. I will continue the custom by delivering my remarks this morning, but I pledge to be briefer.

This is the Association's 100th annual meeting. The first meeting was held in August, 1896, at Blue Mountain House in Washington County, Maryland. In thinking about our 100th birthday, I remembered a story that I heard once about a reporter who was asked to write an article about one of the local residents who was celebrating his 100th birthday. The young and eager reporter was told that not only had the resident achieved this milestone in age, but he also had maintained amazing vigor and mental strength. Somewhat skeptical, the young reporter proceeded to the man's home. Upon his arrival, he was surprised by what he saw. But if he understood one of the keys to healthy longevity, he shouldn't have been surprised.

This Association also remains vigorous and strong, as it begins its 100th year. The mission of the Association, as originally stated in Article Two of our Constitution, is: "To advance the science of jurisprudence, to promote reform in the law, to facilitate the administration of justice, to uphold the standard of integrity, honor and courtesy in the legal profession, to encourage legal education, and to cultivate a spirit of cordiality and brotherhood among the members of the Bar."

If we had to formulate our mission today, we could do little to improve upon that original statement. The means used to achieve these objectives have varied, depending on the developments and circumstances of the times, but the funda-mental priorities remain constant. While our profession today faces many new challenges, our history demonstrates that we share several recurring issues with our predecessors.

What concerns led the original founders to create this Association? Our first President, the Honorable James McSherry, then Chief Judge of the Court of Appeals of Maryland, said, "I confess I feel a deep humiliation, admitting before an audience of intelligent and honorable Maryland lawyers that there is need of drastic measures to protect the Bar of our State from the contamination of incompetent and unworthy practitioners. My friends, let us bring the whole Maryland Bar back to the exalted standard of former days. . . ."

From the outset, the Founders recognized that for the public to have faith and confidence in the judicial system, they must also have faith in the skills and abilities of those entrusted with the role of "gate-keeper" to the system. One of the Association's very first accomplishments was the creation by Legislative Act, in 1898, of the State Board of Law Examiners. Individual lawyer skill and competency became a critical focus of the Association, and this Association took the leadership role in this effort and we continue that leadership today.

In 1920, the Bar Association was twenty-five years old. The members met in Atlantic City. The Bar had a membership of 528, and a total budget of $7,900.00. America had emerged from the "War to End All Wars" and was in the throes of the American Industrial Revolution. Legal education was again foremost in the minds of the Association members. One of the questions of the day was whether a college education should be required for admittance to the Bar. Legal reform and the administration of justice, specifically, were also debated. President Soper's address focused on reform of judicial administration in the State of Maryland. He said, "[We] will welcome any well considered plan that will tend to restore the Courts to their former dignity. . .. When the Judges are charged with the responsibility and are given the power to improve the system by which they operate. . ., and public discussion of changes that are needed and reforms that should be made - then we may expect the Judicial System to be re-established to occupy its rightful place."

The attendees were cautioned by a lawyer named John Lord O'Brian against the "Menace of Administrative Law." Mr. O'Brian deplored the acts of the Federal Government with regard to the deportation of aliens. In his address, he warned of the dangers inherent in the exercise of autocratic powers in the hands of Federal administrators. He decried the growth of the Federal Government and warned against the erosion of individual liberties at the hands of administrative law. He called on the lawyers of Maryland to assert their power and stand up for individual rights and liberties. The American public today calls for smaller government and less involvement and intrusion into their lives. The legal system has not been exempted from this call. In the halls of Congress and in Annapolis, legal reform is a major topic of legislative action, just as it was in 1920, and your Association takes an active part in today's debate.

In 1945, the MSBA convened its Fiftieth Annual Meeting at The Belvedere Hotel in Baltimore. The Association had 750 members; the budget was $17,800.00. World War II was ending. America was poised to assume its role as the dominant military and industrial power in the world. Of particular concern to the Association was the return of lawyer-veterans. It was proposed that the Bar Association take the lead in planning and developing an educational refresher program for these veterans.

The transcripts disclose that one of the speakers, Charles M. Dickson of the Texas Bar, gave a humorous address in which he told a rather derisive lawyer's joke. What was ironic to me about this lawyer's joke was that I heard the same joke repeated verbatim at a meeting less than three weeks ago. Apparently, bad lawyer jokes never seem to go out of style nor are they a freshly minted product of the current anti-lawyer culture.

At that same meeting, President Frederick W. C. Webb called for the creation of a mandatory Bar for the State of Maryland, as a means to combat the erosion of the "lawyer's image." Mr. Webb argued that the public welfare would be best served if every practicing lawyer in the State was required to maintain membership in and to uphold the principles of the Bar.

The call for mandatory membership in the Association faded, but concerns about the lawyers' public image persist. Lawyer jokes, as we have discovered, are not new, and criticism of our profession has been a thread that has woven itself throughout the history of this Association. This situation, I believe, is inevitable. No other profession has the ability or the necessity to involve itself so deeply in the people's lives. We are called upon in moments of crisis and moments of personal loss. We are often called to serve as the advocates and mediators for those who can find no other way to resolve

their problems. We operate in a judicial system that is severely under-funded, leading to a general frustration among the lawyers who use the system as well as the public. Our society, which is based on a belief in the rule of law and the fundamental premise that every person is entitled to his or her day in court, is using the judicial system to a greater extent than it has ever done in the past. Our role as lawyers in this process is destined to be a controversial one and, sometimes, a thankless one. But, at least, we should not be misled by an erroneous impression that all was "fine" in the good old days.

One of the most esteemed lawyers in the history of America, Abraham Lincoln, set a standard for handling criticism, when he wrote:

> "If I were to try to read, much less answer, all the attacks made on me, this shop might as well be closed for any other business. I do the very best I know how, and I mean to keep doing so until the end. If the end brings me out all right, what is said against me won't amount to anything. If the end brings me out wrong, ten angels swearing I was right would make no difference."

In my view, this approach applies to current lawyer criticism. If an unflattering image is the price to be paid for the pursuit of justice, then it is a price that must be paid. However, if some of the unflattering image is the result of undesirable practices, then we must do the very best we know how to correct those.

In 1970, the Bar Association held its 75th Annual Meeting in Atlantic City, New Jersey. Many of you here today were in attendance then. At that meeting the Code of Professional Responsibility was debated and adopted. So, too, was a resolution in support of a statewide district court system. In his address, President E. Dale Adkins, Jr., focused on what he called, "A Crisis of Confidence in Our Judicial System." He remarked that " . . . public discontent and distrust of the judicial process had been fanned into roaring flames by a recent series of controversial and highly publicized events relating to the Court System . . . ." He made particular reference to a sensational and prolonged trial receiving national coverage. That trial was the trial of the "Chicago Seven." He urged the members of the Bar to use their teaching abilities to explain the judicial system to the public and to become an interpreter and defender of the Courts and of the rule of law. In the face of today's current headlines and debate of the effectiveness of the judicial process, we can well heed the same advice.

Even this limited "look back" shows that many of the issues which affected our predecessors, e.g., legal education and competency, protection of the public, legal and judicial reform, and public perception of lawyers, are still very much with us today.

Indeed, many of these same issues were raised at the Vision 2000 Conference held in March of this year. At that Conference, over 100 attorneys and judges tackled the challenges of addressing these issues and others, in today's context and charting the Association's course into the next century.

The preliminary report identifies several areas in which our members want the Association to continue to play a major role. Two received high priority rating and are of particular importance to me: (1) dissemination of information concerning practitioner technology, law office management, computer training and technological assistance; and (2) broadening member participation in this Association, creating an all inclusive membership.

In selecting these two, I was influenced by my belief that the single most important professional responsibility any lawyer has is to represent his or her clients well. Nothing transcends that duty. I also believe that the single most important responsibility that any bar association has to its members is to help its lawyers achieve their maximum potential in meeting their number one responsibility. Nothing transcends that duty.

Effective client representation in today's "information revolution," especially in a mature market, is a daunting task for many of our members. Whether in private practice, government service or as house counsel, a lawyer's need for office management and technology training is critical in order to serve the client well. I have proposed to the Board of Governors that the Association add a law practice management consultant to the Bar Staff. Based on a program now existing in North Carolina, this individual would offer to lawyers assistance in assessing and improving their management practices and procedures. The primary focus will be on voluntary "in-house" law office reviews of lawyers' practices and procedures. In a review, management practices and procedures are evaluated and recommendations for improvement are made. There is an educational component as well as a follow-up to ensure that the recommendations are working. The consultant reviews systems for docket control and conflicts checking, maintenance of excellent client relations, quality control, confidentiality, supervision and training of support staff, file management, billing and timekeeping, and effective internal and external communications. This service will be within the financial reach of each member of the Association, including solo and small-firm practitioners, as well as public service attorneys.

In its duty to help each member of the Association reach his or her maximum potential, this Association must provide the opportunity of full participation to each of its members. A review of this Association's history would be incomplete if it did not recognize that such participation was not always encouraged and, in many cases, denied. Progress has been made in recent years, and it is appropriate that as we celebrate our Centennial Year, I will have the privilege of sharing this 100th Anniversary with Judge Barbara Howe, the second woman President of this Association. Perceptions remain, however, that the leadership of this Association may still be closed to some.

Our Bar Association cannot succeed in the future without using the talents and energy of our diverse membership. I believe that such participation must be aggressively pursued and sustained as a policy of the Association. However, we must set our goals beyond participation. We must make it clear that such participation is a prelude to leadership. I am proposing the creation of a leadership academy. I will be working with the Young Lawyers Section, the Special Committee on Minorities in the Profession, and other sections and minority Bars in the development of the academy. For the first class of the academy, we will recruit younger lawyers who have demonstrated leadership abilities, with an emphasis on diversity. This leadership class will be educated in the management and operation of the Association, will be invited to participate in our events throughout the year, and encouraged to serve on our committees and sections.

Also, from my own experience, I can attest to the value of a mentor. In my years with the Association, I have been fortunate to have received the interest and advice of several Bar leaders. I have spoken with some of our Past Presidents and have asked them to serve as mentors to members of the Academy. I have received their enthusiastic support, and I will be speaking to the remaining Past Presidents in the future. I believe the Past Presidents' interest in the individual will be a key factor in the development of these potential leaders.

Remember the reporter interviewing the gentleman? When the reporter arrived at the gentleman's home, the gentlemen was planting trees along his driveway. The reporter was struck by the fact that the trees were only a foot in height. He was compelled to ask the gentleman why he would take the time to plant the trees, with such little expectation of watching them grow to maturity. The gentleman looked at the reporter and replied, "Think how beautiful they will be in 100 years."

As our Bar Association celebrates its 100th year, let all of us take an interest in the programs that not only benefit us today, but also plant the seeds for improvement for those who follow us, and allow us to say, "Think how good they will be in 100 years."

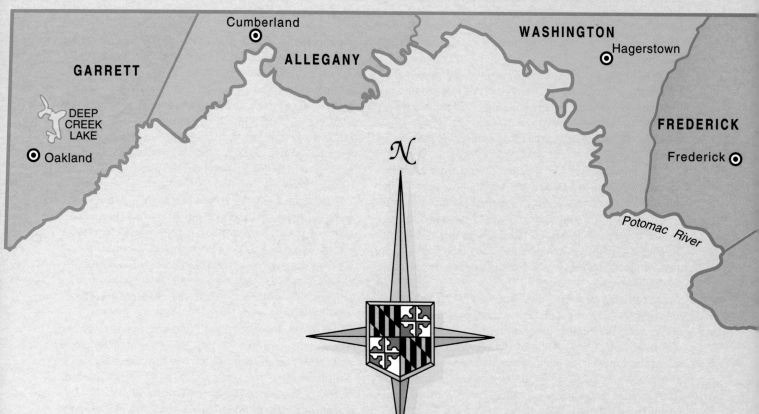

A TOUR THROUGH MARYLAND AND THE DISTRICT OF COLUMBIA

FEATURING MARYLAND LAWYERS, CASES AND COURTHOUSES

"In the courthouses every person stands equal in the eyes of the law and it doesn't matter who the opponent is. Ordinary citizens have a chance to communicate and be heard. . . .

"We know there are immunities, there are special privileges, and there are burdens that can be placed on various litigants, but we also know that in the eyes of judges and juries, people who are parties to judicial proceedings all bear the same name. They're all plaintiffs and defendants, they're the government and the defendant. We all know that all parties, no matter where they work outside of court, how successful or unsuccessful they may have been outside of court, their power with respect to the Judicial Branch of government depends not on wealth, not on station, but on the strength of their cases. It depends on their evidence. If they have enough evidence, they will win, and if they do not have enough, they will lose. And that's the essence of equal justice under law.

"I believe this with all my heart. That's why I'm proud to be a lawyer, prouder even to be a trial lawyer, and so especially proud to train young law students to be trial lawyers. It is in the courtroom where they will appear, more than anywhere else in this country, that equality is clearest. When a plaintiff or a defendant appears in court, each is automatically given the stature of a litigant. For every complaint, there is an answer; for every motion, there is a response; for every charge, there is a plea. And as in no other place, every litigant has an equal chance to be heard."

— Professor Stephen Allan Saltzburg, Howrey Professor of Trial Advocacy, Litigation, and Professional Responsibility, National Law Center of the George Washington University, from a speech delivered at the 64th Annual Fourth Circuit Judicial Conference, June 30, 1994.

Great Falls of the Potomac,
Montgomery County.

Skipjack races on the
Chesapeake Bay.

Inset: Skipjack near Greenbury
Point, where the Severn River
meets the Chesapeake Bay,
Anne Arundel Country.

The wooden dome on Maryland's historic State House, Annapolis.

Chesapeake Bay Maritime Museum, St. Michaels, Talbot County.

Sunset at Crisfield, Somerset County.

Old cemetery and church,
St. Mary's City.

Parallel spans over the Chesapeake Bay connect the Western and Eastern Shores of Maryland.

Calvert Cliffs, Calvert County.

The Pocomoke River at
Milburn Landing State Park,
Worcester County.

The Department of Agriculture,
Prince George's County.

Kent Island Sunset,
Queen Anne's County.

Along the C&O Canal,
Montgomery County,
Maryland.

The beach on
Assateague Island,
Worcester County.

Aerial view of Cambridge and the old Emerson Harrington Bridge, Dorchester County, May, 1976.

Aerial view of Fort McHenry,
Baltimore, Maryland.

Swallow Falls,
Garrett County.

Sugarloaf Mountain from the
front yard of the Comus Inn,
Montgomery County.

Governor William Preston Lane
Memorial Bridge at sunset on
the Chesapeake Bay.

ABOVE: The large circuit courtroom in the Allegany County courthouse.
Photograph by Linda Johnson.

RIGHT: The Allegany County Courthouse, Cumberland, Maryland.
Photograph by Linda Johnson.

June 2, 1970. On the occasion of his investiture as U.S. Attorney for the District of Maryland, George Beall (R) is congratulated by his father, former U.S. Senator J. Glenn Beall, Sr., and U.S. Senator Charles McC. Mathias, Jr. Photograph by Francis DeGennaro.

PRESIDENTS OF THE MSBA - No. 2
1897-98
ROBERT R. HENDERSON (1858-1921)

At his nomination in 1897 as the second President of the MSBA, Robert R. Henderson was called "the father of this Association." The speaker, Judge David W. Sloan, explained: "Some two years ago a movement was made in the Allegany Bar Association looking to the establishment of a State Bar Association, but it was not at that time pressed. When Mr. Henderson was elected the President of that Association, he took the matter up and following out the instructions of the resolution, he appointed a committee, and while the committee worked faithfully, and honestly, it was working under the pressure and push of Mr. Henderson."

His maternal great-grandfather was Captain David Lynn, one of the founders of Cumberland, who commanded a company in the American army during the Revolutionary War. His father was superintendent of the Cumberland Coal and Iron Company, with headquarters at Eckhart Mines, the town where Judge Henderson was born. At Princeton University, he was a classmate of Woodrow Wilson, who was a lifelong friend, although the two differed politically. He graduated from the University of Maryland Law School in 1881 and studied law in the office of A. Hunter Boyd, another MSBA President from Cumberland and later Chief Judge of the Court of Appeals. He was elected Associate

Judge of the Fourth Judicial Circuit (Garrett, Allegany and Washington Counties) as a Republican in 1903 and reelected in 1919. Judge Henderson resigned from the bench in 1921 and died a few months later on December 20, 1921. His son, George Henderson, was also a Cumberland lawyer who served as a Circuit Judge from Allegany County.

PRESIDENTS OF THE MSBA - No. 7
1902-03
BENJAMIN A. RICHMOND (1849-1922)

Mr. Richmond's obituary in the 1922 *Maryland Bar Transactions* said that he was "the recognized leader of the Western Maryland Bar." He was born at Libertytown, Frederick County, and after his admission to the bar in 1873, practiced law for a short time in Indianapolis, Indiana. He settled in Cumberland in 1874 and soon took his place as the leading attorney there. A Republican, he was elected State's Attorney for Allegany County. He also served as President of the State Board of Law Examiners for ten years before his death on February 22, 1922.

PRESIDENTS OF THE MSBA - No. 13
1908-09
WILLIAM C. DEVECMON (1861-1939)

Mr. Devecmon was an accomplished Shakespearean scholar who taught Latin and Greek at St. John's College in Annapolis, his *alma mater*. Born in Cumberland on February 2, 1861, he was one of the lawyers from Allegany County who promoted the establishment of a state bar association. Indeed, it was he who called to order the founding meeting of the Maryland State Bar Association at the Blue Mountain House on Friday, August 28, 1896. Twenty years later he moved to Baltimore, where he died on May 22, 1939, at the age of 78.

PRESIDENTS OF THE MSBA - No. 17
1912-13
A. HUNTER BOYD (1849-1925)

Andrew Hunter Boyd was born in Winchester, Virginia, July 15, 1849. He was educated at private schools in Winchester and at Washington & Lee University and the University of Virginia. He graduated from the law school of the Washington & Lee University in June, 1871. He settled in Cumberland, Maryland, in August, 1871, and began the practice of law there. In November, 1875, he was elected State's Attorney for Allegany County. On May 1, 1893, he was appointed Chief Judge of the Fourth Judicial Circuit by Governor Frank Brown, and was elected to that position the following November. He later became Chief Judge of the Court of Appeals of Maryland.

Robert Randolph Henderson

Benjamin Armstrong Richmond

William C. Devecmon

A. Hunter Boyd

PRESIDENTS OF THE MSBA - No. 36
1931-32
D. LINDLEY SLOAN (1874-1962)

Judge Sloan served as Chief Judge of the Fourth Judicial Circuit and Associate Judge of the Court of Appeals from his election in 1926 until he reached the mandatory retirement age of 70 in 1944. (In those days, Chief Judges of the various judicial circuits also served on the Court of Appeals of Maryland.)

The following story was told by William Gunter, a personal friend of Judge Sloan, at the January, 1961, MSBA Midwinter Meeting:

Judge Sloan's first day on the Circuit Court bench took place at the Garrett County Court House in the December Term 1926. There was an impressive ceremony with Judges Wagaman and Doub present. The ceremonies included the presentation to the new Judge of a homemade gavel hued from an old oak tree from the lands of Meshach Browning, Garrett County's most noted hunter. Immediately after the ceremony, the elder Judges departed, leaving the new Judge to hold the bag. The first case was a murder case. The prisoner was a woman who had the entire sympathy of the crowded courtroom. As the jury retired from the courtroom to begin deliberations, the audience was warned by the new Judge against making any demonstrations upon the return of the jury, which came back in ten minutes. The jury's baldheaded rotund foreman, Senator McCulloh, arose and announced the verdict of "not guilty."

Pandemonium immediately broke loose in the courtroom, whereupon the new Judge excitedly grabbed the new gavel, gave it a bang on the desk, which caused the head to fly off and violently strike the foreman of the jury on his bald head.

He served as Chief Judge of the Court of Appeals upon the death of Carroll T. Bond in 1943. During his tenure on the Court, he participated in the decision of some 3,000 cases, running from 152 Md. to 182 Md. He was born in Pekin, Allegany County, and read law in the Cumberland office of his cousin, Judge David W. Sloan, one of the charter members of the MSBA. He died May 13, 1962, at the age of 88.

PRESIDENTS OF THE MSBA - No. 47
1940-41
WALTER C. CAPPER (1885-1962)

In his 1941 President's Address to the MSBA, entitled *The New Nationalism,* Walter Capper deplored much of the New Deal legislation enacted over the preceding eight years by Congress to deal with the Depression, and criticized recent decisions of the Supreme Court upholding it. "The Constitution was not intended to create a Federal Government which would completely submerge the States," he said. "The equilibrium of our dual form of Government has been disturbed and its purpose rendered obscure by these enactments and decisions."

He was born on January 5, 1885, on a farm near Winchester, Virginia, and rose to become one of Western Maryland's foremost trial attorneys. He began his career at the bar in association with Benjamin A. Richmond, his predecessor as President of the MSBA. At various times he

D. Lindley Sloan   Walter C. Capper   William C. Walsh

represented the Commissioners of Allegany County, the Western Maryland Railway, and the First National Bank and Trust Company of Cumberland. In 1944, he was appointed Chief Judge of the Fourth Judicial Circuit, and thereby became a member of the Court of Appeals of Maryland. He served on the Bond Commission that resulted in the reorganization of the Court of Appeals, and thereby helped legislate himself out of a seat on the appellate court. He was then appointed Associate Judge of the Fourth Judicial Circuit, a position he held until November, 1946. After leaving the bench, Judge Capper returned to the practice of law as a member of the firm of Capper, Jenkins and Berry. He died on January 21, 1962.

PRESIDENTS OF THE MSBA - No. 55
1948-49
WILLIAM C. WALSH (1890-1975)

William C. Walsh was a Judge of the Maryland Court of Appeals, Attorney General of Maryland, and a major figure in the State Democratic Party. He was born in Cumberland on April 2, 1890, the eldest son of William E. Walsh, attorney and charter member of the MSBA. Judge Walsh earned his law degree from Catholic University Law School in 1913. He served in G Company of the Maryland National Guard during General Pershing's 1916 Mexican campaign against Pancho Villa. During World War I he was a first lieutenant in a machine gun company in the 113th Infantry Regiment of the 29th Division in France. In 1921, Judge Walsh was appointed to the Circuit Court bench to fill the vacancy caused by the resignation of Judge Robert Henderson, his predecessor as President of the MSBA. Defeated in the fall election by Albert L. Doub, he was appointed Chief Judge of

the Fourth Judicial Circuit, and also served at the same time on the Court of Appeals, from 1924 to 1926. He was elected Attorney General of Maryland in 1938. While serving in that capacity, he addressed the MSBA in January, 1941, and proposed restructuring the Court of Appeals to limit its members to strictly appellate functions. The proposal, endorsed by the Association, resulted in the creation of the Bond Commission which formulated a constitutional amendment that the voters of Maryland approved in November, 1944.

At the 1961 MSBA convention aboard the cruise ship VICTORIA, William C. Walsh gave what President William J. McWilliams called "probably the most unusual address that has ever been delivered to the Maryland State Bar Association." It was a poignant, yet inspiring report of his visit to Shanghai the previous year to visit his brother, Bishop James Edward Walsh, a Roman Catholic missionary, who was imprisoned in Communist China from 1958 to 1970.

Judge Walsh practiced law in both Cumberland and Baltimore. With Senator Millard E. Tydings, he was a member of the Baltimore firm of Tydings, Walsh, Levy and Archer, and later Miles, Walsh, O'Brien and Morris. In Cumberland he practiced with his son, William, in the family firm of Walsh & Walsh. He died in Cumberland on June 17, 1975.

ANNE ARUNDEL COUNTY

Anne Arundel County was established in 1650, a year after the death of the wife of Cecil Calvert, second Lord Baltimore, and was named in her memory. Her ancestors came to England with William the Conqueror in 1066. Her family name was derived from the swallows of Normandy, the French word *l'hirondelle* meaning "swallow." Annapolis, the county seat and capital of the State, was originally known as Anne Arundell's Towne before it was renamed in honor of Queen Anne. To Kunta Kinte, Alex Haley's great-great-great-great-grandfather, it was *"Naplis,"* the port of entry to which he was brought as a slave from Africa on September 29, 1767. At the close of the American Revolution, the city served briefly as the capital of the United States, when the Continental Congress met in the old State House to receive Washington's commission and ratify the Treaty of Paris. The Maryland State House is the oldest building in the United States in continuous legislative use. St. John's College, renowned for its great books curriculum, was founded there as King William's School in 1695. Annapolis has been the site of the U.S. Naval Academy since 1845, except for the brief period during and after the Civil War when the Academy was relocated in Newport. Annapolis exudes the hustle and bustle of a modern city, while retaining the charm and flavor of a colonial seaport.

For the past three centuries, the appellate courts of Maryland have been conducted in various locations in Annapolis. In colonial times, Annapolis was the center of the legal profession in Maryland. The lawyers followed the provincial courts there when the capital was moved from St. Mary's City in 1695. At each term of court, the city's taverns and inns overflowed with the judges, lawyers and litigants who came to conduct or attend the proceedings. Today, the Court of Appeals, and the intermediate appellate court, the Court of Special Appeals, are housed in a modern building located on Rowe Boulevard on the northern approach to the city. Across the highway in a gleaming new building, the Maryland State Archives contains the records of government that date back to Maryland's beginning as an English colony.

Royal G. Shannonhouse, III, who practices law in Annapolis with the firm of Dalnekoff & Mason, came to the Maryland bar by an unlikely route. Born in North Carolina in 1929, he was admitted to the bar of his home state in 1955 after graduating from the University of North Carolina School of Law and passing the bar examination. In the fall

of 1969, he became one of the first three full-time professors at the new day school of the University of Baltimore School of Law.

From its founding in 1925 until 1969, the law school had been strictly a part-time operation, staffed by lawyers and judges who lived the law by day and taught it at night. Even though it had turned out generations of fine Maryland lawyers, the school was accredited only by the State, but not by the American Bar Association or the American Association of Law Schools. To achieve accreditation, the trustees recruited Dean Joseph Curtis (1914-1987) from the Marshall-Wythe School of Law at the College of William and Mary. One of the first things he did was hire Mr. Shannonhouse to teach legal research and writing, property, and criminal law. In just three years, by August, 1972, the University of Baltimore School of Law had achieved provisional accreditation by the ABA, with full accreditation in 1978.

Royal Shannonhouse was the quintessential law professor, who demanded much, but who gave 150% of himself to the task of teaching. He inspired his students to want to be the best lawyers they could be. By 1983, Mr. Shannonhouse had become a part-time adjunct professor at the school, having joined the Annapolis law firm of Blumenthal, Wayson, Downs & Offutt, P.A., on a full-time basis as "of counsel." His duties included drafting pleadings, conferring with members of the firm on litigation strategies in given cases, and performing legal research, but not appearing in court. In December, 1986, he applied to the Board of Law Examiners under Bar Admission Rule 14 that allowed out-of-state attorneys to take an abbreviated bar examination, if they have practiced law, taught in an accredited law school, or been a judge of a court of record for five of the preceding seven years. He took the exam in February, 1987, was notified that he passed, but that he had not been qualified to sit for the short test. While stating the obvious that Mr. Shannonhouse was "a distinguished lawyer and law professor who has contributed to the law profession in this State and who performs superior work for his firm," the Board denied his application on the alternative grounds that his work at the law firm did not amount to practicing law, but that if it did, it was unauthorized practice.

In an opinion bearing the thinly-disguised style of *In re Application of R.G.S.*, 312 Md. 626, 541 A.2d 977 (1988), the Court of Appeals, by a bare majority, reversed. It held that his work at the firm qualified as the authorized practice of law, found that the combined total of seven years spent

GEORGE WASHINGTON'S FINEST HOUR

In his delightful book, *Washington Bowed,* the late Theodore R. McKeldin (1900-1974), twice Governor of Maryland and Mayor of Baltimore, told the story of George Washington's finest hour. The date was December 23, 1783, the place, the old Senate Chamber in the Maryland State House in Annapolis where the U. S. Congress was convened. Washington came there that day to tender his resignation as Commander-in-chief of the Continental Army. The War of Independence with England had been won, and Washington was universally hailed as the savior of his country. But the members of Congress, jealous of their prerogatives and intent on preserving civilian authority over the military, designed the ceremony of resignation to humiliate the General. It was ordained that they should sit with their heads covered during Washington's remarks, and only upon the conclusion of his address would they stand and lift their hats. The rules stated that they were not to bow to him under any circumstances. And that is what happened. But at the dramatic moment when Washington relin-

Washington resigning his commission as Commander-in-Chief of the Continental Army. From the painting by Edwin White in the State House at Annapolis.

Governor Theodore R. McKeldin. Photograph by Guill Photo.

quished his power and office, when he was once again a private citizen, *he* bowed to *them,* as a gesture of what Mr. McKeldin called his "affirmation of government by the elected representatives of the people." There was not a dry eye in the house. Here was the greatest man in America, who, if he had so desired, might have seized power and set himself up as dictator. But he was not so inclined.

Governor McKeldin related this story to President Eisenhower on one of his visits to Maryland in the 1950s. It was Ike's opinion that the greatest event in Washington's life was his command of the troops at Valley Forge. It was only natural for one who had been Supreme Allied Commander in Europe during the Second World War to hold such a belief. Ike had had his own Valley Forge during the Battle of the Bulge in 1944. Washington's ultimate victory and his own must have seemed providential to him.

Washington initially decided not to attend the Philadelphia Convention in 1787. His health was not good and he longed to remain in retirement at Mount Vernon. Without his prestige and popularity, there might have been no Convention and no Constitution. Luckily for this nation and the cause of democratic government, George Washington changed his mind and went to Philadelphia. There he performed his most indispensable service, as President of the Constitutional Convention.

practicing law and teaching at an *accredited* law school satisfied the requirements of Rule 14. It turned out that the standards he had set for his students and the accreditation he had helped achieve for the University of Baltimore School of Law helped to make Royal Shannonhouse a *Maryland lawyer.*

The Anne Arundel County Courthouse has always been

the center of the local bar. It was there on January 2, 1931, that 17 lawyers founded the Bar Association of Anne

RIGHT: Statue of Chief Justice Roger Brooke Taney in front of the Maryland State House.

Right Insets: Governor Parris N. Glendening; Lieutenant Governor Kathleen Kennedy Townsend. Photographs courtesy of Richard Tomlinson.

William Paca, Maryland Governor and its first U.S. District Judge.

The William Paca House at 186 Prince George Street, was built by the young Harford County lawyer during 1763-65. It was saved from demolition and restored by Historic Annapolis, Inc. Photograph by Coos Hamburger.

Arundel County. Today, the Bar Association has a membership of 775 lawyers who practice law in every part of the county. The association's archives are carefully preserved by Melvin Hoffman, Esquire, historian of the bar.

The landmark decision of the U.S. Supreme Court in *Brady v. Maryland*, 373 U.S. 83, 83 S. Ct. 1194, 10 L.Ed.2d 215 (1963), resulted from a murder conviction rendered by a jury sitting in the Anne Arundel County Courthouse. The prosecution did not inform the accused that his accomplice in a robbery had confessed to killing the victim. The Supreme Court agreed with the Maryland Court of Appeals that the State had a duty to disclose exculpatory evidence to the defense and that the failure to do so was a denial of due process.

Fifteen years before *Brown v. Board of Education*, 347 U.S. 483, 74 S.Ct. 686, 98 L.Ed. 873 (1954). Thurgood Marshall represented Walter S. Mills, an African-American high school principal, in a class action suit for equal pay brought in the Federal court in Maryland. In a history-making decision rendered in *Mills v. Board of Education of Anne Arundel County*, 30 F.Supp. 245 (D.Md.1939), U.S. District Judge W. Calvin Chesnut enjoined the board from paying black educators less than their white counterparts, holding that the difference in salaries paid to white and black public school teachers was unlawful discrimination based solely on race and color.

CHIEF JUDGE ROBERT C. MURPHY

Upon his retirement in 1996, Robert C. Murphy will have served as Chief Judge of the Court of Appeals of Maryland for 24 years—longer than any other Chief Judge in the history of the court, (with the exception of Chief Judge Benjamin Rumsey, the very first Chief Judge, who served 28 years, 1778-1806). For the five years before he assumed the position in 1972, he was Chief Judge—the first—of the Court of Special Appeals. He selected kelly green as the color of the volumes containing the reports of cases decided by the newly-created court. His tenure on both courts was marked by innovation guided with stability. He will rank as one of the great Judges in the history of Maryland.

Chief Judges Robert C. Murphy (R) and Alan M. Wilner (L). Photograph by Susan M. Marzetta.

Severn Teackle Wallis, first President of the Bar Association of Baltimore City.

tion that reformed the structure of the city's courts. The Maryland Constitution of 1867 created for Baltimore a cumbersome judicial system known as "The Supreme Bench of Baltimore City." Within the Supreme Bench were six separate courts, each with its own clerk, having specialized functions and overlapping authority, confusing to the Bar and the public. In 1980, reform legislation drafted by the City Bar allowed the voters of Maryland to abolish this arcane system by their approval of a constitutional amendment. In 1983, the Circuit Court for Baltimore City came into being, its various functions and jurisdiction united in one clerk's office. Saundra E. Banks, an African-American woman, was the first person elected clerk of the new court, and continues to serve in that position today.

In 1986, Circuit Judge John Carroll Byrnes led the movement to create The Baltimore Courthouse and Law Museum Foundation, Inc., to restore the building. In 1991, members of the Bar Association of Baltimore City and the Monumental

City Bar Association raised $400,000 to renovate Courtroom 400, the ceremonial courtroom in which investitures and memorial proceedings have always been conducted. In 1988, the Bar Association honored Administrative Judge Joseph H.H. Kaplan for his leadership in this effort and for creating six modern courtrooms in the former U.S. Courthouse and Post Office.

THE TWO LAW SCHOOLS IN MARYLAND ARE LOCATED IN BALTIMORE CITY

The University of Maryland School of Law

The University of Maryland School of Law is the oldest law school in Maryland and one of the oldest in the nation, dating from the year 1813 when David Hoffman was appointed the first Professor of Law in the history of the school. It took him 11 years before the curriculum he was preparing was ready for

Professor David Hoffman, LL.D. Photograph of cameo portrait from Cordell, *The University of Maryland* (1907).

use. He began giving lectures in 1824 under the auspices of the medical faculty of the University. He directed the school until 1833, after which legal instruction was suspended for 37 years. In February, 1870, the law school was revived

The Edward A. Garmatz Federal Building and U.S. Courthouse opened in 1976 and was named in honor of the veteran Maryland Congressman. Photograph by Linda Johnson.

The Clarence M. Mitchell, Jr., Courthouse, with the Battle Monument in the foreground. Photograph by Linda Johnson.

when 20 students enrolled in classes held in a building on Mulberry Street. The first law class of six students graduated in June, 1871. From these humble beginnings, the University of Maryland School of Law grew into a nationally-known institution of legal learning. By 1930 the law school was accredited by the American Bar Association and the following year by the American Association of Law Schools.

Today the School of Law is housed in William Preston Lane Hall at 500 West Baltimore Street, built in 1967 during the deanship of William P. Cunningham. The Thurgood Marshall Law Library, located on Paca Street, was dedicated in 1982. The old Westminster Presbyterian Church, was acquired in trust and restored as "Westminster Hall," to use for academic and social events. The adjoining cemetery contains the graves of Edgar Allan Poe (1809-1849) and many of Baltimore's foremost citizens.

The progress of the school has continued under the able leadership of Dean Donald Gifford. The University of Maryland School of Law remains a national leader in providing quality legal education.

The University of Baltimore School of Law

The University of Baltimore was a private, non-profit institution of higher learning for nearly the first 50 years of its existence until it joined the State system in 1974. Evening schools of law and business founded in 1925 were joined by a two-year Junior College in 1937 and a full-time College of Liberal Arts in 1961. In 1969, a day law program was begun and the first full-time law faculty was hired. The law school achieved provisional accreditation by the ABA in

August, 1972, full accreditation in 1978, and was later accredited by AALS. In 1982, under the stewardship of Dean Laurence M. Katz, a new law school building was completed on the corner of Mt. Royal and Maryland Avenues. The building was recently renamed The John and Frances Angelos Law Center in honor of the parents of Peter G. Angelos, graduate and benefactor of the school, and owner of the Baltimore Orioles.

Dean John A. Sebert, at the helm of the law school since 1993, recently announced the establishment of the Center for International and Comparative Law and a comprehensive revision of the upper-class curriculum. The goal is to continue to improve the quality of the academic program so that it will "graduate students who are effective, reflective and responsible attorneys." The University of Baltimore School of Law continues to enjoy a reputation as the provider of sound legal training with a practical flavor.

In 1988, when Judge Solomon Baylor wrote an article for the *Maryland Bar Journal* in which he paid tribute to the African-American Judges in Maryland, he omitted one of the best — himself! He has devoted his professional life to

The John and Frances Angelos Law Center at the University of Baltimore School of Law.

The Thurgood Marshall Law Library of the University of Maryland School of Law.

SUPERMAN OF THE LAW: LUTHER MARTIN (1748-1826)

History has given little credit to Maryland's most outstanding delegate to the Philadelphia Convention that produced the Constitution of the United States in 1787. His name was Luther Martin, perhaps America's greatest lawyer from before the Revolution to the Federal Period. At the time of the Constitutional Convention, although he was only 39 years old, Luther Martin had already been Attorney General of Maryland for nine years, described by Henry Adams as "rollicking, witty, audacious, drunken, generous, slovenly and grand."

He had a dramatic impact on the final document, opposing a number of provisions which, had they been incorporated in the Constitution, would have prevented ratification. One of these was James Madison's proposal that the President sit with the Supreme Court as a council of revision for the purpose of vetoing state laws. To Luther Martin, Americans owe the equal representation of states in the U.S. Senate, the later addition of a Bill of Rights for which Martin clamored, and the Supremacy Clause in Article VI, Clause 2, which is the keystone of Federalism.

After his unsuccessful fight against ratification, Luther Martin became one of the Constitution's staunchest supporters. He successfully defended Justice Samuel Chase from impeachment and Aaron Burr on a treason charge and appeared before the Supreme Court as counsel for the State in the landmark case of *McCulloch v. Maryland*, 4 U.S. 415 (4 Wheat. 316), 4 L.Ed. 579 (1819).

In Luther Martin's old age, the Maryland General Assembly assessed a $5 fee for his support from members of the legal profession. On July 10, 1826, he died in New York at the home of Aaron Burr, who befriended him. He was buried in an unmarked grave in the churchyard of St. John's Chapel that has long since been paved over. There is no monument to him in Maryland either.

Luther Martin - portrait attributed to Cephas Thompson - Courtesy Baltimore Bar Library.

---

representing the less fortunate and to preserving the history of the African-American lawyers of Maryland. Born in King William County, Virginia, on April 25, 1922, he graduated from Baltimore's Frederick Douglass Senior High School, Coppin State College and the University of Maryland School of Law (LL.B. 1951). He served as Assistant City Solicitor and member of the Zoning Board before his appointment to the District Court of Maryland for Baltimore City in 1970. In 1978, he became the 100th Judge to serve on the Supreme Bench of Baltimore City (now the Circuit Court). After his retirement in 1985, he led campaigns to raise funds for the commissioning of portraits of Justice Thurgood Marshall, Juanita Jackson Mitchell and Clarence M. Mitchell, Jr., to be hung in the city courthouse. One day his portrait will undoubtedly join theirs.

It was the exclusion of African-American attorneys from membership in the Bar Association of Baltimore City and the Maryland State Bar Association that led to the founding of the Monumental City Bar Association in the early 1930s. The organization was incorporated on April 2, 1935, by Thurgood Marshall, Warner T. McGuinn, George J. Evans, Emory R. Cole, W. Ashbie Hawkins, Robert McGuinn and Karl F. Phillips. That year some of its members scored

a victory in the successful prosecution of a lawsuit demanding an end to segregation at the University of Maryland School of Law. Gradually doors formerly closed were opened, and African-American lawyers gained justified recognition for their competence and ability. Today, decades after the demise of "whites-only," the Monumental City Bar Association continues to have relevance, its members actively engaged in the work of the Maryland State and Baltimore City Bar Associations.

Everett J. Waring (1859-1915) became the first African-American attorney to practice before the State courts of Maryland when the Judges of the Supreme Bench of Baltimore City admitted him to the bar in October, 1885. He soon rose to prominence, and is believed to be the first African-American lawyer to argue before the U.S. Supreme Court, in the case of *Jones v. U.S.*, 137 U.S. 202 (1890), in which he had also appeared at trial for the defense.

Linwood G. Koger, Sr. (1889-1973) and John R. Hargrove (1923-) were the first African-American members admitted to the Maryland State Bar Association on June 24, 1960. Mr. Koger, the son of a freed slave, was born in North Carolina but grew up in the District of Columbia. He served in France during World War I and was

Judge Joseph H. H. Kaplan, Administrative Judge of the Circuit Court for Baltimore City.

Judge Joseph C. Howard. Photograph from a portrait by Simmie Knox.

Kurt L. Schmoke, Mayor of Baltimore.

George L. Russell, Jr. Photograph by Kenneth L. Brooks Studios, Inc.

wounded in action. After receiving his law degree from Howard University, Mr. Koger was admitted to the Maryland bar in 1923. He served as Assistant City Solicitor from 1944-48, and as a police magistrate from 1955-59. He served five terms as President of the Monumental City Bar Association. A Republican, he ran unsuccessfully for the Baltimore City Council, House of Delegates and Maryland Senate.

John R. Hargrove, a graduate of Howard University and the University of Maryland School of Law, was admitted to the Maryland bar in 1950. He practiced law in Baltimore for five years with Benjamin Forman, David Mason and W.A.C. Hughes. In October, 1955, he was appointed Assistant U.S. Attorney by George C. Doub, and thus became the first African-American to hold that position in the District of Maryland. He was First Assistant by 1962 when he left the office to accept a judgeship on the People's Court, to succeed Judge E. Everett Lane, the first African-American judge appointed in Maryland. Judge Hargrove later served on the Municipal Court, as Administrative Judge of the District Court of Maryland for Baltimore City, Associate Judge of the Supreme Bench of Baltimore City, and currently, as Senior Judge on the U.S. District Court.

George L. Russell, Jr., became the first African-American to serve as a Circuit Judge in Maryland when he was appointed to the Supreme Bench of Baltimore City by Governor Tawes in 1966, the first black City Solicitor of Baltimore from 1968-74, and the first black President of the Bar Association of Baltimore City in 1974. He was a partner in the law firm of Russell and Thompson, P.A., which merged with Piper & Marbury in 1986. He was one of the first four African-American attorneys to be elected to the American College of Trial Lawyers. He was recently honored by the Fellows of the Maryland Bar Foundation for professional legal excellence. In August, 1995, he was honored by his induction into the Hall of Fame of the National Bar Association at its convention held in Baltimore.

Judge Joseph C. Howard was the first African-American to be elected a Circuit Judge in the State of Maryland without first having been appointed when he was elected to the Supreme Bench of Baltimore City (now the Circuit Court for Baltimore City) in 1968. He served there for more than a decade before his appointment by President Carter to the U.S. District Court for the District of Maryland in 1979, the first African-American Judge to adorn that bench.

During his senior year at Morgan State University, future Judge Harry A. Cole first came to public attention as President of the Student Council. On April 24, 1942, he organized a "March on Annapolis," in conjunction with Dr. Carl Murphy, publisher of the *Baltimore Afro-American* newspaper; Lilly May Carroll Jackson, head of the N.A.A.C.P. in Baltimore; and her daughter, future lawyer Juanita Jackson Mitchell. Nearly 2,000 African-American citizens converged on the State capital to demand repeal of Maryland's Jim Crow laws. They came to the State House where they had a cordial audience with Governor Herbert R. O'Conor. The nation had just entered the Second World War and the time was ripe for reform. As the *Afro-American* reported the next day:

Robert B. Watts

Charles H. Dorsey, Jr.

After the war, he enrolled at the University of Maryland School of Law. He was inspired to become a lawyer by W.A.C. Hughes, the Baltimore legal giant of an earlier generation. He graduated in 1949, passed the Maryland bar examination the same year and joined his mentor, Mr. Hughes, and lifelong friend Robert Watts in working for the N.A.A.C.P. Harry Cole also plunged into Republican politics in Baltimore City. He became the first African-American appointed Assistant Attorney General of Maryland in May, 1953, in the office of Attorney General Edward D.E. Rollins. In 1954, he won election to the Maryland Senate by a mere 37 votes! He thus became the first African-American elected to the Maryland General Assembly, where he worked to change the laws.

In 1967 he was appointed a Judge on the Municipal Court of Baltimore City. Eight months later, he was elevated to a judgeship on the Supreme Bench of Baltimore

Everett J. Waring
Photograph courtesy of Museum of Baltimore Legal History.

Judge Robert M. Bell
Photograph by Guill Photo.

Judge Solomon Baylor at the dedication of a portrait of Justice Thurgood Marshall by the noted artist Simmie Knox, October 16, 1991. Photograph by Guill Photo.

Harry Cole, a student at Morgan State College, was to tell the Governor that he, as a young person, was anxious that there be democracy at home for him to defend if he were to go abroad and fight to preserve democracy.

In 1943, after graduating *magna cum laude* from college, Harry Cole enlisted in the U.S. Army and spent 17 months overseas, in France and Belgium and later in the Pacific on Okinawa.

May 20, 1980 - Governor Harry R. Hughes signs into law Chapters 523, 524, 525 and 526, Acts of 1980, consolidating the courts of Baltimore City. Pictured (seated): Governor Hughes; Benjamin L. Cardin, then-speaker of the House of Delegates; (standing, L-R): James H. Langrall, President, Bar Association of Baltimore City; Theodore S. Miller, immediate Past President; Judge Meyer M. Cardin, co-chair of Bar Consolidation Committee; State Senator J. Joseph Curran, Jr. and Robert Ashman, Executive Director of the Bar Association of Baltimore City.

ETTA HAYNIE MADDOX (1860-1933)

Etta H. Maddox was born in East Baltimore in 1860 and graduated from Eastern High School and the old Baltimore University Law School in 1901. She applied for admission to the bar, but because she was not a "male citizen," her application was refused by the Court of Appeals of Maryland. *In re Maddox*, 93 Md. 727, 50 A. 487 (1901). The opinion, written by Chief Judge James McSherry, held that the use of the masculine pronoun in the Act providing for admission to the bar prevented women from being attorneys, but suggested that she take her case to the Legislature. This she did. At her request, a bill was introduced in the General Assembly of 1902 by State Senator Jacob M. Moses. Opponents made strenuous efforts to kill the bill in committee, but Ms. Maddox replied, "It will never die while I live." She persevered in having a hearing, and the committee, favorably reported the bill, after being addressed by some of the leading women of Maryland. She spent the last night of the session in the State Senate fighting the opponents of the bill, who tried to kill it with amendments. Just before the session ended at one o'clock in the morning, it enacted Chapter 399, Laws of 1902, which provided: "Women shall be permitted to practice law in this State upon the same terms, conditions and requirements and to the same extent as provided in this article with reference to men." Etta Haynie Maddox passed the next bar examination with distinction, thus becoming the first woman in modern times to be admitted to the bar of Maryland in September, 1902. Ms. Maddox practiced law in Baltimore and helped lead the fight for women's suffrage and equal rights until her death on February 19, 1933.

City (now the Circuit Court for Baltimore City). In December, 1977, he was appointed to the Court of Appeals of Maryland by Governor Blair Lee, III. He took the oath of office in Annapolis on December 12, 1977, the 199th anniversary of the Court. It was a little more than 35 years since he had gone there as a college student to protest the legal status of his fellow citizens. He served as a Judge on the State's highest court for 13 years, until his mandatory retirement on January 1, 1991.

Robert B. Watts was Judge Cole's classmate at the University of Maryland and his law partner after they graduated in 1949. In 1957, Governor McKeldin appointed him Traffic Court Magistrate and in 1963, he was appointed Judge of the Municipal Court by Governor Tawes. He served for 17 years as a Judge on the Circuit Court for Baltimore City, from 1968-85. Since leaving the bench, he has practiced law with the firm of Piper & Marbury.

Milton B. Allen was also a former law partner of Judge Watts. He enjoyed a long and successful career as a criminal defense attorney. In 1970, he became the first African-American elected State's Attorney for Baltimore City. He served as Judge of the Circuit Court for Baltimore for 10 years, from 1976-86. His son, David B. Allen, served as a Judge of the Orphans' Court for Baltimore City.

Charles H. Dorsey, Jr. (1930-1995) was a giant in the Maryland legal community, serving as Executive Director of the Legal Aid Bureau for 25 years. Under his direction, the organization expanded from three Baltimore offices to 13 locations throughout the State, with a staff of more than 100 lawyers. The bureau recently opened a new headquarters building in Baltimore. Mr. Dorsey was President of the Bar Association of Baltimore City, Chairman of the State Board of Law Examiners, and served for many years as a Director of the Baltimore Bar Library. Chief Judge Robert

William Donald Schaefer, attorney, was Mayor of Baltimore from 1971-1987, and led the City's first Renaissance. He was Governor of Maryland from 1987-1995. Photograph by Kenneth Brooks Studio.

TOP RIGHT: Judge Harry A. Cole and some of his law clerks, November 10, 1990. Photograph by Guill Photo.

BOTTOM RIGHT: Dedication of the portrait of Everett Waring, April 18, 1995, in the centennial year of his admission to the bar as the first African-American attorney to practice in the Maryland State Courts. Photograph by Guill Photo.

of the Court of Appeals. When the voters approved the changes, including the addition of a new seat on the Court from Baltimore, he was unexpectedly appointed to fill it by Governor O'Conor in December, 1944. He served briefly as Chief Judge before his mandatory retirement from the Court in 1952. He later returned to the private practice of law with his old firm, until his death.

PRESIDENTS OF THE MSBA - No. 50
1943-44
ELI FRANK, SR. (1874-1958)

In the middle of his term as President of the MSBA, Judge Frank reached the mandatory retirement age of 70 as Associate Judge of the Supreme Bench of Baltimore City, and returned to private practice with the firm later known as Frank, Bernstein, Conaway & Goldman. He was born in Baltimore on February 8, 1874, and was an honors graduate of both the Johns Hopkins University (A.B. 1894) and the University of Maryland Law School (LL.B. 1896). He was a founder of the Hebrew Hospital, later known as Sinai Hospital, the Associated Jewish Charities, and the Park School. Judge Frank was appointed to the Supreme Bench of Baltimore City in 1922 by Governor Ritchie. He was President of the Bar Association of Baltimore City, an early member of the American Law Institute, and a member of the law faculty of the University of Maryland for 40 years. After World War II, he taught some of the refresher courses sponsored by MSBA for returning veterans. He was a noted author of treatises on title, property and procedure. Judge Frank died in Baltimore on July 25, 1958. His son, Eli Frank, Jr., served as President of the MSBA in 1969-70.

PRESIDENTS OF THE MSBA - No. 52
1945-46
W. CALVIN CHESNUT (1873-1962)

It is not surprising that Judge Chesnut's first job after graduating from John Hopkins University in 1892 was as a reporter for ten weeks with the *Baltimore American*. Although he opted out of a career in journalism in favor of a life immersed in the law, he spent that life as a writer of opinions and historical tracts about the law that have enriched and informed the legal literature of Maryland. He practiced with the firm of Gans and Haman from 1899 until his appointment as U.S. District Judge in 1931. When he took qualified retirement in 1953 at the age of 80, he was honored by the Bar Association of Baltimore City with a testimonial dinner attended by the largest gathering of Maryland lawyers and judges up to that time. Heading the list of 800 attendees was Chief Justice Earl Warren, who called the guest of honor "one of the most distinguished

Eli Frank, Sr.
From the portrait in the Clarence
M. Mitchell Courthouse by R.
McGill MacKall.

W. Calvin Chesnut

judges to grace the bench in this generation."

His notable books include *A Federal Judge Sums Up* (1947) and *Sixty Years in the Courts* (1958). His memorable address as President of the Association in 1946 recounted the 1893 Evening News Libel Case that he witnessed in Baltimore as a law student.

PRESIDENTS OF THE MSBA - No. 54
1947-48
FREDERICK W. BRUNE (1894-1972)

Judge Frederick William Brune, fourth member of his family to bear the name, was born in Baltimore on October 15, 1894. His grandfather was a founder of one of Maryland's first law firms, Brown & Brune, in Baltimore in 1838. His father, Frederick W. Brune, III, was a charter member of the MSBA in 1896. Judge Brune graduated from Harvard University in 1916 and the Harvard Law School in 1920. In between he served in World War I with the Ambulance Corps and with Army Intelligence. In 1921, he achieved a perfect score on the Maryland bar examination. He was an Assistant U.S. Attorney in 1923-24, leaving to form a law partnership with William C. Coleman, Edgar T. Fell and Edwin F.A. Morgan. In 1927, he formed a partnership with Mr. Morgan under the name Morgan & Brune. The following year, the firm was absorbed into Semmes, Bowen & Semmes. He remained a partner there until 1954, when he was appointed Chief Judge of the Court of Appeals of Maryland by Governor McKeldin. He served until 1964, when he retired at the mandatory age of 70. The Brune

Frederick W. Brune

Frank B. Ober

John S. Stanley

Reuben Oppenheimer

Room at the University of Maryland School of Law was dedicated in his memory.

PRESIDENTS OF THE MSBA - No. 56
1949-50
FRANKLIN B. OBER (1889-1981)

At his death at the age of 91 on January 20, 1981, Frank B. Ober was the senior partner of Ober, Grimes and Shriver, successor to the Baltimore law firm founded by Albert Ritchie and Stuart S. Janney in 1903. A graduate of Princeton and the Harvard Law School, he joined Ritchie & Janney in 1913. Mr. Ober saw action in World War I as a captain in the 315th Field Artillery in the Meuse-Argonne Campaign, later attaining the rank of major. When he returned to the firm in 1919, it was known as Janney, Ober, Slingluff & Williams.

Frank Ober was a recognized leader at the bar in the areas of litigation and corporate reorganization. He handled the Mortgage Guaranty case, which Judge Chesnut called the most complex reorganization case in his experience.

Mr. Ober was a dedicated anti-Communist. In the late 1940s, he was appointed Chairman of the Maryland Commission on Anti-subversive Activities by Governor Lane and the Maryland General Assembly. He submitted legislation that came to be known as the "Ober Law," patterned after the Smith Act, which prescribed loyalty oaths by State employees.

PRESIDENTS OF THE MSBA - No. 58
1951-52
JOHN S. STANLEY (1897-1962)

John Snowden Stanley was born in Laurel, Maryland, the fifth generation lawyer in his family. His father, Charles H. Stanley, was counsel to the Baltimore & Ohio Railroad,

Mayor of Laurel, and a charter member of the MSBA.

Mr. Stanley was a graduate of the Boys' Latin School, Johns Hopkins University and the University of Maryland School of Law. During World War I, he served in the infantry as a second lieutenant. He was admitted to the bar in 1922. From 1927 until his death, he practiced law in Baltimore with the firm of Hershey, Donaldson, Williams and Stanley. His wife, Elizabeth Gillingham Rich, was the daughter of Charles S. Rich, also a member of the bar. One of his sons, J. Snowden Stanley, Jr., is a partner in the Baltimore firm of Semmes, Bowen and Semmes.

PRESIDENTS OF THE MSBA - No. 62
1955-56
REUBEN OPPENHEIMER (1897-1982)

Reuben Oppenheimer was President of the Maryland State Bar Association in 1955 when he was appointed by Governor McKeldin to a new judgeship on the Supreme Bench of Baltimore City. He was born in Baltimore on October 24, 1897, attended city public schools and graduated from Johns Hopkins University in 1917. He served in the U.S. Navy in World War I. He graduated with honors from Harvard Law School in 1921, having served as law review editor in his senior year, graduating with honors from Harvard Law School in 1921. He joined the law firm of Frank, Emory, Beeuwkes & Skeen as an associate in February, 1921. Eli Frank left in 1922 to become a judge, and the next year Mr. Oppenheimer became a partner. By 1927, the name was changed to Emory, Beeuwkes, Skeen & Oppenheimer. Governor Tawes appointed him to the Court of Appeals of Maryland in 1964, to succeed Judge Brune. He retired at the mandatory age of 70 in 1967. Judge Oppenheimer died on July 10, 1982, at the age of 84.

James A.C. Bond   F. Neal Parke

Bar Association. Its most distinguishing features are its original antique furniture, including oak windsor chairs in the jury box. An assortment of jackets is stored in the clerk's desk, a reminder of bygone days when witnesses were required to be properly attired.

One of the most important cases tried there was the prosecution for robbery of an indigent farm worker named Smith Betts, that resulted in the famous decision of the U.S. Supreme Court in *Betts v. Brady*, 316 U.S. 455, 62 S.Ct. 1252, 86 L.Ed.1595 (1942). Chief Judge William Henry Forsythe (1874-1951) of Howard County denied Mr. Betts' request to have counsel appointed to represent him. After the Judge convicted him in a bench trial and sentenced him to eight years in prison, the defendant sought a writ of *habeas corpus* on the ground that he had been denied his Sixth Amendment right to "assistance of counsel" made applicable to the states by the Fourteenth Amendment. By a 6-3 majority, the Supreme Court affirmed the decision of Chief Judge Carroll T. Bond rejecting Mr. Betts' argument. The Court held that the Sixth Amendment was not applicable to the states and that there was no clear constitutional right to counsel in non-capital state court criminal trials. Over the next 20 years, subsequent decisions chipped away at *Betts v. Brady*, until it was completely overruled in 1963 by the landmark decision of *Gideon v. Wainwright*, 372 U.S. 335, 83 S.Ct. 792, 9 L.Ed.2d 799.

On February 24, 1898, the corporate charter of the Bar Association of Carroll County was executed by Charles B. Roberts, Charles T. Reifsnider, James A.C. Bond, David N. Henning, Charles E. Fink, William H. Thomas, George L. Stocksdale, John Milton Reifsnider, Michael E. Walsh, John M. Roberts, Edward O. Weant, Francis Neal Parke, Charles

T. Reifsnider, Jr., Guy W. Steele, Ivan D. Hoff, and J. Frank Long. It was incorporated for the purpose of "maintaining the honor and integrity of the profession of law, of cultivating social intercourse among its members, of maintaining its usefulness in promoting the due administration of justice, of procuring and maintaining a library for the use of its members, and of educating its members to a high standard of professional knowledge." The beautiful law library on the ground floor of the Historic Courthouse is maintained by the Carroll County Bar Foundation. A full-length standing portrait of Judge Edward O. Weant, Jr., former Judge of the Circuit Court and the Court of Special Appeals, surveys the splendid room.

Mary Gray Clemson (1886-1953) was almost 60 years old when she became the first woman to practice law in Carroll County in 1946. Born in Calvert County, she was the daughter of attorney John B. Gray, Sr., and worked as a secretary in his law office until her marriage. In 1915, she married Charles O. Clemson (1875-1951) of the Carroll County bar, and lived in Westminster for the rest of her life. Her obituary published in the 1953 *Maryland Bar Transactions* was the first ever for a woman attorney.

PRESIDENTS OF THE MSBA - No. 9
1904-05
JAMES A.C. BOND (1844-1930)

Judge Bond's house in Westminster still stands at 202 East Main Street facing Court Street and the Carroll County Courthouse. Next door is the tiny law office he shared with F. Neal Parke, where Judge James E. Boylan, Jr., read law as a young man.

James A.C. Bond was born on September 3, 1844, in Calvert County, and died at his residence in Westminster on August 17, 1930. He graduated from Princeton in 1866, and read law with James T. Briscoe and William Meade Allison. He was admitted to the bar at Baltimore in 1867 and moved to Westminster the following year. He was appointed Associate Judge of the Fifth Judicial Circuit on May 1, 1890, and served until the fall of 1891, when he was defeated for the nomination by Charles B. Roberts. In 1899, he was appointed Chief Judge of the Fifth Judicial Circuit by Governor Lloyd L. Lowndes, but was defeated by I. Thomas Jones. He returned to private practice and became counsel to the Baltimore & Ohio Railroad, a position he held until his death.

PRESIDENTS OF THE MSBA - No. 29
1924-25
F. NEAL PARKE (1871-1955)

Judge Parke lived in Westminster in the beautiful brick house that now serves as the rectory next to the

ABOVE: The Carroll County Courthouse. Photograph by Linda Johnson.

LEFT: The beautiful old Circuit Courtroom in the Carroll County Courthouse. Photograph by Linda Johnson.

Charles O. Fisher, Sr.

Episcopal Church of the Ascension on Court Street, down from the courthouse. He was a cadet at West Point from 1889-91, but was forced to withdraw because of ill health. He returned home, studied law in the office of Chief Judge William H. Thomas, and was admitted to the bar at Westminster on December 3, 1893. He entered the practice of law in the office of his grandfather, Joseph Maxwell Parke. In 1898 he entered into partnership with Judge James A.C. Bond, that continued until 1924 when he was appointed Associate Judge of the Court of Appeals by Governor Ritchie. This was in the days when judges on the appellate bench also sat as trial judges. While sitting as a trial judge in Carroll County in 1925, he upheld the shield law enacted by the General Assembly in 1896 that protects newspaper reporters and editors from being forced to disclose their confidential sources. He served until 1941, when he reached the mandatory retirement age of 70, and returned to law practice in Westminster. As a member of the Bond Commission on the reorganization of the Maryland Court of Appeals, he dissented from the Commission's report. He died on June 2, 1955.

PRESIDENTS OF THE MSBA - No. 87
1980-81
CHARLES O. FISHER, SR. (1917-   )

Charles O. Fisher, Sr., was born in Washington, D.C., on June 15, 1917, and came to Westminster with his family at the age of four. When he began practicing law in 1946, there were only ten other members of the Carroll County bar. He went into practice with the late Eugene Walsh (1895-1980) and together they later formed the partnership of Walsh & Fisher on April 1, 1953. Mr. Fisher is truly a general practitioner, handling every kind of case except custody and divorce. He has tried cases all over the State. "I'm happy to get up in the morning. There's something new all the time. As long as the good Lord gives me the strength, I hope to continue to practice law. The advantage of practicing in a small town is that everyone knows each other. You become part of the community."

CECIL COUNTY

Cecil County (pronounced "Sessel" by the natives) was established by proclamation dated June 6, 1674, from Baltimore and Kent Counties as a buffer against the land claims of William Penn. By mistake, the boundaries set forth in the proclamation contained all of Kent County, and therefore a corrective order restoring Kent County was issued on June 19, 1674. The county was named for the second Lord Baltimore, Cecil Calvert. (He in turn was named after Sir Robert Cecil, the famous lawyer and English Secretary of State by whom Sir George Calvert, Cecil's father, was employed as secretary.) The county seat of Elkton was known originally as Head of Elk and later as Elktown, in the days when George Washington and Lafayette passed through on their way to Yorktown. Until 1938, when the law changed requiring a longer waiting period, Elkton was the marriage capital of the east coast, the streets of town lined with wedding chapels. As the Maryland county seat closest to Pennsylvania, New Jersey and New York, it continues to attract thousands of couples each year who want to get married without the legal requirement of a blood test. When the old 1787 courthouse with its quaint belfry was torn down in 1940 to make way for a new town building, the only feature retained was the brick floor.

The design of the next Cecil County Courthouse at Elkton was considered very *avant garde* at its dedication on July 26, 1940. The edifice of Port Deposit granite and limestone was said to be the first air conditioned public building in Maryland. The 1940 courthouse was dwarfed by a huge addition in 1966. The unusual facade on the modern wing features an interesting bas relief of ducks and fish, wildlife symbols from the Cecil County seal.

Perhaps the most famous case to be tried in the Cecil County Courthouse was the murder prosecution of a Buddhist named Lidge Schowgurow. The members of the grand jury that indicted him and the petit jury that convicted him of first degree murder had been required to swear an oath that they believed in the existence of God. Article 36 of the Maryland Declaration of Rights provided that none should be barred from serving as jurors on account of their religious beliefs as long as they believed in a Supreme Being. Schowgurow, whose religion did not include a belief in God, challenged the constitutionality of his indictment and conviction on the basis of the First and Fourteenth Amendments to the U.S. Constitution. On appeal, the Court of Appeals reversed the conviction and

149

remanded the case for a new trial, holding as unconstitutional the requirement of a belief in God as a condition for serving on grand and petit juries. The Court also held that its decision would not be given retroactive effect, so as not to invalidate convictions that had become final before the opinion was rendered. Nevertheless, a consequence of the opinion was the invalidation of all pending state court indictments that had been issued by grand juries from which non-believers were excluded. The result was the reindictment of some criminal defendants or the waiver of defects in their indictments by many others. *Schowgurow v. State*, 240 Md. 121, 213 A.2d. 475 (1965).

Cecil County State Senator Walter Baker was the prosecutor in the *Schowgurow* case. After the conviction was reversed by the Court of Appeals, Schowgurow was retried in Oakland, Garrett County, before Judges James Getty and Harold Naughton sitting with a jury, Fred Thayer prosecuting. The jury could not decide between verdicts of first degree murder and first degree murder without capital punishment. At four o'clock in the morning, the foreman, DeCoursey Boulden, later a three-term member of the House of Delegates, summoned the bailiff, told him that the jury was hung 10-2, and asked for coffee. The case resulted in a mistrial. By the third trial, the Supreme Court had decided *Miranda v. Arizona,* 384 U.S. 436, 86 S.Ct. 1602, 16 L.Ed.2d. 694 (1966), casting doubt upon the admissibility of Schowgurow's confession. As a result, plea negotiations resulted in a guilty plea and the defendant received an 18-year sentence.

An interesting sidelight to the *Schowgurow* case is that one of the judges specially assigned to hear it on appeal was Judge Shirley B. Jones, Associate Judge of the Supreme Bench of Baltimore City. When the case came on for hearing in October, 1965, it was the first time in the history of the State that a woman sat on the Court of Appeals of Maryland.

Phil Sherman and I visited Elkton to meet with Judge Edward D.E. Rollins, Jr., of the Circuit Court for Cecil County. He was born into the legal profession, the son and namesake of his father, who was an attorney, circuit judge, Attorney General of Maryland, and President of the MSBA. Attending the annual meetings of the State Bar in Atlantic City as a young boy with his family, he met and became friends with lawyers from every part of Maryland. His classmate at the University of Maryland Law School was Cornelius Sybert, when their fathers were running against each other for Attorney General. Neal Sybert became Judge of the Circuit Court for Howard County, while Ed Rollins became Judge of the Circuit Court for Cecil County. After graduating and passing the bar in 1956, Judge Rollins

entered his father's law office in Elkton. There were then only 13 lawyers practicing there. Today, there are five times that number, about 40 lawyers practicing in offices on Main Street alone. One of them is Edward D.E. Rollins, III, the Judge's son, whose law office and title company are located in the old Mitchell House, one of Elkton's many historic landmarks. The Cecil County Bar Association, founded in 1904, presently has about 80 members.

John S. Wirt

Judge Rollins presides in Courtroom No. 1, the same courtroom his father occupied, where the *Schowgurow* case was tried. The walls are lined with photographs of former Judges Albert Constable, Frederick Stump, Austin L. Crothers, and Edward D.E. Rollins, Sr.

PRESIDENTS OF THE MSBA - No. 6
1901-02
JOHN S. WIRT (1851-1904)

John S. Wirt was a leading Democratic politician in turn of the century Maryland, as well as a charter member of the Maryland State Bar Association and its sixth President. He was born near Cecilton on November 16, 1851, the son of Dr. John W. Wirt, a prominent physician, and Margaret Biddle, his wife. He graduated from St. John's College in 1868 and the University of Maryland School of Law in 1872. He practiced in Baltimore with L. Allison Wilmer, whom he had met in college. In 1878, he took the advice of U.S. Supreme Court Justice David Davis, a relative, and went to Chicago to practice law with the firm of Judd & Whitehouse. He returned to Maryland and opened an office in Elkton upon the death of his brother, Henry B. Wirt, in 1881. He was an ardent supporter of Grover Cleveland and a delegate to the 1884 and 1892

RIGHT: The 1787 Cecil County Courthouse at Elkton was enlarged in 1884-86 by a third story, a new roof, and a tower in front that contained a balcony, a clock, a semi-onion dome and a weathervane in the shape of a fish. The building was torn down in 1940. Courtesy of the Maryland State Archives, MSA SC 2117-107.

Edward D.E. Rollins

Democratic National Conventions. He represented Cecil County in the Maryland Senate and House of Delegates. He was one of the first three members of the Board of Law Examiners chosen by the Court of Appeals to administer the new written bar examination in 1898, Mr. Wirt was a contender for the Governorship in 1899, but was defeated for his party's nomination by John Walter Smith. He died childless on May 17, 1904, and thus, as his obituary stated, "this family name has become extinct in Maryland."

PRESIDENTS OF THE MSBA - No. 63
1956-57
EDWARD D.E. ROLLINS (1899-1976)

Edward Dorsey Ellis Rollins was named for Dr. Edward Dorsey Ellis, the physician who brought him into the world on November 15, 1899, in Baltimore, Maryland. (Judge R.

Dorsey Watkins was also named after Dr. Ellis.) He grew up in Baltimore and attended public school there. After graduating from City College, he enlisted in the U.S. Navy at the outbreak of World War I in April, 1917. In 1919, at war's end, he entered the University of Maryland School of Law, graduating and passing the bar in 1922. For the next five years he practiced law in Baltimore before moving to Elkton in 1927. In 1930, he was elected State's Attorney for Cecil County as a Republican, and served three consecutive terms. During World War II, he was chief air raid warden for Cecil County, and later became director of civil defense. In October, 1952, he was appointed Attorney General of Maryland by Governor McKeldin, succeeding W. Hall Hammond whom McKeldin had appointed to the Court of Appeals. As the Republican candidate for Attorney General in 1954, he was Governor McKeldin's running mate, but was defeated by Democrat C. Ferdinand Sybert. In 1957, McKeldin appointed him Associate Judge of the Second Judicial Circuit, succeeding Judge Floyd J. Kintner. He was elected in his own right in the 1958 election and served until his mandatory retirement at the age of 70 in 1969. Judge Rollins died on July 5, 1976.

The 1940 Cecil County Courthouse (L) and the 1966 addition (R). Photograph by Linda Johnson.

Courtroom No. 1 in the Cecil County Courthouse, where the *Schowgurow* case was tried the first time. Photograph by Linda Johnson.

CHARLES COUNTY

Charles County was established on May 10, 1658, and named for Charles Calvert (1637-1715), third Lord Baltimore. There is nothing in the early records to indicate where the first session of the county court was held when it convened on May 25, 1658. Some of the earliest cases concerned citations for contempt of court. On August 19, 1658, Thomas Baker was charged with contempt for referring to Justice Job Chandler as "a spindel-shanked Doge." Later records indicate that Baker later became a Justice himself and was removed from the bench after being convicted of hog-stealing. On May 12, 1659, the Justices inquired of Robert Troop, Edmund Linsey and Joseph Linton as to whom called Justice John Jenkins "Captain Grindstone," a derogatory term probably based upon his heavy sentences.

Inns and private homes appear to have served as makeshift courthouses before 1674. In that year the county paid John Allen 20,000 pounds of tobacco to build a courthouse and prison about three miles south of LaPlata and three miles east of Port Tobacco. It was not until 1727 that Port Tobacco became the county seat. The name was a corruption of its Indian name, and has no connection with tobacco or shipping. It original name was Charlestown, until 1820 when it was officially changed to Port Tobacco.

The reconstructed Charles County Courthouse at Port Tobacco. Photograph by Coos Hamburger.

The selection of LaPlata as the county seat came much later in the county's history, as the result of its preeminence as a railroad town. During the American Revolution, the county was a center of patriotic fervor. Thomas Stone of Charles County signed the Declaration of Independence; Daniel of St. Thomas Jenifer, also of Charles County, signed the Constitution of the United States. They both attended the Mt. Vernon Conference at the home of George Washington in March, 1785, the purpose of which was to reach agreement with Virginia regarding navigation on the Potomac. The conference led to the calling of the Annapolis Convention and later, the Philadelphia Convention that produced the Constitution. The economic difficulties of the post-Revolutionary period are evident from the fact that a mob threatened the life of the attorney for creditors who filed hundreds of collection suits at the courthouse in Port Tobacco in 1786.

The Price of Nationhood: The American Revolution in Charles County, (W.W. Norton & Co., 1994), written by Jean B. Lee, Professor of history at the University of Wisconsin at Madison, debunks the myth that American independence produced only beneficial results for the country. Professor Lee makes a solid case for the proposition that the disruption of trade with England brought economic stagnation to Charles County and retarded its development for more than a century. For Charles County, in her view, the price of nationhood was financial ruin.

Many remnants of the 18th Century survive there to this day. Tobacco is still a major cash crop in the area. The plantations and estates established there by the colonial gentry may yet be visited and enjoyed, as well as the unspoiled beauty of the land. The county has 150 miles of shoreline on the Potomac, Wicomico, Port Tobacco and Patuxent Rivers.

Charles County gained notoriety after the assassination of Abraham Lincoln on April 14, 1865, as the hiding place of the assassins. Early on the morning after the murder, John Wilkes Booth and David Herold arrived at the home of Dr. Samuel A. Mudd at Bryantown, seeking medical attention for Booth's broken leg. Dr. Mudd claimed that Booth was disguised and used an assumed name, and that the Doctor set the broken leg not knowing Booth's true identity or that the President was dead. Because it was later asserted that Dr. Mudd was acquainted with Booth, and that he had had numerous opportunities to turn him over to the authorities, Dr. Mudd was charged as a conspirator in the President's death. He was arraigned on May 10,

The 1896 Courthouse at LaPlata, 1928-30. The architect was Joseph C. Johnson; the contractor, James Haislip. Courtesy of the Maryland State Archives, Hayman Collection, MSA SC 1406-270.

1865, and went on trial before a military commission. Frederick Stone (1820-1899), prominent Charles County lawyer, later Circuit Judge, and charter member of the MSBA, joined Dr. Mudd's defense team behind lead counsel Thomas Ewing, Jr., and he also represented Herold. At the end of the trial, on May 30, 1865, the commission convicted the defendants and sentenced all of them to death, except Dr. Mudd, who was sentenced to life imprisonment at hard labor at Dry Tortugas prison in the Florida Keys. After serving four years, he was pardoned by President Andrew Johnson for his heroism in rendering medical aid to victims of a yellow fever epidemic.

Judge Stone later agreed with the judgment against his client. In 1883, after Dr. Mudd's death, he told the New York *Tribune* in an article published on April 17, 1883: "The court very nearly hanged Dr. Mudd. His prevarications were painful. He had given his whole case away by not trusting even his counsel or neighbors or kinfolks. It was a terrible thing to extricate him from the toils he had woven about himself. He had denied knowing Booth when he knew him well. He was undoubted accessory to the abduction plot, though he may have supposed it would never come to anything. He denied knowing Booth when he came to his house when that was preposterous. He had been even intimate with Booth." Judge Stone did not give any details as to how he formed his opinion. The Mudd family has been

The Charles County Courthouse at La Plata as it appears today contains the old 1896 structure inside an addition constructed in 1954. Photograph by Linda Johnson.

The Circuit Courtroom in the Charles County Courthouse. Photograph by Linda Johnson.

trying for years to clear the Doctor's name.

In 1993, the School of Law of the University of Richmond conducted a mock trial of an imaginary appeal of Dr. Mudd's conviction. The participants were actual lawyers and judges. Dr. Mudd was represented by F. Lee Bailey, and Candida Ewing Steel, the great-great-granddaughter of Thomas Ewing, Jr., Dr. Mudd's lead counsel at his trial. Counsel for the Army included Rear Admiral John S. Jenkins, Associate Dean of George Washington University's National Law Center. The trial was attended by more than 500 spectators, including 25 members of the Mudd family.

The outcome was a unanimous decision by a three-judge panel in favor of Dr. Mudd. Two judges held that he should have been tried in a civil court, not by a military tribunal, in conformity with the decision of the Supreme Court in *Ex parte Milligan*, 71 U.S. (4 Wall.) 2, 18 L.Ed. 281 (1866). One judge decided that the evidence was insufficient to convict Dr. Mudd.

LaPlata, the century-old county seat of Charles County, appears to have gotten its name from "Le Plateau," the Chapman family farm where the town sprang up. The decline of steamboat travel and the rise of the railroad spelled the end of Port Tobacco. In the 1890s, the determination of which town would be the center of local government became an important issue in county politics that split both political parties. After the courthouse at Port Tobacco mysteriously burned on August 3, 1892, the voters of Charles County selected LaPlata over Chapel Point as the new county seat at a referendum in June, 1895. The following year, a new courthouse was built at LaPlata. In 1996, the Charles County Bar Association, 85 members strong, will celebrate the centennial anniversary of the Charles County Courthouse at LaPlata.

The first electricity to reach Charles County came in the late 1920s over the Potomac Electric Power Company line to LaPlata and Waldorf. In February, 1936, the Charles County Electric Cooperative was organized under the auspices of the Rural Electrification Administration, and inexpensive electric power was brought to the majority of the population two years later. The Potomac River Bridge was built in the 1930s on the site of an 18th century ferry. It now bears the name of Harry W. Nice (1877-1941), in memory of the Maryland lawyer who served as Governor of Maryland from 1935-39. The bridge fostered commercial development in Southern Maryland by connecting Baltimore and Washington via Route 301. Located just 18 miles from the nation's capital, Charles County today is one of Maryland's fastest growing subdivisions.

155

W. Mitchell Digges   J. Dudley Digges

PRESIDENTS OF THE MSBA - No. 39
1934
W. MITCHELL DIGGES (1877-1934)

Judge W. Mitchell Digges was born at "Hydromont," the family homestead in Charles County, Maryland, on February 17, 1877, and died at his home in LaPlata on October 15, 1934, at the age of 57, four months after taking office as President of the MSBA. He was a member of the Maryland House of Delegates (1910-12) and naval officer of the port of Baltimore (1913-21). He was elected Chief Judge of the Seventh Judicial Circuit in 1923, serving in that capacity and simultaneously as Associate Judge of the Court of Appeals of Maryland until his death.

PRESIDENTS OF THE MSBA - No. 12
1907-08
L. ALLISON WILMER (1849-1932)

General L. Allison Wilmer was born on September 17, 1849, in Charles County, Maryland, and died on March 19, 1932, in Newark, New Jersey. He graduated from St. John's College in 1871 and then undertook the study of law. He was appointed Adjutant General of the State of Maryland by Governor Lloyd Lowndes on February 19, 1896, and was a charter member of the Maryland State Bar Association.

PRESIDENTS OF THE MSBA - No. 75
1968-69
J. DUDLEY DIGGES (1912-1983)

"When the history of the Maryland State Bar Association is written, the figure of the Honorable J. Dudley Digges will be seen to have cast a long shadow." So prophesied Norman P. Ramsey in a 1982 tribute that was published in the *Maryland Law Review* upon Judge Digges' retirement from the Court of Appeals. As President-elect of the MSBA during the presidency of Rignal W. Baldwin (1967-68), Judge Digges chaired a committee that recommended drastic changes in the structure of the Association to conform to the model of the American Bar Association. As part of this "quiet revolution," outmoded committees were swept aside, including the Admissions Committee that passed upon applications for membership, in favor of more

La Plata, Charles County, in the 1930s. Photograph courtesy of the Maryland State Archives, Merrick Collection, MSA SC 1477-6759.

television stations beamed in from nearby Pittsburgh carried only news of local elections in Pennsylvania. Oakland is actually closer to Canada than it is to Salisbury. As it turned out, access to Maryland television would not have told us very much. Because the race was so close, its outcome remained in doubt for weeks, and Mrs. Sauerbrey's challenge to Mr. Glendening's narrow victory was not decided until January in a courtroom in Annapolis.

The day after the election, Susan and I visited the Garrett County Courthouse, where we were greeted by an old friend, Jim Sherbin, the county State's Attorney. He and his wife, Linda S. Sherbin, who serves as a master and examiner in chancery and practices law with the firm of

ABOVE: The Circuit Courtroom in the Garrett County Courthouse. Photograph by Linda Johnson.

RIGHT: The Garrett County Courthouse at Oakland, Maryland. Photograph by Linda Johnson.

171

James L. Sherbin, State's Attorney for Garrett County.

John W. Garrett, for whom Garrett County was named. From *Baltimore-American Illustrated Edition, The State of Maryland* (1896).

Stover & Sherbin, live on a farm north of Oakland. Jim currently serves on the MSBA Board of Governors. In his years as a prosecutor, first in Baltimore City and in Garrett County since 1975, Jim has tried literally thousands of criminal cases. Perhaps his most famous was the trial of Richard Danny Tichnell for the 1979 murder of a Garrett County Deputy Sheriff. The defendant was the first to be sentenced to death under Maryland's current statute. The sentence was later vacated on appeal. *Tichnell v. State*, 290 Md. 43, 427 A.2d 991 (1981).

Obviously tired but elated by his reelection victory, Jim treated us to a personally guided tour of the courthouse and introduced us to Circuit Judge Fred A. Thayer. Judge Thayer's grandfather, Fred A. Thayer (1854-1942), was one of the pioneer lawyers in the county. Judge Thayer has done a remarkable job of restoring and renovating the circuit courtroom.

Our tour guides through the town of Oakland were local attorney Leonard J. Eiswert and Mayor Asa M. McCain, Jr. Among the many points of interest we visited were the 1884 B & O Railroad Station and Cornish Manor, now a restaurant, but formerly a resort outside of town. Many famous visitors have come to Oakland over the years, including President and Mrs. Grover Cleveland, who arrived at the railroad station bound for their honeymoon at nearby Deer Park in June, 1886.

The natural wonders of Garrett County are its greatest attractions. Muddy Creek Falls is the highest in Maryland, some 52 feet in height. In August, 1918, and again in July, 1921, Henry Ford, Thomas A. Edison and Harvey Firestone stayed at a campsite near the falls identified by an historical marker. Deep Creek Lake is not a natural wonder, but was created by the Youghiogheny Hydroelectric Corporation of the Associated Gas and Electric System Lake by damming up Deep and Cherry Creeks, North and Green Glades, Meadow Mountain, Piney, Poland, Pawn, Gravley, Marsh, Smith and Bull's Arms Runs. Garrett County is one of the State's most beautiful places, a skier's paradise in winter, a center for water sports in the summer, and a year-round delight to those who love the healthy outdoor life.

As Maryland's westernmost subdivision, Garrett County shares a border with Preston County, West Virginia. Disputes over the boundary from the headwaters of the Potomac River to the Pennsylvania line led to the filing of suit in the U.S. Supreme Court by the Attorney General of Maryland in 1891. In a series of decisions in the case of *Maryland v. West Virginia*, 217 U.S. 1, 30 S.Ct. 268, 54 L.Ed. 645 (1910) and 225 U.S. 1, 32 S.Ct. 672, 56 L.Ed. 955 (1912), the Court held that West Virginia's claim to the north bank of the Potomac River was not justified. Citing the Maryland Charter granted by King Charles I to Cecil Calvert in 1632, the Court confirmed Maryland's claim to the entire Potomac River, extending to its southern shore. Commissioners were appointed who ran and marked the permanent boundary along the so-called "Deakins Line."

HARFORD COUNTY

Harford County was the last county in Maryland to be established before the American Revolution, and the last to be named for a member of the Calvert family. Carved out of Baltimore County in 1773, it was named for Henry Harford (1759-1834), the last proprietor of Maryland. He was the illegitimate son of Frederick Calvert, the sixth and last Lord Baltimore.

The town of Bush, also known as "Harford Town," on the Philadelphia Road, was established as the first county seat. It was there that an assembly of elected representatives met in a tavern on March 22, 1775, and endorsed independence from England in what came to be known as "The Bush Declaration." The town, little more than a village crossroads, remained the county seat for only nine years, until Bel Air was chosen as the new site of the county

James W. Rouse. Photograph by Carol Anstett.

Judge of the Court of Appeals, Attorney General of Maryland, a Howard County lawyer, and father of Judge Cornelius (Neal) F. Sybert, Jr.

I first met Judge Neal Sybert in July, 1994, in his chambers at the Howard County Courthouse. He was a former State's Attorney for Howard County, and practiced law with his late father and Lewis S. Nippard on Lawyers' Row across the street. He took me on a tour of the courthouse in which he has practiced law and served as a prosecutor and jurist his entire professional life. He retired from the Court in May, 1995.

The week Judge Sybert left the bench, he introduced me to the oldest lawyer in Howard County, retired District Judge John L. Clark, at his home in the beautiful farm country near Marriottsville. The rambling manor house in which he lives was built about the year 1810. A well-stocked library betrays his knowledge and love of history. Surprisingly, he is an expert on prehistoric stone sculpture of the Incas and Mayas of South and Central America. Over lunch in his spacious dining room, with a fire crackling in the hearth, Judge Clark recounted for us some of his experiences at the bench and bar. One of two sons of Circuit Judge James Clark, (his brother is former State Senator James Clark), his career began in 1938 when he was admitted to the bar, developed as he practiced law for 30 years in Ellicott City, and culminated as a Judge on the then-new District Court of Maryland. He reckons that he heard about 10,000 cases in his six years on that court.

The history of the bar of Howard County predates the founding of the county itself. Charles Carroll of Carrollton (1737-1832), Maryland attorney and last surviving signer of the Declaration of Independence, resided at Doughregan

Manor near Ellicott City and is buried there. The Howard County Bar Association was founded in June, 1941, by Judge James Clark, then President of the Maryland State Bar Association. In 1995 approximately 500 lawyers lived and worked in Howard County. Of that number, 375 are members of the Howard County Bar Association. Today, Ellicott City reflects the quiet charm of bygone days. On the more modern side is the beautiful city of Columbia, a well-proportioned community built in the 1960s and '70s by the Rouse Company midway between Baltimore and Washington. The lawyers of Howard County are clustered in both locations.

James W. Rouse (1914-1996), the visionary responsible for building Columbia, was a 1938 graduate of the University of Maryland School of Law. His father, Willard G. Rouse, was a Maryland lawyer and businessman, and was also a charter member of the Maryland State Bar Association. Jim Rouse was born in Easton, Maryland, and built his first shopping center in nearby Talbottown. Other notable Maryland projects pioneered by the Rouse Company over the years are Harundale Mall, Maryland's first enclosed shopping center (1958), Charles Center (1959), the Village of Cross Keys (1964), and Harborplace (1980). His dream was to build communities that enhance the quality of life; to create cities and suburbs that are not only pleasant places in which to live, but that are designed to bring people together in an environment that celebrates individuality. The concept of a planned community was his antidote for suburban sprawl. In 1995, he was honored for his many achievements by being awarded the Presidential Medal of Freedom.

The fascinating story of how Columbia became a reality was related to this author by John Martin Jones, an attorney who helped Mr. Rouse overcome the legal problems that stood in the way of the project. The first thing the Rouse Company did was to create a corporation, the Howard Research & Development Corporation ("HRD"), to acquire the land and design the new town. By August, 1965, in 165 separate purchases, HRD had acquired 14,000 acres in central Howard County, some 22 square miles, slightly larger than the island of Manhattan. Connecticut General Life Insurance Company and Chase Manhattan Bank were the joint lenders that furnished $50 million in long-term mortgage notes to HRD. (Wilde Lake was named for Frazar B. Wilde, the canny Scotsman who was chairman of Connecticut General's board.) The planning of the new town took 18 months. In 1965, Howard County approved special zoning for the project as a "New Town District." It was a radical departure from traditional Euclidean zoning that would have required 165,000 separate hearings.

Judge Diane O. Leasure

Judge Donna Hill Staton

Objections to the zoning approvals were overruled by Judge Macgill at the circuit court level and construction proceeded.

In 1968, General Electric Corporation took an option to purchase nearly 1,100 acres adjacent to Columbia to build a plant that was calculated to employ 10,000 people in the manufacture of appliances. The biggest hurdle to overcome in persuading G.E. to exercise its option was obtaining county zoning approval. Another new type of zoning, the "Industrial Development Zoning District," was created by Rouse lawyers and approved by Howard County. Without knowing precisely where the factory was going to be built, because G.E. itself did not yet know, the zoning established environmental controls on the plant that G.E. hoped to construct. Proper notice of the zoning change was given. A few residents who feared a loss of property values if the project succeeded fought the zoning approval granted to G.E. before the County Commissioners, in the Circuit Court, and all the way to the Court of Appeals. In the case of *Bowie v. Board of County Commissioners of Howard County*, 253 Md. 602, 253 A.2d 727 (1969), their suit was rejected. A unanimous Court, speaking through Judge William J. McWilliams (a former President of the MSBA), approved the zoning, holding that there was sufficient evidence before the Board of County Commissioners to justify its decision, even though the Court disagreed with the Board's rationale. The Rouse victory in the Court of Appeals assured the success of Columbia.

Diane Gail Schulte became the first woman jurist in Howard County when she was appointed to the District Court by Governor Hughes in 1980. She was admitted to the Maryland bar ten years earlier, served as law clerk to U.S. District Judge James R. Miller from 1970-71, and was Assistant State's Attorney for Baltimore City from 1971-73.

She later served as Assistant County Solicitor and member of the State Board of Law Examiners, and was named Howard County Woman of the Year in 1979.

On October 24, 1995, Governor Parris N. Glendening appointed a new generation of Circuit Judges for Howard County with an emphasis on diversity of race and gender. Diane O. Leasure was named to succeed Judge Sybert and Donna Hill Staton was appointed to a newly-created fifth seat on the Circuit Court. They are the first women Circuit Judges in the history of Howard County. Judge Staton is also Howard County's first African-American Circuit Judge.

They were opposed in the primary election of March 5, 1996, by District Judge Lenore R. Gelfman and attorneys Jonathan Scott Smith and Jay Fred Cohen. Judges Leasure and Staton won nomination in the Democratic primary, but lost to Judge Gelfman and Mr. Smith in the Republican primary. As a result, there will be a contested election for the Circuit Judgeships in November, 1996.

PRESIDENTS OF THE MSBA - No. 49
1942-43
JAMES CLARK (1884-1955)

James Clark was born in Howard County on his parents' farm, "Fairfield," and received his early education at a nearby one-room schoolhouse. In 1907 he began the practice of law in Ellicott City, the same year he graduated from the University of Maryland Law School and passed the bar examination. Even as a busy lawyer, he stayed close to the land, operating several farms and breeding cattle. He served two terms as State's Attorney for Howard County, 1920-24 and 1929-34. In 1942, the year he began his term as President of the Maryland State Bar Association, he was appointed Associate Judge of the Circuit Court for Howard County. One

James Clark   P. Dennis Belman

of the most unusual cases that came before him occurred in Anne Arundel County in 1945, when, sitting with Chief Judge James E. Boylan, Jr. (1899-1965), they heard the criminal prosecution of 37 prisoners charged with rioting at the Maryland House of Correction at Jessup. Thirty-two defendants were convicted. Judge Clark served until his retirement on October 22, 1954, his 70th birthday, when he resumed the practice of law. His death occurred only five months later on March 25, 1955. In 1959, his widow purchased the old First Presbyterian Church building across the street from the courthouse and presented it to the Howard County Historical Society in his memory.

PRESIDENTS OF THE MSBA - No. 101
1993-94
P. DENNIS BELMAN (1942-   )

Since 1982, P. Dennis Belman has been a partner in the Columbia law firm of Levan, Schimel, Belman & Abramson, P.A., where he specializes in business and corporate law. He is a former Securities and Exchange Commission lawyer; former partner at Smith, Somerville & Case; and former vice president of and associate general counsel to the Rouse Company. One of the major projects sponsored by the MSBA during his year as President was *Law Links,* a program that provides summer internships for 50 high school students in area law firms while educating them about the justice system. Mr. Belman championed mandatory continuing legal education for lawyers, the development of legal services delivery systems to the working poor, and the creation of a commission by the General Assembly to improve the State judicial system.

KENT COUNTY

William Claiborne, the Virginia agent who founded on Kent Island the first English settlement within the present boundaries of Maryland, was responsible for giving Kent County its name. The island upon which he established a small fort and trading post he named the "Kentish Isle," and the Calverts who dispossessed him referred to the entire upper portion of the Eastern Shore as the "Isle of Kent." The exact date of its founding is undocumented, but the date of August 2, 1642, is assumed, based upon a reference to the "Sheriff of Kent County" bearing that date in the provincial records. The earliest courts of Kent County were the manorial courts presided over by large landowners on their own plantations. The first Kent County Courthouse was built at New Yarmouth before 1680 on land owned by Major James Ringgold, the owner of Huntingfield, a plantation of 1,000 acres. In 1707, the county seat was moved to its present

GEORGE VICKERS

George Vickers was born in Chestertown, Maryland in 1801. He opposed secession in 1861, assisted Governor Hicks to raise an Eastern Shore regiment and attained the rank of major general of militia. In the trial of President Johnson, Senator Vickers voted for acquittal.

Photo: U.S. Senator George Vickers.
From *Baltimore-American Illustrated Edition, The State of Maryland* (1896).

location at Chestertown The town on the Chester River became the center of trade and social life of the upper Eastern Shore. Its historic charm and beauty come alive every September when it opens its oldest homes to an evening tour by candlelight.

Chestertown is profiled in the opening chapter of *Remembering Main Street,* a recent book by native-born author Pat Ross (Penguin Books, 1994). She writes in praise of the small town way of life as only one could who grew up in that atmosphere and moved away to New York City. The book has all the charm of a postcard from home, and indeed, it is filled with old postcard pictures of the college town on the shores of the Chester River.

Historical markers succinctly recount the town's history:

Chestertown, Maryland,
County seat of Kent County, established in 1706, situated on the most travelled highway between south and north during the revolutionary period. George Washington made eight known visits here between 1756 and 1793. Rich in colonial history.

Memorial Park
From this point, on May 23, 1774, a group of Chestertown citizens, undisguised and in broad daylight, boarded the brigantine GEDDES and threw its cargo of tea into the Chester River.

Washington College
Founded in 1782.
George Washington gave to its founding, granted use of his name and served on its board of visitors and governors. He attended public exercises here in 1784 and received degree of Doctor of Laws in 1789.

Bridge over the Chester River, Chestertown, Maryland, 1906. Photograph courtesy of the Maryland State Archives, Merrick Collection, MSA SC 1477-6469.

The Kent County Courthouse at Chestertown. Photograph by Linda Johnson.

EZEKIEL FORMAN CHAMBERS (1788-1867)

"One of the most distinguished Associate Judges of the Maryland Court of Appeals, he was born in Chestertown, Maryland, on February 28, 1788. After his admission to the bar, he entered at once into a large practice, which in the course of a few years extended over the whole of the Eastern Shore of Maryland. For 50 years, beginning in 1817, he was one of the leading lawyers in the State. In 1826 he was elected to the United States Senate, and served in that body until 1834, when he was elected to the Court of Appeals. He retired in 1851 upon the adoption of the new Constitution, under which the entire judiciary of the State was reorganized. He again returned to the practice of law, which he continued until the Civil War. Judge Chambers was an able speaker as well as a learned jurist. One of his most remarkable speeches was on the Judiciary Tenure, which was delivered at the Maryland Convention, in April, 1851. He said the necessary elements in the character of a judge were first, a consciousness of perfect independence; a freedom from all motive to do wrong; an exemption from all fear to do right. These principles guided his own career on the bench."

— From *The Green Bag*, 1894

Photo: Ezekiel Forman Chambers. Autographed carte de visite from the collection of the Library Company of the Baltimore Bar.

The name of George B. Rasin has been practically synonymous with Kent County. For more than a quarter century, he was resident Judge of the Circuit Court, to which he was appointed by Governor Tawes in December, 1960. He was born at Worton, Kent County, on May 28, 1917, attended its public schools, and graduated from Washington College in 1937. From there it was on to the University of Maryland School of Law, from which he graduated in 1941, and was admitted to the bar the same year. He served during World War II in military intelligence in the U.S. Army, 1941-43, and the Army Air Force, 1943-45. Discharged in 1945 with the rank of captain, he served with the European Headquarters of the U.S. Foreign Aid Program from 1950-52. He was elected State's Attorney for Kent County in 1954, and served one term. In 1956, he was

U.S. Senator James Alfred Pearce, Sr. From Steiner, *Men of Mark in Maryland* (1907).

James Alfred Pearce, Jr.

elected State Senator from Kent County. He is Kent County's leading citizen. His dignified demeanor on the bench symbolized the majesty of the law for a generation of Kent Countians. His daughter, Gail Rasin Caplan, is a Judge on the District Court of Maryland for Baltimore City.

There are only about 30 members of the Kent County Bar Association, making it one of the friendliest in the State. In 1948, the Association was reactivated by Harrison W. Vickers, Jr. (1877-1958), who served as President from 1948 until his retirement in 1951. Mr. Vickers was also responsible for organizing the Second Judicial Circuit Bar Association and presided at the organizational meeting, at which Governor William Preston Lane, Jr., was the principal speaker.

PRESIDENTS OF THE MSBA - No. 16
1911-12
JAMES ALFRED PEARCE, JR. (1840-1920)

Chestertown remembers its native son, James Alfred Pearce, Jr., on two prominent memorials. A plaque dedicated to his memory was affixed to the front of the old Kent County Courthouse during the County's tercentenary celebrations in 1942. As Chief Judge of the Second Judicial Circuit, he presided at trials there from 1897 to 1912, while also serving as an Associate Judge of the Court of Appeals of Maryland. He served as President of the MSBA the same year he retired as a Judge.

At nearby Memorial Park, on High Street, is a large granite stone bearing his name, which he erected in June, 1917, commemorating "the patriotism and valor of a once-divided but now reunited country." This Civil War monument is inscribed to the South on the southern side, and to the Union on the northern side, with the names of fallen heroes on both sides.

MONTGOMERY COUNTY

Montgomery County was established in 1776 and named for General Richard Montgomery, a Revolutionary War hero who lost his life while fighting in Canada. A central site for the county seat was chosen on the road from Frederick to Georgetown where the first county court met in a tavern on May 22, 1777. The town that grew up around the court was known first simply as Montgomery County Courthouse, then Williamsburg, and since 1804, the name it bears today of Rockville, after Rock Creek, the source of which is nearby.

The old Red Brick Courthouse in the center of the city is the third Montgomery County Courthouse and stands on the site of its predecessors. When the courthouse opened in October, 1891, Montgomery County had a population of only

27,000. This imposing Romanesque building reflects the grave importance Montgomery Countians of that day ascribed to the functions of law and government. The circuit courtroom on the second floor measured 50 x 60 feet with a vaulted ceiling 24 feet high and two large stained glass windows. The building also housed the county school board, sheriff, county commissioners, orphans' court and register of wills, in addition to the circuit court clerk.

It was perhaps in the judges' chambers of the old Red Brick Courthouse that 13 Rockville lawyers assembled on an afternoon in 1894 and founded the Bar Association of Montgomery County, Maryland. The founders were Thomas Anderson, H. Maurice Talbott, Philip D. Laird, William Viers Bouic, Jr., Charles W. Prettyman, Robert B. Peter, Edward C.

The 1891 Red Brick Courthouse, Rockville, Maryland. Photograph by Linda Johnson.

Peter, Thomas L. Dawson, James B. Henderson, Frank Higgins, Alexander Kilgour, and Samuel Riggs of R.

Clara Barton (1821-1912), the nurse who founded the American National Red Cross as an aid to the 1864 *Geneva Convention for the Amelioration of the Condition of the Wounded and the Sick of the Armies of the Field,* lived in Montgomery County at Glen Echo. Albert Bouic filed a case concerning her estate that was tried in the old courthouse:

Dr. Julian R. Hubbell sued Mrs. Mabelle R. Hirons in the [Circuit Court for Montgomery County, in equity], claiming she had obtained land in Glen Echo from him by undue influence. Dr. Hubbell had been the secretary to Clara Barton, and had been entertained along with Miss Barton by the crowned heads of Europe. Miss Barton was anxious that her property at Glen Echo be used as a monument to her memory, as Mount Vernon is to the memory of George Washington. For that purpose she deeded the property to Dr. Hubbell.

Soon afterwards Clara Barton died. Sometime thereafter Mrs. Hirons came to see Dr. Hubbell. She knew that both Dr. Hubbell and Clara Barton believed in spiritualism and [she] claimed to be a medium. Within ten days after she arrived at the Doctor's home, she had a deed from Dr. Hubbell for all the land. Mrs. Hirons was a young woman, about 40, attractive, and Dr. Hubbell was an elderly man and unmarried. She went into a seance with Dr. Hubbell in which she told him the spirit of Clara Barton said, "You are getting old and Mrs. Hirons is young. Turn all the property over to her. She will be better able to use it for the purposes for which I have given it to you."

About five years went by and the old gentleman realized she was selling some of the property and he filed a bill to set aside the conveyance on the grounds of undue influence...

During the trial Mrs. Hirons claimed she gave Dr. Hubbell ten thousand dollars for the land, but she never could trace the ten thousand dollars. She said it was cash given her by some man who was dead. There wasn't any evidence of the money being deposited in any bank, nor was there any evidence that Dr. Hubbell ever entered into his bank account any such sum.

The presiding Judge of the Circuit Court [Judge Hammond Urner] set aside the conveyance to Mrs. Hirons. She appealed and the Court of Appeals sustained the decision of

ALBERT M. BOUIC
(1882-1969)

In 1901, Albert M. Bouic began the study of law at the age of eighteen in the office of his father, William Viers Bouic, Jr., in Rockville. Included in the curriculum his father selected for him were Macauley's *History of England*, Hallam's *Middle Ages,* and Blackstone's *Commentaries.* When Mr. Bouic was admitted to the bar in July, 1906, there were only about 20 lawyers practicing in Montgomery County. Fifty years later he reminisced about those halcyon days:

When I went into my father's office to study, the same office where I now practice, there were two little rooms in it, each heated by its own little coal stove. I had to make these stoves up in the mornings when I went to work. There was a little johnny house out in the back but we had no running water. We had oil lamps and when we went to the office at night for any purpose, such as to examine *Maryland Reports* in cases we were trying, the chimneys of the oil lamps would be so dirty we could hardly read by them.

When there was a sale of land in the County conducted by my father, we would have to go there by horse and buggy. I remember going to Damascus with my father and it took all day. We left Rockville early in the morning and didn't get back until late the same day. The roads were dusty and it was a forty mile round trip...

Photo: Albert M. Bouic. Photograph from Andrews, *Tercentenary History of Maryland.*

the lower Court. What was left of the property was returned to Dr. Hubbell.

The case is reported as *Hirons v. Hubbell*, 149 Md. 593, 132 A. 645 (1926). The Clara Barton homestead is now

The 1931 Montgomery County Courthouse (now the District Courthouse). Photograph by Linda Johnson.

The Montgomery County Judicial Center. Photograph by Linda Johnson.

"Glen Echo," the home of Clara Barton, Montgomery County, Maryland. (By special permission of the U.S. Park Service.) Photograph by Coos Hamburger.

a National Historic Site, administered by the National Park Service.

A new courthouse built next door to the Red Brick Courthouse in Rockville in 1931 was the scene of a contemptuous act perpetrated upon the Circuit Court. David Lee and Pat Frank, two reporters from the *Washington Herald* who published information overheard from a private conversation between Judges Urner, Woodward and Willard, were jailed for criminal contempt. The published information related to a decision that the Judges intended to render in a pending criminal case in which the defendant was charged with conspiracy to commit murder. On appeal, the conviction of Lee was sustained, that of Frank reversed for lack of proof. *In re Lee*, 170 Md. 43, 183 A. 560 (1936).

The lawyer who represented Lee and Frank at their contempt trial was legendary Rockville lawyer Vivian V. Simpson. As a sophomore at the University of Maryland a dozen years earlier, she had filed suit to obtain a *mandamus* requiring the undergraduate school to readmit her as a third year dormitory student. She had been transferred instead to George Washington University because of her alleged lack of discipline. The suit was brought in Baltimore, and was tried before Judge Eugene O'Dunne, who issued the *mandamus*. On appeal, the decision was reversed, Chief Judge Carroll T. Bond espousing the position that "The maintenance of discipline, the upkeep of the necessary standards of behavior in a body of students in a college, is, of course, a task committed to its faculty and officers, not the courts." *Woods v. Simpson*, 146 Md. 547, 551, 126 A. 882, 883 (1924). Ms. Simpson spent a lifetime in

Judge James R. Miller, Jr. (R) joined Maryland's U.S. District Court on November 16, 1970. (L-R): Judge Frank A. Kaufman, Senior Judge Roszel C. Thomsen, Chief Judge Edward S. Northrop, Senior Judge R. Dorsey Watkins, Judge Alexander Harvey, II, and Judge James R. Miller, Jr. Judges Northrop and Miller were the first Federal Judges appointed to the bench from Montgomery County.

the courts challenging authority. She was the first woman member of the Montgomery County Bar Association and in 1949, became its first woman President. She died in 1987.

Another woman made history on the Montgomery County bench. Kathryn J. DuFour became the first woman in Maryland to serve as a Circuit Court Judge. She was appointed to the Montgomery County Circuit Court by Governor McKeldin in April, 1955, and served until 1970. The law library at Catholic University in Washington D.C., was named in her honor at the dedication of the Columbus School of Law on October 1, 1994.

The late Judge Rita C. Davidson was the first woman to serve on both the Court of Special Appeals (1972) and the Court of Appeals of Maryland (1979). In 1994, Judge Irma S. Raker became the second woman to serve on the Court of Appeals of Maryland. Judge Rosalyn Bell was the first woman appointed to the District Court of Maryland for Montgomery County (1978), the second woman appointed to the Circuit Court for

Elizabeth Tennery, Historian of the Montgomery County Bar Association. Photograph by Guill Photo.

Judge Kathryn J. DuFour. Portrait by Joyce Birkenstock. Photograph by Matthew Barrick.

Peter Messitte, U.S. District Judge. Photograph by Brooks, Bethesda, Maryland.

General Richard Montgomery

Montgomery County (1980), and the second woman to serve on the Court of Special Appeals (1983).

Torcaso v. Watkins was a mandamus action brought in the Circuit Court for Montgomery County that went all the way to the U.S. Supreme Court. Roy R. Torcaso, a resident of Montgomery County, was appointed a notary public by the Governor, but declined to subscribe to the oath of office that the clerk of court was required by law to give to him. The oath, prescribed by Article 37 of the Declaration of Rights of the State Constitution, required every person holding a public "office of profit or trust" in Maryland to declare a belief in the existence of God. Mr. Torcaso said that he would take an oath of office, but not declare his belief in God. He sued Clayton K. Watkins, the clerk of court, to require him to deliver Mr. Torcaso's notary commission, charging that the requirement of a belief in God as a condition of holding public office violated the First and Fourteenth Amendments. Judge Ralph Shure

dismissed the petition, and an appeal was taken to the Court of Appeals, which affirmed. Judge William L. Henderson's opinion stated: "The Fourteenth Amendment does not prevent the states from establishing qualifications for office, at least where the qualifications are not based on such an unreasonable and improper classification as to be discriminatory. . . [W]e find it difficult to believe that the Supreme Court will hold that a declaration of belief in the existence of God, required by Article 37 of our Declaration of Rights as a qualification for State office, is discriminatory and invalid." *Torcaso v. Watkins*, 223 Md. 49, 58, 162 A.2d 438, 443-44 (1960). An appeal was taken to the U.S. Supreme Court, which reversed, stating that "[t]his Maryland religious test for public office unconstitutionally invades the appellant's freedom of belief and religion and therefore cannot be enforced against him." In holding the test oath unconstitutional, Justice Hugo Black recalled the early history of Maryland:

There were, however, wise and far-seeing men in the Colonies — too many to mention — who spoke out against test oaths and all the philosophy of intolerance behind them. One of these, it so happens, was George Calvert (the first Lord Baltimore), who took a most important part in the original establishment of the Colony of Maryland. He was a Catholic and had, for this reason, felt compelled by his conscience to refuse to take the Oath of Supremacy in England at the cost of resigning from high governmental office. He again refused to take that oath when it was demanded by the Council of the Colony of Virginia, and as a result he was denied settlement in that Colony. A recent historian of the early period of Maryland's life has said that it was Calvert's hope and purpose to establish in Maryland a colonial government free from the religious persecutions he had known — one "securely beyond the reach of oaths. . ."

Torcaso v. Watkins, 367 U.S. 488, 490-91, 81 S.Ct. 1680, 1681-82, 6 L.Ed.2d 982, 984-985, 987-988 (1961).

Montgomery County retained its rural character as a farming community until the demand for new housing after World War II brought land development, industry and technology. The economic boom made Montgomery County the richest in the State, and it became a vital part of the Washington Metropolitan area. By 1990, the county had a population of 757,027!

The phenomenal growth of the county led to the construction of a modern Judicial Center and Executive

Replica of the 1708 Queen Anne's County Courthouse, Queenstown, Maryland.
Photograph by Coos Hamburger.

Courtroom in the reconstructed colonial courthouse of Queen Anne's County at Queenstown, Maryland. Photograph by Coos Hamburger.

once wrote that Judge Nicholson was 'another of those half-forgotten personalities who wait by the way to reward historical investigation.' The Courthouse remained in its original state until after the Civil War. In 1876, plans were made to rebuild that structure 'on a scale which will change it from one of the most inconvenient to one of the most desirable of our county buildings.' Aside from this reconstruction, which was accomplished for $6,800, the exterior of the courthouse is virtually the same as it was when originally constructed. An interesting and often overlooked feature is the gold eagle which appears in the pediment of the main portion of the building. It is undoubtedly a reflection of the fervent patriotism of the early citizens of the county, who were less than a decade from the ratification of the Federal constitution."

My wife, Susan Marzetta, and I encountered Judge Sause in front of the courthouse in Centreville on a Friday afternoon as he was returning to chambers from lunch. We informed him of our quest for information and he kindly obliged by recounting for us some of the interesting history of the area. By coincidence, it was October 14, 1994, the Judge's 60th birthday.

Judge Sause graduated from Williams College with honors (A.B. 1955) and from the University of Virginia (J.D. 1958) and was admitted to the bar in 1958. He served as law clerk to Judge William L. Henderson on the Court of Appeals, then went to work as an Assistant State's Attorney for Baltimore City, and later entered into private law practice on the Eastern Shore. In 1964-65, he was chairman of the

Young Lawyers' Section of the MSBA. He has been a Circuit Judge since 1988. He told us what it was like to practice law in Queen Anne's County when he arrived there a generation ago.

At the beginning of each term of court, all the lawyers in the county would meet in the courthouse library, in the presence of the judge and the county assessor. The county assessor would have in his possession all of the county tax assessment records. Someone would suggest the name of a person to serve as a juror, and the assessor would examine the books to make sure the person was a property owner. Then the lawyers would debate the merits of that person to perform jury duty. Each juror was selected individually by a vote of the lawyers, grand jurors and petit jurors alike. On the first day of court, the three Circuit Judges would meet, and one would charge the grand jury, after which all the lawyers were required to be in attendance. Each case on the docket would be called, and each would either be passed for settlement or assigned for trial during the following two weeks. It was not until 1942 that an office in the courthouse was provided for the use of the judges. Until then, judicial duties, including the signing of orders, were performed at the judges' homes. Judge Thomas J. Keating, Jr. (1872-1951), lived in a house down the street from the courthouse, and was the last judge in Queen Anne's County who had his chambers in his home. Today, the Queen Anne's County Bar Association numbers about 30 members who gather for their annual meeting every November. On June 6, 1996, the bench and bar

Clarence W. Miles

of Queen Anne's County will celebrate the bicentennial of the Centreville Courthouse with appropriate festivities.

Speaking at the 1905 meeting of the Maryland State Bar Association, John H.C. Legg of Centreville, a charter member of the Association, said: "[W]hen Adam and Eve had to leave the Garden of Eden, they were allowed the privilege of selecting a place to go, and wherever they went would be called Paradise, and they went to the Eastern Shore of Maryland."

PRESIDENTS OF THE MSBA - No. 60
1953-54
CLARENCE W. MILES (1897-1977)

Clarence W. Miles was born in Cambridge, Maryland, on June 29, 1897, the son of Alonzo L. Miles, a charter member of the MSBA. He was admitted to the Maryland bar in 1920, and practiced law in Salisbury for five years with his brother, Hooper S. Miles. In 1925, he came to Baltimore and was appointed People's Counsel before the Public Service Commission of Maryland. That year, he founded the University of Baltimore, with Eugene A. Edgett, Assistant State's Attorney for Baltimore City, and Howell A. King, of the University of Maryland School of Business. For a brief period, Mr. Miles and Mr. Edgett were law partners. In the early 1930s, he and Seymour O'Brien entered into a partnership that later became the firm of Miles, Walsh, O'Brien & Morris. In 1953, the firm merged with Mullikin, Stockbridge and Waters to become Miles & Stockbridge.

During World War II, Mr. Miles served as a colonel in the Judge Advocate General's Corps on the staff of General Dwight D. Eisenhower in North Africa and Europe. He won the Bronze Star for his wartime service. After the war, he organized the Greater Baltimore Committee and served as its first chairman. He served on the Bond Commission to reorganize the State's judiciary and was Chairman of the Miles Commission to restructure the State laws controlling horse racing.

The year 1953-54 witnessed two of the greatest achievements of his life, his attainment of the Presidency of the Maryland State Bar Association and the purchase of the

St. Louis Browns baseball team that became the Baltimore Orioles. He chaired the Cambridge Racial Commission to combat racial tensions during 1963-64. Mr. Miles was active in Democratic Party politics and ran unsuccessfully in the 1966 gubernatorial primary.

Judge Robert L. Karwacki praised him in 1976 when he received the Distinguished Alumnus of the Year Award from the University of Maryland School of Law:

Clarence Miles is a lawyer who contributes over and above his professional expertise; he gives his time to affairs for the benefit of his city, state and country. He has set an ideal for community involvement.

Clarence W. Miles died at "White Banks," his home near Queenstown, Maryland, on October 8, 1977, at the age of 80.

SAINT MARY'S COUNTY

The principles of religious freedom and the separation of Church and State were born in the New World at a place called St. Mary's City. Founded in 1634 by a handful of English settlers, it served for the next sixty years as the capital of the Maryland colony, its seat of justice and representative government. Here the first lawyers and judges in the province began a venerable legal history. One of them, Margaret Brent, took her place as the first woman to practice law on the North American continent.

Governor Leonard Calvert and his advisors, including Captain Henry Fleete, a guide from Virginia who was well acquainted with the ways of the native Americans, met with the friendly chiefs of the Yaocomico tribe and purchased a former village as the site of the new town. Farm tools and cloth were bartered for land and lodgings, and the meeting was concluded with a treaty of peace that was never broken. The settlement was named in honor of the Virgin Mary by the colonists, many of whom were Roman Catholics.

In sending them forth from England, Governor Calvert's brother, the Lord Proprietor, Cecil Calvert, Second Lord Baltimore, was carrying out the design of their father, Sir George Calvert, of establishing the colony as a haven for their fellow Catholics. When they came ashore, in addition to their meager possessions, the colonists brought with them their personal religious convictions and the precious heritage of the English common law, including due process and trial by jury.

his youth working on the plantation owned by Edward Lloyd V. He learned to read and escaped to freedom in the North. Embracing the cause of abolition, he lectured widely and published an anti-slavery newspaper, *The North Star.* After the Civil War, he served as U.S. Marshal of the District of Columbia.

One afternoon Susan and I had lunch with Alexander Gordon, IV, who has practiced law in Easton since 1981. His father, the late Alexander Gordon, III (1909-1963), was also a lawyer, and served as the first full-time Executive Director of the Maryland State Bar Association in 1962-63. Alex became a lawyer with Niles, Barton & Wilmer after clerking for a year with Judge Frederick J. Singley (1912-1988) on the Court of Appeals of Maryland. He holds a degree in economics from Oberlin College, an M.B.A. in finance from the Wharton School, a J.D. from the University of Maryland, and, as if all that were not enough, he is a Certified Public Accountant! Although Alex appears before most of the circuit courts on the Eastern Shore. he estimates that 75% of his practice is devoted to bankruptcy cases. He is a member of the panel of standing trustees in the Baltimore division of the U.S. Bankruptcy Court.

Today he is known throughout the State as the foremost authority on the law of mortgages in Maryland, having written volumes and taught courses for MICPEL on that subject and on Chapter 7 bankruptcy. *Gordon on Mortgage Foreclosures* (1994) is in its third edition. The

Alexander Gordon, IV.

time and effort he has devoted to continuing legal education in Maryland is all the more remarkable when one considers that he is not paid for his work and earns no royalties from the sale of his publications. He does all this for the pride of authorship and for the sheer pleasure he gets out of rendering valuable service to his fellow lawyers. He is the only recipient of MICPEL's Award for Outstanding Contribution to the Bar, having received it in 1986 and 1995. In 1992, he was elected to the Board of Trustees for MICPEL, and has served since then as a member of its Executive Committee and as its Treasurer.

Alex extols the pleasures of practicing law in Easton, where the bar numbers about 45-50 active practitioners, and another 15 who are semi-retired. The Talbot County Bar Association, of which he is a member, appears to date from the year 1907, when its existence was first noted

The 1794 Talbot County Courthouse at Easton was enlarged in 1958. Photograph by Linda Johnson.

The Circuit Courtroom in the Talbot County Courthouse. Photograph by Linda Johnson.

W. Mason Shehan

among the records of the Maryland State Bar Association. In the 1907 *Maryland Bar Transactions,* and in every yearly volume up to and including 1917, after which local bar associations and their officers were no longer recorded, the President and Secretary of the Talbot County Bar Association were listed respectively as Joseph B. Seth and T. Hughlett Henry.

PRESIDENTS OF THE MSBA - No. 37
1932-33
W. MASON SHEHAN (1873-1940)

William Mason Shehan was born in Talbot County (conflicting sources say Easton <u>and</u> Oxford) on December 24, 1873. He taught at the Easton High School and read law in the offices of U.S. Senator Charles H. Gibson and Charles C. Carrington. He received a formal legal education at the University of Maryland School of Law, from which he graduated in 1896, after having been admitted to the bar in 1895. He opened a law office in Easton and formed a partnership with General Joseph B. Seth in 1898, known as Seth & Shehan. In 1919, the firm became known as Seth, Shehan & Marshall, when G. Elbert Marshall became a partner. From 1912-19, he was State Insurance Commissioner. He was elected to succeed Judge William H. Adkins as Chief Judge of the Second Judicial Circuit, thereby qualifying him to serve simultaneously as Associate Judge of the Court of Appeals of Maryland. He died on August 25, 1940.

WASHINGTON COUNTY

Washington County was named in honor of General George Washington by the Maryland Constitutional Convention in the fateful year of 1776. The county seat was originally called "Elizabeth Hager's Town" by the city's founder, Jonathan Hager, in honor of his wife. Hagerstown was founded in 1762 on 200 acres that he purchased from attorney Daniel Dulany for 44 pounds in 1739. The family homestead, still standing in what is now the City Park, was a virtual fortress of stone constructed over a spring for protection against attack by marauding tribes. As the frontier grew safer after the French and Indian War, German settlers poured into the valley to establish farms and businesses. The first county court sessions were held there in a markethouse that stood in the town square at the crossroads of what is now Washington and Potomac Streets. Because Hagerstown was the center of converging wagon roads and rail lines, it became known as the "Hub City of the Cumberland Valley."

The guided tour of Hagerstown and its environs was conducted by native-born lawyer William P. Young, Jr., a partner in the firm of Meyers, Young & Grove, P.A. The firm traces its lineage back to the 1930s when John and Charles Wagaman began the practice of law in downtown Hagerstown. Their uncle, Charles D. Wagaman (1864-1922) was a charter member of the Maryland State Bar Association in 1896. Bill Young is a graduate of the Johns Hopkins University and the University of Maryland School of Law, a former President of the University of Maryland Alumni Association, an instructor and author of MICPEL real estate courses, a teacher at the Hagerstown Junior College, and a veteran chairman and member of numerous MSBA committees. He took off an entire day from his busy schedule to show Susan and me some of the region's numerous points of interest.

The tour began at Hagerstown's Maryland Theatre, designed by Scottish-born Thomas Lamb, the best known theatre architect of his day, and built in 1915 on the former site of the building where Jacob Gruber printed his world-famous *Hagerstown Farmer's Almanac*. Originally a vaudeville theatre, it featured such stars as the legendary Will Rogers. Silent movies were shown there with musical accompaniment supplied by a huge organ that also includes a player piano. The Theatre was abandoned after the front of the building was destroyed by fire. A group of concerned citizens, among them Bill Young's law partner, Lynn F. Meyers, organized a consortium that purchased the building, restored it to its former glory, and reopened it as a living reminder of Hagerstown's past. The renovated 1400-seat theatre is now the home of the Maryland Symphony Orchestra and presents many other musical and dramatic productions.

The Theatre is not far from the public square that was the site of Hagerstown's first courthouse. The square is at the intersection of Potomac Street (Route 65) leading north to Pennsylvania, and Washington Street (Route 40, the Old National Pike), running west to Cumberland, the road followed by all of the western pioneers. Hagerstown's predominant character as the hub city was shaped by the railroads. The Shenandoah Valley Railroad, the Norfolk, the Southern, Western Maryland and Pennsylvania Railroads, the Franklin County Railroad all came together here and then separate spurs shot off to other destinations. So Hagerstown was very much a railroad town as well as an agriculturally-based town.

Bill directed us to Hagerstown's Rose Hill Cemetery, where so many of the region's historical figures are remem-

bered in stone. Among them are Maryland Governors William T. Hamilton (1820-1888) and William Preston Lane, Jr. (1892-1967), both of whom were lawyers; many of the charter members of the Maryland State Bar Association from Hagerstown; and a number of Confederate war dead. Every year, a group of Jewish lawyers from Baltimore makes a pilgrimage there to lay a wreath on the grave of a Scots-Irish lawyer named Thomas Kennedy (1776-1832). In 1818, Kennedy, then a delegate to the Maryland General Assembly from Washington County, sponsored legislation to remove from the State Constitution a Christian test oath required for holding public office. The so-called "Jew Bill" failed to pass time after time, and Kennedy himself lost his seat in 1823 to an opponent running on a "Christian ticket." But he won the next election and witnessed the passage of his bill in 1826. His support of the bill was not motivated by self-interest. As he so eloquently stated: "There are few Jews in the United States; in Maryland, there are very few. But if there was only one — to that one, we ought to do justice."

Tenth annual meet of the League of American Wheelmen in the Main Square of Hagerstown, July 4, 1889. Courtesy of the Maryland State Archives, Merrick Collection, MSA SC 1477-5170.

Mules pulling a canal boat on the Chesapeake and Ohio Canal near Hancock, Maryland, circa 1910. Courtesy of the Maryland State Archives, Merrick Collection, MSA SC 1477-6404.

The battle of Antietam was fought not far from Hagerstown on September 17, 1862, the bloodiest single day of the Civil War. Deemed a Union victory, the battle was the cue for Lincoln to issue the Emancipation Proclamation, which he determined must not be seen as a desperate reaction to a military defeat.

After the fighting, Thomas Kennedy's daughter-in-law, Mrs. Howard Kennedy, took into her home a young Union soldier who had been shot through the neck. She probably saved the life of Captain Oliver Wendell Holmes, future Supreme Court Justice. The house, known as "Mt. Prospect," at the corner of Prospect and Washington Streets, was torn down to make way for a parking lot.

We learned from Bill Young that there are more stone bridges in Washington County than in any other county in the United States. A number of them were photographed years ago by David Cottingham, a local photographer, whose work is now on permanent display in the courthouse.

The Washington County Courthouse also features images of some of the great judges and lawyers from Hagerstown's history. The main circuit courtroom was the scene of the 1905 convention of the Maryland State Bar Association.

On June 10, 1828, both the Chesapeake & Ohio Canal Company and the Potomac Company applied to the Circuit Court for Washington County to enjoin the Baltimore & Ohio Railroad Company from acquiring rights of way along the projected route of the canal through Frederick and Washington Counties. Circuit Judge Thomas Buchanan (1768-1847) granted the preliminary injunction against the railroad. The railroad did not file an answer to the suit, but filed three suits of its own against the canal before Theodorick Bland, Chancellor of Maryland. Bland consolidated the cases and ruled in favor of the railroad in 1831. The case went to the Court of Appeals, where it was argued between December 26, 1831 and January 2, 1832. The B & 0 Railroad was represented by Daniel Webster and Reverdy

Johnson; counsel for the C & O Canal were Walter Jones and Alexander C. Magruder. The Court ruled 3-2 in favor of the canal. The opinion is reported as *Chesapeake and Ohio Canal Co. v. Baltimore and Ohio Railroad Co.*, 4 Gill & Johnson 1 (1832) and fills half a volume. H.H. Walker Lewis, legal historian par excellence, commented that it "may well be Maryland's greatest case." *THE GREAT CASE OF THE CANAL vs. THE RAILROAD*, 19 *Md. Law Review* 1 (Winter, 1959). The railroad may have lost the battle, but it won the war, beating the canal on its westward race to the mountains.

Perhaps the most famous case tried in recent history in the Washington County Courthouse was that of *State v. Zantzinger.* The trial was removed to Hagerstown from

RIGHT: After the battle, President Lincoln visits General McClellan at Antietam, Washington County, Maryland. Courtesy of the Maryland State Archives, Merrick Collection, MSA SC 1477-5822.
ABOVE: Wagons crossing the bridge at Antietam, shortly after the battle, September, 1862. Photograph by Alexander Gardner, courtesy of the Maryland State Archives, Merrick Collection, MSA SC 1477-5589.

221

JUDGE RICHARD HENRY ALVEY (1826-1906)

Born in St. Mary's County and admitted to the bar in Charles County, Richard H. Alvey will always be identified with Hagerstown and Washington County, where he lived, practiced law and served as a Judge on the Circuit Court and Court of Appeals from 1867 to 1893. For the last ten of those years, he was Chief Judge of the Court of Appeals of Maryland, before he was appointed Chief Justice of the Court of Appeals of the District of Columbia by President Cleveland in the spring of 1893. For the more than 37 years that he served as a Judge in Annapolis and Washington, D.C., he maintained his residence in Hagerstown, returning home by train on Friday nights and leaving again for work on Monday mornings. His name was mentioned as a possible Chief Justice of the United States to succeed Morrison Waite, but his age and the fact that he was a Southerner militated against his appointment. When he received a cable from Washington at his home in Hagerstown requesting his date of birth, a supporter urged him to make himself younger. His reply: "I will not tell a lie even for a place on the Supreme Court!"

PHOTO: Judge Richard H. Alvey. Photograph from Steiner, *Men of Mark in Maryland* (1907).

Baltimore City, and lasted from June 19-27, 1963. William Zantzinger was charged with first degree murder in the death of Hattie Carroll, an African-American waitress at Baltimore's Emerson Hotel, who died of a stroke after he reportedly hit her with a cane at the so-called "Spinsters' Ball" the previous February. There was no question that the defendant was extremely intoxicated on that occasion and that he had called Mrs. Carroll some offensive names. The issue was whether he had actually hit her and whether his conduct had caused her death. The case was prosecuted by Charles E. Moylan, Jr., the State's Attorney for Baltimore City. The defendant was represented by Frederick J. Green. The three judge panel that heard the case was composed of Chief Judge D. Kenneth McLaughlin, Judge Irvine H. Rutledge, and Judge Stuart F. Hamill. The evidence was conflicting, but the panel convicted the defendant of manslaughter and sentenced him to six months in prison. No appeal was taken and he served his sentence in the Hagerstown Jail. The case was the subject of a bitter ballad by folksinger Bob Dylan, entitled *The Lonesome Death of Hattie Carroll.*

PRESIDENTS OF THE MSBA - No. 31 (1926-27) ALEXANDER ARMSTRONG, JR. (1877-1939)

Alexander Armstrong, Jr.

Alexander Armstrong was born in Hagerstown, Maryland, on June 28, 1877, the son and namesake of attorney Alexander Armstrong (1847-1905) who was a charter member of the Maryland State Bar Association. Unlike his father, he was an ardent Republican who was elected Attorney General of Maryland (1919-23), but was defeated for Governor by Democrat Albert Ritchie in 1923. His mother, Elizabeth Key Scott, was related to Francis Scott Key. He was the class valedictorian at Washington County High School in 1895 and also at Princeton University in 1899. One of his professors was Woodrow Wilson, who offered him the position as his assistant, which he declined in order to pursue a legal career. He received his law degree from the University of Pennsylvania in 1903. He practiced law in Hagerstown continuously from his admission to practice before the Court of Appeals on January 13, 1904, and also in Baltimore after December, 1923, as the senior partner of Armstrong, Machen & Allen. (His partners were Arthur W. Machen, Jr., President of the MSBA in 1939-40, and Wendell D. Allen. H. Vernon Eney, MSBA President in 1963-64, joined the firm in 1934.) Mr. Armstrong was city attorney for Hagerstown from 1904 to 1906, and State's Attorney for Washington County from 1908 to 1912. He served as a member of the State Board of Law Examiners and was one of Maryland's three commissioners to the Conference on Uniform State Laws. Film and television star Bess Armstrong is his granddaughter, who began her acting career as the lead in a Gilbert & Sullivan production by the Young Victorian Theatre of Baltimore.

The Washington County Courthouse. Photograph by Linda Johnson.

RIGHT: The Circuit Courtroom in the Washington County Courthouse. Photograph by Linda Johnson.

John P. Corderman

PRESIDENTS OF THE MSBA - No. 91
1984-85
JOHN P. CORDERMAN
(1942-   )

Ten years after being named "Outstanding Young Man of Washington County" in 1974, John P. Corderman took office as President of the Maryland State Bar Association, at age 42, one of the youngest to be so honored. He was born in Hagerstown, Maryland, on May 14, 1942, educated in the local schools, and earned his A.B. and J.D. degrees from the University of Maryland. He was Deputy State's Attorney for Washington County from 1971 to 1974, and served his county in the Maryland Senate from 1975 to 1977. In 1977, he became a Judge of the Circuit Court for Washington County, the position he held while he also served as MSBA President. His term as President was marked by his defense of the competency of lawyers against

HENRY KYD DOUGLAS
(1838-1903)

The youngest member of Stonewall Jackson's staff, Henry Kyd Douglas recorded his recollections of the Civil War in *I Rode With Stonewall*, published posthumously. He was born in Shepherdstown, West Virginia (then Virginia), and died at his home in Hagerstown, Maryland, having suffered from tuberculosis for a number of years. He was a graduate of Franklin and Marshall College, read law in the offices of two Virginia judges, and was admitted to the bar in 1860. Practicing briefly in St. Louis, he returned home to enlist in the Confederate Army in 1861. He was severely wounded at Gettysburg on July 3, 1863, and was taken captive. After the war, he came to Hagerstown, where he practiced law and served as a Judge. While arguing a case in the Court of Appeals against Severn Teackle Wallis, involving an insurance loss by fire, Wallis referred repeatedly to a firm of actuaries by the name of "Smith, Thomas & Henry." Douglas said, "Mr. Wallis, there is no magic in those names. You might just as well refer to Shadrach, Meshach and Abednego." To which Mr. Wallis replied, "What better witnesses would you want on a fire claim?"

PHOTO: Henry Kyd Douglas. *Baltimore-American Illustrated Edition, The State of Maryland* (1896).

William P. Young, Jr. Photograph by Guill Photo.

attacks by such detractors as Chief Justice Warren E. Burger.

He had the reputation as a tough Judge because of the severe sentences he imposed on some violent criminal offenders. He was the victim of a terrorist bomb that came to his house wrapped as a Christmas present. The bomb exploded in his lap on December 22, 1989, causing shrapnel wounds and loss of hearing that resulted in his early retirement. No one has ever been arrested in the case. After leaving the bench, he returned to the private practice of law in Hagerstown. On April 1, 1996, he began a two-year term as Attorney General of the small island nation of Palau in the western Pacific Ocean.

WICOMICO COUNTY

Wicomico County was the last county to be established on the Eastern Shore, and the only Eastern Shore county to be created by a constitutional convention. The year was 1867, when the present Constitution of Maryland was drafted and ratified. Land from Somerset and Worcester Counties was taken to form the new county, whose population was clamoring for their own county seat. Salisbury was the natural choice, as the largest city on the lower Shore. Division Street in Salisbury had been the aptly-named dividing line for those living on the east side to attend court in Snow Hill, while those on the west side had to go to Princess Anne. A courthouse and jail were not constructed until 1878. Until then, terms of court were held in Jackson's Opera House. The Victorian courthouse was one of the few buildings in Salisbury to survive the disastrous fire of October 17, 1886. The bell of St. Peter's Episcopal Church that sounded the first alarm was later hung in the tower of the courthouse.

Because of responsible leadership, Salisbury was spared much of the racial strife that affected the rest of the Eastern Shore in the 1960s. In 1961, without fanfare, a committee of black and white citizens chaired by attorney John W.T. Webb obtained the agreement of local restaurant owners to integrate their businesses. Theaters and motels soon followed suit, voluntarily opening their doors to all. Mr. Webb and the Salisbury Bi-racial Commission received an award from the Sidney Hollander Foundation in recognition of their successful efforts "in reducing discrimination and promoting equal opportunity."

Phil Sherman and I visited the Salisbury chambers of Administrative Judge Alfred T. Truitt, Jr., who took us on a tour of the Wicomico County Courthouse, its 1936 wing and a more recent addition completed in 1992. The courthouse at Salisbury is the largest on the Eastern Shore. The old ceremonial courtroom has the look and feel of the wood-panelled courtrooms of the 1950s featured in the Perry Mason television series starring Raymond Burr.

On September 8, 1993, the law library contained in the older part of the courthouse was dedicated by the Wicomico County Bar Association as "The Alfred T. Truitt, Jr., Law Library." The Judge's father was Mayor of Salisbury in 1932 at the time the city celebrated its bicentennial. Judge Truitt recounted for us some tales of lawyers, trials and law practice in the counties of the lower Eastern Shore.

One of the many cases Judge Truitt prosecuted when he was State's Attorney for Wicomico County was that of Joseph James Batholomey. On December 8, 1968, in the

After the great Salisbury Fire of 1886, the Wicomico County Courthouse was one of the few surviving buildings. Courtesy of the Maryland State Archives, Merrick Collection, MSA SC 1477-6481.

The Wicomico County Courthouse of 1878. Photograph by Linda Johnson.

U.S. Senator Paul S. Sarbanes

course of escaping from the Wicomico County Jail, on the top floor of the Salisbury Courthouse, the defendant shot and killed Sheriff Samuel A. Graham and Deputy Sheriff Albert Kelly, and shot at another man but missed. The trial was removed to Charles County where he was tried before a jury. The defendant was represented by James F. Garrity. At the conclusion of the trial, the jury deliberated for two hours before rendering verdicts of guilty upon all four indictments charging the defendant with escape, assault with intent to murder and two counts of first degree murder. He was sentenced to death in the gas chamber on the murder convictions by Chief Judge Dudley Digges, who pondered the sentence for six months before imposing it. The Court of Appeals of Maryland upheld the convictions and the sentence in *Bartholomey v. State*, 260 Md. 504, 273 A.2d 164 (1971). The case reached the U.S. Supreme Court with a number of other death penalty cases. The Supreme Court reversed Bartholomey's death sentence in *Bartholomey v. Maryland*, 408 U.S. 938, 92 S.Ct. 2870, 33 L.Ed.2d 759 (1972), based upon its 5-4 decision in the case of *Furman v. Georgia*, 408 U.S. 238, 92 S.Ct. 2726, 33 L.Ed.2d 346 (1972), that held capital punishment to be cruel and unusual punishment in violation of the Eighth Amendment because of the random fashion in which it was imposed.

Salisbury was the birthplace of Maryland's senior U.S. Senator, Paul S. Sarbanes, who was born there above his parents' bakery on February 3, 1933. He graduated from Wicomico County Senior High School and from Princeton University Phi Beta Kappa, *magna cum laude* in 1954. A Rhodes scholar, he graduated with honors from Oxford in 1957 and the Harvard Law School in 1960. His legal career began as law clerk to U.S. Circuit Judge Morris Ames Soper. He was engaged in the practice of law in Baltimore from 1961-62 and 1965-70. In 1962-63 he was administrative assistant to Walter Heller, chairman of President Kennedy's Council of Economic Advisors. After serving in the Maryland House of Delegates from 1966-70, he defeated longtime Maryland Congressman George Fallon in the 1970 Democratic primary by 2,000 votes, and sailed to victory in the general election. As a member of the Judiciary Committee, he gained national prominence as drafter of the articles of impeachment voted by the House against President Nixon in the summer of 1974. Two years later, he was elected to the U.S. Senate, defeating Senator J. Glenn Beall, Jr. Since then, he has been reelected in 1982, 1988 and 1994. In 1986, he was the keynote speaker at a public

The old Circuit Courtroom of the Wicomico County Courthouse. Photograph by Linda Johnson.

Courthouse with Addition of 1936. Photograph by Linda Johnson.

James E. Ellegood
Photograph from Sams and Riley,
Bench and Bar of Maryland (1901).

Frederick W. C. Webb

Levin Claude Bailey

E. Dale Adkins, Jr.

forum known as a "Jefferson Meeting" celebrating the bicentennial of the U.S. Constitution in Annapolis, sponsored by MSBA and the League of Women Voters. Since the advent of the Clinton Administration, he has been responsible for nominating women and minorities to serve on the Federal courts.

The modern addition to the Wicomico County Courthouse. Photograph by Coos Hamburger.

PRESIDENTS OF THE MSBA - No. 25
1920-21
JAMES E. ELLEGOOD (1842-1925)

James E. Ellegood was born in what is now Wicomico County on January 1, 1842. He was educated at Washington College and was admitted to the bar on July 5, 1869. He practiced law for most of his life in Salisbury, except for a few years in Cumberland. He successfully represented Wicomico County in a number of lawsuits for unpaid taxes against the Baltimore, Chesapeake and Atlantic Railway. The cases are reported as *B.C.&A. Ry. v. Ocean City*, 89 Md. 89, 42 A. 922 (1899); *B.C.&A. Ry. v. Wicomico Co.*, 93 Md. 113, 48 A. 853 (1901); and 103 Md. 277, 63 A. 678 (1906). The case of *Wicomico County v. Bancroft*, 203 U.S. 112, 27 S.Ct. 21, 51 L.Ed. 112 (1906), was decided by the Supreme Court in favor of Mr. Ellegood's client, the taxing authority, against the holder of railroad bonds.

With this background as a litigator against railroads, Mr. Ellegood's death was particularly ironic. His automobile was struck by a train while driving across the tracks at Delmar, Maryland, on January 24, 1925, and he was killed instantly.

PRESIDENTS OF THE MSBA - No. 51
1944-45
FREDERICK W. C. WEBB (1889-1956)

Frederick Woolford Conway Webb was born in Vienna, Dorchester County, Maryland, on June 27, 1889, the son of John W.T. Webb and Anna Virginia Conway. He was graduated from the University of Virginia in 1912 and was admitted to the bar the following year. He practiced his entire life in Salisbury, first as an associate in the firm of Ellegood, Freeney and Wailes, then in 1918 as a partner with Amos W.W. Woodcock in the firm of Woodcock and Webb, later known as Webb, Bounds and Travers. In his address as President of the Maryland State Bar Association in 1945, he advocated opening the membership of the Association to all Maryland lawyers, which did not finally happen until another generation had passed. His son, John W.T. Webb (1918-1990), was the Salisbury lawyer who chaired the Bi-racial Commission that integrated the city's public accommodations in 1961. He was a partner in the firm his father founded which is now known as Webb, Burnett, Jackson, Cornbrooks & Wilber.

PRESIDENTS OF THE MSBA - No. 57
1950-51
LEVIN CLAUDE BAILEY (1892-1952)

Judge Levin Claude Bailey was born in Quantico, Wicomico County, Maryland, on February 7, 1892. He graduated with honors from St. John's College in 1911, and the University of Maryland School of Law in 1913. He was admitted to the bar later that year having attained the highest score on the bar examination. He began the practice of law in Salisbury in the office of his uncle, Joseph L. Bailey. He served in the Army in France and Germany during World War I, attaining the rank of Captain. He returned to Salisbury in 1919, where he entered the office of Miles, Bailey & Miles. He served as City Solicitor of Salisbury and was elected twice as State's Attorney for Wicomico County. On May 29, 1943, he was appointed Chief Judge of the First Judicial Circuit by Governor Herbert R. O'Conor, which entitled him to also serve as Associate Judge of the Court of Appeals of Maryland. When the Court of Appeals was reconstituted after the passage of the Bond Amendment in 1944, Judge Bailey became strictly a trial judge in the Circuit Court. From 1946 until a week before his death, he served as Chairman of the Rules Committee of the Court of Appeals. His son, the late James Porter Bailey, practiced law with the Salisbury firm founded by his father and held the position of U.S. Magistrate Judge.

PRESIDENTS OF THE MSBA - No. 77
1970-71
E. DALE ADKINS, JR. (1915-1982)

When E. Dale Adkins, Jr., was awarded an honorary doctor of laws degree by Salisbury State University the year before his death, the citation read in part: "Your name has been synonymous with public service to Maryland for decades. To you our leaders turn for advice and counsel, not only on legal matters, but also on judicial appointments to the federal bench."

He was a leader in the commercial, civic and political life of the Eastern Shore, built upon the heritage of his prominent family. A Republican, he served one term as State Senator from Wicomico County before his appointment to the Circuit Court at the age of 37 in 1952, succeeding Judge Levin Claude Bailey. He served only briefly before leaving the bench to return to private practice. He was chairman of the board of the E.S. Adkins Company, the family lumber and building materials business. In the 1960s he was a member of the Wicomico County Commission on Interracial Problems, bringing peaceful change to the previously segregated public schools and other facilities of the county. The year he stepped down as President of the MSBA, the Association held its first annual convention on the Eastern Shore in 64 years, largely due to his efforts. He was a founder and first president of the Eastern Shore Symphony Society, president of the Wicomico County Library, and trustee of Salisbury's Peninsula General Hospital, where he died on June 15, 1982, at the age of 66. At the time of his death, he was senior partner in the firm of Adkins, Potts & Smethurst. His daughter, Sally Adkins, and son, E. Dale Adkins, III, are members of the Maryland Bar.

WORCESTER COUNTY

Worcester County was created from Somerset County in 1742 by legislative fiat (Chapter 19, Acts of 1742), and named for the Earl of Worcester. Snow Hill has served as the county seat from the beginning. Located inland on the Pocomoke River, the town was founded in 1686 and is believed to have been named after a suburb of London.

Maryland's only Atlantic shoreline is located in Worcester County. The sandy coasts of Assateague Island and Ocean City are part of a barrier reef forty miles long, no more than three miles wide, and separated from the mainland by bays bearing the names Sinepuxent, Chincoteague and Assawoman. The Maryland State Bar Association held six of its first 12 annual conventions at Ocean City, the state's only ocean port and beach resort, in the years 1897, 1899, 1902, 1903, 1906, and 1907. Sixty-four years passed before the MSBA returned to Ocean City in 1971. Since then, it has met there from 1973 to 1981, and every year from 1983 to the present (1995).

After the Civil War, Isaac Coffin opened The Rhode Island Hotel at what is now Ocean City for the benefit of sportsmen and visitors. The idea of developing the narrow strip of beach was first conceived by a group of promoters who laid out plans for a resort in August, 1872. The founders of Ocean City were George W. Purnell, Lemuel B. Showell, D. Jones Taylor, R. Jenkins Henry of Berlin, and Purnell Toadvine of Salisbury. The tract was called "Ladies' Resort to the Sea," on a land patent dated 1868 held by Stephen Taber of Long Island. He favored the idea of developing the area into a resort and deeded the founders the site for a hotel. At a meeting held in Salisbury, they chose the name Ocean City from a number of suggested names, including Beach City and Sinepuxent City. It was not until 1874 that sufficient capital to build Ocean City's first hotel was raised by public subscription and the sale of stock. The three-story Atlantic Hotel at Boardwalk and Wicomico Street opened on July 4, 1875, the date traditionally regarded as the official beginning of Ocean City. The resort's first patrons travelled there by horse and carriage over sandy roads and through salt marshes. They were ferried across Sinepuxent Bay by a scow to the sandy strip of land on which Ocean City stands. Two years later, The Seaside Hotel was erected. A branch of the Eastern Shore Railroad was extended from Berlin to the bay about the year 1880. A little later a bridge was built to carry trains into the town. The Atlantic and The Seaside were destroyed in a million dollar fire that swept the resort in 1925. The Atlantic was rebuilt on the original site and is still in operation at the foot of the southern end of the Boardwalk next to the amusement pier.

Speaking at the annual convention in Ocean City in 1971, Judge Daniel Prettyman recalled the last occasion when MSBA met there in 1907:

> On the day preceding the meeting I remember boarding the steamer in Baltimore. . . [I]t could have been the Emma Giles or the Louise, and we sailed down the Bay to Claiborne. As I recall it was something like a three-hour cruise, and at Claiborne we boarded the train of coaches of the B.C. and A., Baltimore, Chesapeake and Atlantic Railroad. This train was dubbed "The Flyer," I suspect more from the insects that infected the area than the speed of the tour. However, a congenial conductor tried to make life comfortable for us, and we came down the peninsula and through Salisbury, and I remember we arrived in Berlin at 8

o'clock that night, and shortly thereafter we arrived at the waters of the Sinepuxent Bay and came across a narrow trestle bridge into Ocean City. The Station was located at Somerset and Baltimore Avenue. . . We were met at the station by the head station master and we walked with him carrying our baggage by the powerhouse and the Seaside Hotel up to the long porches of the Atlantic Hotel which stretched from the boardwalk to All America, and obtained our accommodations.

On the following morning the convention was called to order by the President, Conway W. Sams of Baltimore City. The first order of business was the Presidential Address, and at that time President Sams' address was entitled "The Law and Its Enforcement," and in his stentorian oration Mr. Sams discussed the problem of law enforcement and attributed at least some of the problem to "the enormous output of laws by the Legislature" [Laughter] and the ponderous number and increasing publication of the decisions of the courts [Laughter]. . . Mr. Frank G. Turner of Baltimore was Treasurer, and based

RIGHT: The Worcester County Courthouse at Snow Hill. Photograph by Linda Johnson.

Snow Hill, Worcester County, Maryland, Washington Street, in the days of the horse and buggy, circa 1915. Courtesy of the Maryland State Archives, Merrick Collection, MSA SC 1477-4862.

upon the annual dues of $5 a year, the total disbursements for the Association in the year1906-07 was in the amount of $1,975.75. As has been reported there were 500 members of the Association, and there were eleven local bar associations here in the State.

After these brief ceremonies we then adjourned to engage in some of the recreation and pleasures of the resort . . . and went to the end of the boardwalk at the south end of South Second Street and there watched the fishermen put their heavy boats out to the water and row through the surf out to the pound net, and there they would gather the fish and row back through the surf in the evening, and when they reached the beach a team of mules was taken down and pulled the heavy boats back up onto the high land and to the sheds where the fish were prepared for the commercial market. . .

We then returned to the hotel and enjoyed some of the delicious and very rich food at the famous Atlantic Hotel kitchen, and if we needed it we could go down Coughlan's Drug Store and get some Sal Hepatica or baking soda.

On the following day we saw quite a sight. It was the Fourth of July, and the excursion train came on out, car after car on the train, and the men all in their high starched collars and skimmer straw hats, ladies with their ankle-length dresses and beautiful broad-brimmed hats, all carrying their parasols and the little ones following along in their best bib and tucker, each one with a basket heavily laden with fried chicken and baked country ham. That was to be the food for the day in picnic fashion, and they would then race to the porches of the Casino to stake out a claim on a table and bench which would be the focal point for the family's activity for that day. In

Kathleen E. Smith.

the Casino there was an auditorium for theatrical productions. There were bowling alleys and pool tables on the second floor, and the first floor had concessions and games of various kinds.

But those who were venturesome went over to the bath house operated by Gil Cropper and John Raine, and there they could rent a bathing suit for 25 cents for all day, keep it as long as you wanted. . . There was a long rope, and I might say my personal recollection is sufficient to remember this, that extended from the boardwalk out into poles in the beach, and you didn't dare venture into the surf unless you had firm hold on that rope to bring you ashore if you couldn't make it otherwise. . . For my own sake, the 1907 convention is memorialized forever because I could sit on the sweeping porches of the Atlantic Hotel in a rocking chair and have the white coated delivery man deliver me a mint julep, one after the other, at 25 cents apiece.

Kathleen E. Smith is one of the new breed of lawyers on the Eastern Shore. A sole practitioner, her law office is located in Ocean City on heavily-travelled Ocean Highway. Hers is mostly a civil trial practice, including insurance defense, although she also handles criminal and domestic cases. Born in Easton, raised in Federalsburg, educated on Shakespeare and James Joyce at Mary Washington College, she clerked in Towson for the late James H. Cook at Cook, Howard, Downes & Tracy, (later Venable, Baetjer & Howard), while studying law at the University of Maryland. (Mr. Cook was President of the MSBA in 1976-77.) He taught by example how to practice law with civility, while zealously representing clients. His courtliness was an inspiration. After graduation, she returned to the Eastern Shore in 1989 to clerk for Judge Dale Cathell on the Court of Special Appeals, where she developed an interest in the history and lore of the legal profession. As a new lawyer with the Salisbury firm of Banks, Nason, Hickson &

Circuit Courtroom in the Worcester County Courthouse. Photograph by Linda Johnson.

Sullivan, she tried her first case before Judge Marvin Smith (no relation) of the Court of Appeals, who was sitting by special assignment in the District Court. As if that were not intimidating enough, she knew him from the time she was a mischievous eight-year-old, having attended the same Methodist Church in Federalsburg. (When the Judge disclosed for the record his acquaintance with Ms. Smith, she was apprehensive that he was about to disclose as well the time he caught her pitching quarters in church.) She went on to work at the Ocean City firm of Williams, Hammond, Moore, Shockley & Harrison, before going out on her own this year (1995). She was instrumental in assembling a group of lawyers and judges from Somerset, Worcester, and Wicomico Counties who agreed to be interviewed by Phil Sherman and me in preparation for this book.

PRESIDENT OF THE MSBA - No. 33
(1928-29)
JOHN W. STATON (1873-1932)

John W. Staton was born in Berlin, Maryland, on January 4, 1873, and died in Snow Hill, Maryland, on February 17, 1932. "Chanceford," his residence in Snow Hill, was built by James Rounds Morris, clerk of the Worcester Circuit Court before 1800. After his father's death in 1889, he was appointed deputy clerk of the Circuit Court. While serving in that capacity, he began reading law, and was admitted to the bar upon oral examination on January 18, 1898. He continued to serve

231

John W. Staton

Samuel K. Dennis

as deputy clerk until October 1, 1903, when he resigned to engage in the practice of law. He became senior partner in the firm of Staton, Whaley & Price. His eulogy in the 1932 Maryland Bar Transactions said in part:

> Mr. Staton's long training in the Clerk's office, combined with the associations he had formed, and the contacts he had established, served him to admirable purpose when he first engaged in the practice of law. He was successful from the beginning. The painstaking care with which he prepared his cases, his conservative opinions and his judicial discernments were attributes of such high quality as to attract and command a large clientele.

PRESIDENT OF THE MSBA - No. 38
(1933-34)
SAMUEL K. DENNIS (1874-1953)

Samuel K. Dennis was born at "Beverly," the ancestral home of the Dennis family in Worcester County, Maryland, on September 28, 1874. His uncle, Henry Page, was also President of the MSBA and a judge on the Court of Appeals of Maryland. While working as personal secretary to Governor John Walter Smith, he attended the University of Maryland School of Law, where he graduated in 1903 near the top of his class, completing the three-year course in just two years. He scored high on the bar examination and was admitted to practice that year. In 1904 he ran as a Democrat for the House of Delegates from Worcester County and was elected. He also went into private practice with his cousin, James Upshur Dennis, who served as secretary of the MSBA from 1903 to 1908. He was U.S. Attorney

for Maryland from 1915 to 1920. While in private practice in the 1920s, he devoted much of his time to the cause of fighting tuberculosis. With Dr. Victor Cullen, he helped found the Henryton Hospital and Mt. Wilson Sanitarium. At his investiture as Chief Judge of the Supreme Bench of Baltimore City (now the Circuit Court for Baltimore City) on August 27, 1928, he was presented with judicial robes by Randolph Barton, Jr., President of the Bar Association of Baltimore City. This marked the first occasion that a Baltimore City judge ever wore a robe. The same year, his motion to admit women members to the City Bar Association was defeated.

On March 1, 1940, Judge Dennis was named chairman of the committee that drafted the first Maryland Rules of Procedure that went into effect on September 1, 1941.

Although he was a resident of Baltimore City and the last Dennis to live on the family homestead at Beverly, Samuel K. Dennis never lost his identification with the Eastern Shore. The fact of his birth there is recorded on his gravestone in Baltimore's Druid Ridge Cemetery. And author Katherine Scarborough, in her *Homes of the Cavaliers,* wrote:

> . . .[O]ne of the beams in the cellar of Beverly shows a scar, scarcely healed since it was made several years ago. From the beam a generous piece of wood was cut away, not with wanton intent, but to be made into the gavel used constantly by Judge Samuel K. Dennis to maintain "order in the court."

WASHINGTON, D.C.

Marylanders share a special pride in the fact that the nation's capital was built on land ceded to the Federal government by the State in 1791. Washington, D.C. has had a most profound impact on

The White House. Photograph by Coos Hamburger.

The U.S. Capitol. Photograph by Coos Hamburger.

Maryland's political, social, economic and legal history. Our national institutions, cultural and governmental, are located there. It was in Washington that countless members of the Maryland bar were born, lived and died, were educated or taught others, practiced law, or pursued careers in statecraft, politics or private business. Some of Maryland's greatest lawyers argued cases before the Supreme Court. Others held important judicial office, including service as Justices on the high court. Still other Marylanders were elected by their fellow citizens to represent the State in the halls of Congress. Maryland's legal history does not end at the District line.

On September 8, 1791, the name of the first President of the United States was given to the proposed capital city, and the territory in which the city would be built was designated the District of Columbia. Why? The sale of lots was about to commence, and the project had to have a name so that it could be used on the maps that were about to be printed. The names were selected by three commissioners appointed to superintend the sale of lots and the construction of public buildings. Two of the commissioners were Marylanders. Thomas Johnson of Frederick was a lawyer, first Governor of the State, and Associate Justice of the United States. Daniel Carroll of Upper Marlboro was a signer of the Constitution.

How the District of Columbia came to be selected as the location of the capital of the new nation is a story unto itself. It will be remembered that in the year 1790, this country's first Secretary of the Treasury, Alexander Hamilton, prepared a financial plan that called for the new government to assume the unpaid debts contracted for by the states during the war for independence, amounting to about $54 million. The assumption bill went down to defeat in the House of Representatives on April 12, 1790, by a vote of 28-22. Maryland, Virginia, Georgia and New Hampshire had been most strongly opposed to the bill, while the Middle States were split on the issue. The other hot issue on everyone's mind was the question of where the national capital would be located. Various sites on the Susquehanna, Potomac, and Delaware Rivers had been proposed, but no consensus had been reached. Hamilton used this controversy as the means to an end. At a dinner given by Secretary of State Thomas Jefferson and attended by Hamilton and James Madison, an agreement was brokered by which the capital would be established on a ten miles square site on the Potomac to be chosen by the President in return for southern support for assumption. On July 16, 1790, the law was enacted which provided for the capital to be located on the Potomac River. On August 4, a law providing for the assumption and payment of debts was approved. Thus, the very existence of Washington, D.C. was born of political compromise.

George Washington chose the peninsula formed by the Potomac and Anacostia Rivers as the site for the capital city. On October 13, 1792, he attended the laying of the cornerstone for the President's House, the city's first public building. Washington did not live to see the White House completed nor the city that bears his name rise above the swamps near the banks of the Potomac.

THE CAPITOL

The laws of the nation are enacted by the Congress of the United States in the marble chambers of the U.S. Capitol. Since 1800, momentous decisions have been made here on Capitol Hill, including declarations of war, the enactment of social legislation, the ratification of treaties and the confirmation of Federal judges and other officials. When the light on the top of the Capitol dome is lit at night, it signifies that Congress is in session.

Television news commentator Roger Mudd, brother of the late John Mudd of the Maryland bar, said this about Congress in remarks to the MSBA at its Mid-year Meeting on January 12, 1968:

> The American Parliament is called Congress. It consists of 535 members who are housed in six enormous buildings on Capitol Hill, which is always referred to in Washington as "The Hill."
>
> The Capitol itself is a sprawling, three-story marble and limestone structure, topped by a cast-iron dome and honeycombed with miles of corridors and subterranean passageways. . .
>
> Congress is divided into two branches. Each branch is divided into committees, which are ruled by old men called "chairmen." To become a chairman, one need only to have been in office longer than anyone else on the committee, who also wants to be chairman. . .
>
> There are a great many differences between the House and the Senate. In the House, a member may talk for only five minutes, unless he has everyone's consent to go longer. In the Senate, a member may talk forever, and some have. . .

The Capitol has not only been the home of the House of Representatives and the Senate. The U.S. Supreme Court sat in a first floor committee room from 1801-08. It was there that Chief Justice John Marshall established judicial review in the case of *Marbury v. Madison,* 5 U.S. (1 Cranch) 137 (1803). In 1808 the Court moved to another room, and during construction in 1809 it held sessions in a tavern. From 1810 until the British burned Washington in August, 1814, and later, from 1819-60, the Court sat in the Old Supreme Court Chamber located in the Capitol basement. It was there on May 24, 1844, that Samuel F. B. Morse sent the first telegraph message over the wire to Baltimore: "What hath God wrought!" In the same room freedom was denied to Dred Scott by Chief Justice Roger Brooke Taney and a divided Supreme Court in 1857 in the

---

WILLIAM M. MERRICK (1818-1889)

Born near Faulkner, Charles County, Maryland, on September 1, 1818, he was a graduate of Georgetown University in 1831 and received a law degree from the University of Virginia Law School. He was appointed to the Circuit Court of the District of Columbia by President Buchanan in 1855. Because he ordered the Army to discharge some underage recruits in *habeas corpus* proceedings at the start of the Civil War, he was placed under house arrest for two months as a suspected Southern sympathizer and his salary withheld by order of Secretary of State William Seward. In 1863, the court upon which he sat was abolished by Act of Congress, the Supreme Court of the District of Columbia was created in its place, and he was turned out of office. Judge Merrick took up teaching law at the Columbian College (now George Washington University), practiced law in Howard County, Maryland and was elected to Congress in 1870. In 1885, President Cleveland appointed him to a judgeship on the Supreme Court for the District of Columbia. It took a year to confirm him by the Senate because of his age and the persistent, unfounded rumor that he had been disloyal. He served on the court until his death on February 4, 1889.

PHOTO: Judge William M. Merrick from a *carte de visite* owned by the Baltimore Bar Library.

Washington College of Law Dean Elliott Millstein (L) and Claudio Grossman, (R), Dean of Graduate Studies, honor alumni Judge John McAuliffe and Judge Irma Raker, of the Maryland Court of Appeals.

infamous decision that heralded the Civil War. From 1860 until 1935, the Court occupied the Old Senate Chamber upstairs on the first floor of the Capitol.

Statuary Hall is the nation's Hall of Fame, located in the former chamber where the House of Representatives met from 1807-57. Maryland chose two native sons for immortality among the assembled statues: Charles Carroll of Carrollton, Maryland attorney, U.S. Senator and signer of the Declaration of Independence, and John Hanson, "first President of the United States in Congress Assembled," 1781. Both statues were the creation of sculptor Richard E. Brooks.

LAW SCHOOLS LOCATED IN THE DISTRICT OF COLUMBIA

AMERICAN UNIVERSITY WASHINGTON COLLEGE OF LAW

"The Washington College of Law, part of The American University since 1949, is located on the university's 76-acre campus in one of the city's safest and most beautiful residential neighborhoods. The university, chartered in 1891 and incorporated by an act of Congress in 1893, was founded as a Methodist-related graduate school of history and public affairs . . . .The Washington College of Law is the result of a vision of two remarkable women, Ellen

TOP RIGHT: First building owned by the Washington College of Law at 1315 K Street, home of the law school from 1920-26.

BOTTOM RIGHT: 4400 Massachusetts Avenue, N.W., John Sherman Myers Hall, on the American University campus.

235

Columbus School of Law Building, Catholic Uninversity of America.

Spencer Mussey and Emma M. Gillett, who in 1896 established a coeducational school to ensure that women, as well as men, had the opportunity to study law. This extraordinary history has formed the foundation for the college's long commitment to increasing opportunities for those who traditionally have not been in the mainstream of the profession."
— 1993-94 *Bulletin*

CATHOLIC UNIVERSITY OF AMERICA
COLUMBUS SCHOOL OF LAW

Catholic University was founded in 1889 by James Cardinal Gibbons of Baltimore as a Roman Catholic school of theology with a constitution approved by Pope Leo XIII. The campus was built upon the 60-acre estate of James Middleton, and features the National Shrine of the Immaculate Conception. Schools of law, engineering, architecture, social work, social science and nursing were added over the years. On October 1, 1994, a number of striking new buildings were dedicated to encompass the Columbus School of Law, including the Judge Kathryn DuFour Law Library, named for Maryland's first woman Circuit Judge from Montgomery County.

GEORGE WASHINGTON UNIVERSITY
THE NATIONAL LAW CENTER

"The National Law Center of the George Washington University is the oldest law school in the District of Columbia. It was founded in 1865 and has grown to become

one of the largest law schools in the country. Its total student population numbers over 1,600 . . . The Law Center is one of eight academic units of The George Washington University, which was originally established by charter of

The George Washington University National Law Center. Photograph by Bob Narod.

Congress in 1821 as The Columbian College . . . As an institution, the National Law Center is characterized by the richness and diversity of its curriculum. It prepares men and women to meet the needs of society in various fields of law and encourages scholarly research and writing in the law. As a national school, the Law center prepares students to practice law in any geographic area of the country." — National Law Center *Catalogue*.

GEORGETOWN UNIVERSITY LAW CENTER

Georgetown University is the oldest Roman Catholic college in the United States, founded in 1789. It traces its beginnings to the Georgetown Academy, founded two years earlier by John Carroll (1735-1815), America's first Bishop and Archbishop, who was born in Upper Marlboro. It has been a Jesuit institution since 1805. The School of Law opened in 1870. "Georgetown University Law Center prepares its graduates to excel in a range of legal careers from private practice to teaching and public service of all kinds. It is an educational institution dedicated to the principle that law is but the means, justice is the end. With this in mind, Georgetown has built an environment that is at once conducive to the exchange of practical ideas and the pursuit of academic excellence." —Georgetown University Law Center Catalogue.

HOWARD UNIVERSITY SCHOOL OF LAW

In 1866, Howard University, named for its founder, Major General Oliver Otis Howard, a white Civil War veteran, began as a theological seminary for African-American men. The following year, the university's purposes were enlarged when it received a charter from Congress. The charter mandated the creation of seven departments, including schools of law, medicine, theology and agriculture. "The Howard University School of Law is proud of its tradition as an advocate for justice as it looks ahead to a future as exciting as its past . . . . What sets this school apart from others is its ability not only to teach, but to nurture lawyers, to train them to think critically and independently, to explore new ideas, to examine and make use of the past. Here, from the first day of class, the law student is handed the tools to shape his or her own professional life under the guidance of a distinguished and experienced faculty in a broad-based program that stresses fundamentals . . . ." — Howard University School of Law *Bulletin*, 1994-96.

Edward Bennett Williams Law Library, Georgetown University Law Center. Photograph by Michael Milkovich.

Howard Uiniversity School of Law.

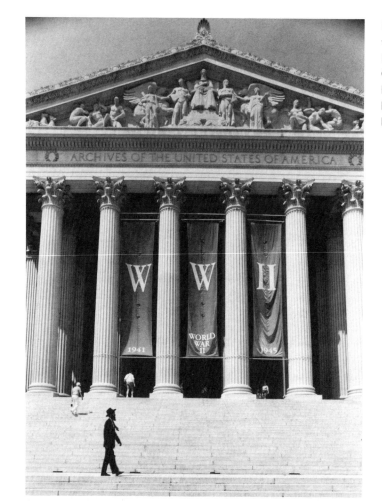

LEFT: The National Archives, where the Declaration of Independence, the Constitution and the Bill of Rights are displayed. Photograph by Coos Hamburger.

The Thurgood Marshall Federal Judiciary Building at One Columbus Circle is the headquarters of the Administrative Office of the U. S. Courts and the Federal Judicial Center.

EPILOGUE

By James F. Schneider

Iwill always remember the past two years as a time of intense devotion by many to the production of this first centennial history of the MSBA. Throughout this endeavor I have been sustained by the belief that this book will help to preserve the precious heritage of our bar and inspire future generations of lawyers to continue to strive for justice. One hundred years from now, the Maryland State Bar Association will be preparing to celebrate a second century of striving for justice. It is my fervent hope that historians yet unborn will be laboring on a bicentennial history of our Association. To such persons I offer my encouragement and best wishes. We must begin now to preserve our "future history."

The advent of the Information Age presents a golden opportunity for preserving much of our current history using high capacity computers. Technology not yet invented no doubt will assist even more. Our Association's Historian, Philip Sherman, is taking steps to save MSBA memorabilia in a documentary and photographic archive at the Maryland Bar Center, including the research and drafts of this book. He hopes to catalogue and shelve all MSBA publications, including old *Maryland Bar Transactions* and past issues of the *Maryland Bar Journal* and the *Bar Bulletin*. There must be a renewed effort to fill the void that resulted from the discontinuation of the Committee on Legal Biography in 1971. It is not too late to resume the compilation of biographies of pivotal people in the current history of the MSBA. The inspiring stories of past heroes of the Maryland Bar will enliven the practice of law for future generations of lawyers. The chroniclers of the future should be able to satisfy their thirst for knowledge about the history of the MSBA at its headquarters.

Videotaped interviews and programs will be valuable to future historians. Wouldn't it have been wonderful if such technology had existed in the past? It is available today and ought to be used. Important current events of this Association should be recorded and preserved for future reference. How wonderful it would have been if a videotape could been made of the founding meeting of the MSBA at the Blue Mountain House in 1896 for viewing in 1996!

I never had the pleasure of meeting S. Vannort ("Norty") Chapman (1905-1992), whose 18 years of service as Secretary of the MSBA, when combined with those of his father, James W. Chapman (1871-1943), totalled some 53 years; but I feel that I knew him because of a videotaped interview that Phil Sherman conducted with him in March, 1985.

He had just closed his law office three months earlier at the age of 79. For 38 minutes, Mr. Chapman talked to Phil about growing up at the annual MSBA conventions, and growing into the practice of law at his father's right hand. He loved the Association and reminisced about how awe-inspiring it was for a young lawyer to be in the presence of some of Maryland's greatest legal lights. It was a rare moment captured for posterity on videotape when Mr. Chapman uttered this bit of homespun philosophy to coming generations of Maryland lawyers:

S. Vannort ("Norty") Chapman (1905-1992).

> The way to be happy is to be successful in creating things that will live beyond you. What you create is more important than what you acquire and build up in worldly goods.

By his own standard, Norty Chapman was a successful person. He left behind a Maryland State Bar Association dedicated to the purposes for which it was founded 100 years ago: To advance the science of jurisprudence, to promote reform in the law, to facilitate the administration of justice, to uphold the standard of integrity, honor and courtesy in the legal profession, to encourage legal education and to cultivate a spirit of cordiality and brotherhood among the members of the Bar. The Maryland State Bar Association:

A CENTURY OF STRIVING FOR JUSTICE!

	PRESIDENTS OF THE MARYLAND STATE BAR ASSOCIATION		
1.	JAMES McSHERRY (1842-1907)	FREDERICK FREDERICK COUNTY	1896-97
2.	ROBERT RANDOLPH HENDERSON (1858-1921)	CUMBERLAND ALLEGANY COUNTY	1897-98
3.	JOHN PRENTISS POE (1836-1909)	BALTIMORE CITY	1898-99
4.	HENRY PAGE (1841-1913)	PRINCESS ANNE SOMERSET COUNTY	1899-1900
5.	STEVENSON A[RCHER] WILLIAMS (1851-1932)	BEL AIR HARFORD COUNTY	1900-01
6.	JOHN SLUYTER WIRT (1851-1904)	ELKTON CECIL COUNTY	1901-02
7.	BENJAMIN ARMSTRONG RICHMOND (1849-1922)	CUMBERLAND ALLEGANY COUNTY	1902-03
8.	GEORGE WHITELOCK (1854-1920)	BALTIMORE CITY	1903-04
9.	JAMES A[LEXANDER] C[HESLEY] BOND (1844-1930)	WESTMINSTER CARROLL COUNTY	1904-05
10.	JOHN PARRAN BRISCOE (1853-1925)	PRINCE FREDERICK CALVERT COUNTY	1905-06
11.	CONWAY W[HITTLE] SAMS (1862-1909)	BALTIMORE CITY	1906-07
12.	L[EMUEL] ALLISON WILMER (1849-1932)	LA PLATA CHARLES COUNTY	1907-08
13.	WILLIAM C[OOMBS] DEVECMON (1861-1939)	CUMBERLAND ALLEGANY COUNTY	1908-09
14.	DAVID G[REGG] McINTOSH (1836-1916)	TOWSON BALTIMORE COUNTY	1909-10
15.	WILLIAM L[UKE] MARBURY (1858-1935)	BALTIMORE CITY	1910-11
16.	JAMES A[LFRED] PEARCE, JR. (1840-1920)	CHESTERTOWN KENT COUNTY	1911-12
17.	A[NDREW] HUNTER BOYD (1849-1925)	CUMBERLAND ALLEGANY COUNTY	1912-13
18.	WALTER I[RELAND] DAWKINS (1858-1936)	LEONARDTOWN ST. MARY'S COUNTY	1913-14
19.	N[ICHOLAS] CHARLES BURKE (1854-1923)	TOWSON BALTIMORE COUNTY	1914-15
20.	HAMMOND URNER (1868-1942)	FREDERICK FREDERICK COUNTY	1915-16
21.	JOSEPH C[HALMERS] FRANCE (1862-1938)	BALTIMORE CITY	1916-17

	PRESIDENTS OF THE MARYLAND STATE BAR ASSOCIATION		
22.	JOHN B[ROWN] GRAY, SR. (1853-1937)	PRINCE FREDERICK CALVERT COUNTY	1917-18
23.	EDWARD C. PETER (1862-1923)	ROCKVILLE MONTGOMERY COUNTY	1918-19
24.	MORRIS A[MES] SOPER (1873-1963)	BALTIMORE CITY	1919-20
25.	JAMES E[DWARD] ELLEGOOD (1842-1925)	SALISBURY WICOMICO COUNTY	1920-21
26.	SYLVAN HAYES LAUCHHEIMER (1870-1955)	BALTIMORE CITY	1921-22
27.	ALBERT C[ABELL] RITCHIE (1876-1936)	ANNAPOLIS ANNE ARUNDEL COUNTY	1922-23
28.	T[HIEMANN] SCOTT OFFUTT (1872-1943)	TOWSON BALTIMORE COUNTY	1923-24
29.	F[RANCIS] NEAL PARKE (1871-1955)	WESTMINSTER CARROLL COUNTY	1924-25
30.	JOHN C[ARTER] ROSE (1861-1927)	BALTIMORE CITY	1925-26
31.	ALEXANDER ARMSTRONG (1877-1939)	HAGERSTOWN WASHINGTON COUNTY	1926-27
32.	CHARLES McHENRY HOWARD (1870-1942)	BALTIMORE CITY	1927-28
33.	JOHN W. STATON (1873-1932)	SNOW HILL WORCESTER COUNTY	1928-29
34.	WALTER L[OANE] CLARK (1878-1941)	BALTIMORE CITY	1929-30
35.	JAMES W[ILKINSON] CHAPMAN, JR. (1871-1943)	BALTIMORE CITY	1930-31
36.	D{UNCAN] LINDLEY SLOAN (1874-1962)	CUMBERLAND ALLEGANY COUNTY	1931-32
37.	W[ILLIAM] MASON SHEHAN (1873-1940)	EASTON TALBOT COUNTY	1932-33
38.	SAMUEL K[ING] DENNIS (1874-1953)	SNOW HILL WORCESTER COUNTY	1933-34
39.	W[ALTER] MITCHELL DIGGES (1877-1934) (Died in office)	LA PLATA CHARLES COUNTY	1934
40.	T. HOWARD DUCKETT (1880-1967)	HYATTSVILLE PRINCE GEORGES COUNTY	1934-35
41.	GEORGE WEEMS WILLIAMS (1874-1937)	BALTIMORE CITY	1935-36
42.	JOHN S[HAW] NEWMAN (1870-1940)	FREDERICK FREDERICK COUNTY	1936-37

PRESIDENTS OF THE MARYLAND STATE BAR ASSOCIATION

43.	JESSE N[ICHOLAS] BOWEN (1879-1938) (Died in office)	BALTIMORE CITY	1937-38
44.	ROBERT F[IELD] STANTON (1869-1956)	BALTIMORE CITY	1938
45.	FRANK I. DUNCAN (1858-1946)	TOWSON BALTIMORE COUNTY	1938-39
46.	ARTHUR W[EBSTER] MACHEN, JR. (1877-1950)	BALTIMORE CITY	1939-40
47.	WALTER C. CAPPER (1885-1962)	CUMBERLAND ALLEGANY COUNTY	1940-41
48.	CHARLES MARKELL (1882-1955)	BALTIMORE CITY	1941-42
49.	JAMES CLARK (1884-1955)	ELLICOTT CITY HOWARD COUNTY	1942-43
50.	ELI FRANK, SR. (1874-1958)	BALTIMORE CITY	1943-44
51.	FREDERICK W[OOLFORD] C[ONWAY] WEBB (1889-1956)	SALISBURY WICOMICO COUNTY	1944-45
52.	W[ILLIAM] CALVIN CHESNUT (1873-1962)	BALTIMORE CITY	1945-46
53.	OGLE MARBURY (1882-1973)	LAUREL PRINCE GEORGES COUNTY	1946-47
54.	FREDERICK W[ILLIAM] BRUNE (1894-1972)	BALTIMORE CITY	1947-48
55.	WILLIAM C[ONCANNON] WALSH (1890-1975)	CUMBERLAND ALLEGANY COUNTY	1948-49
56.	FRANKLIN B[ENEDICT] OBER (1889-1981)	BALTIMORE CITY	1949-50
57.	LEVIN CLAUDE BAILEY (1892-1952)	SALISBURY WICOMICO COUNTY	1950-51
58.	JOHN S[NOWDEN] STANLEY (1897-1962)	BALTIMORE CITY	1951-52
59.	EDWARD H[AMILTON] BURKE (1886-1955)	REISTERSTOWN BALTIMORE COUNTY	1952-53
60.	CLARENCE W[ILLIAM] MILES (1897-1977)	QUEENSTOWN QUEEN ANNE'S COUNTY	1953-54
61.	STEDMAN PRESCOTT (1896-1968)	ROCKVILLE MONTGOMERY COUNTY	1954-55
62.	REUBEN OPPENHEIMER (1897-1982)	BALTIMORE CITY	1955-56
63.	EDWARD D[ORSEY] E[LLIS] ROLLINS (1899-1976)	ELKTON CECIL COUNTY	1956-57

	PRESIDENTS OF THE MARYLAND STATE BAR ASSOCIATION		
64.	G[EORGE] C[ARL] A[RVID] ANDERSON (1898 -1985)	BALTIMORE CITY	1957-58
65.	JOHN B[ROWN] GRAY, JR. (1894-1989)	PRINCE FREDERICK CALVERT COUNTY	1958-59
66.	JOSEPH BERNSTEIN (1897 -1972)	BALTIMORE CITY	1959-60
67.	WILLIAM J[AMES] McWILLIAMS (1904-)	ANNAPOLIS ANNE ARUNDEL COUNTY	1960-61
68.	EMORY H[AMILTON] NILES (1892-1976)	BALTIMORE CITY	1961-62
69.	KENNETH C. PROCTOR (1907-)	TOWSON BALTIMORE COUNTY	1962-63
70.	H. VERNON ENEY (1908-1980)	BALTIMORE CITY	1963-64
71.	J. DEWEESE CARTER (1904-1977)	DENTON CAROLINE COUNTY	1964-65
72.	WILLIAM L[UKE] MARBURY, JR. (1901-1988)	BALTIMORE CITY	1965-66
73.	BENJAMIN B[RAFMAN] ROSENSTOCK (1902-1979)	FREDERICK FREDERICK COUNTY	1966-67
74.	RIGNAL W[OODWARD] BALDWIN, JR. (1902-1986)	BALTIMORE CITY	1967-68
75.	J. DUDLEY DIGGES (1912-1983)	LA PLATA CHARLES COUNTY	1968-69
76.	ELI FRANK, JR. (1903-1983)	BALTIMORE CITY	1969-70
77.	E[LIJAH] DALE ADKINS, JR. (1915-1982)	SALISBURY WICOMICO COUNTY	1970-71
78.	ROSZEL C[ATHCART] THOMSEN (1900-1992)	BALTIMORE CITY	1971-72
79.	DAVID E. BETTS (1911-1982)	ROCKVILLE MONTGOMERY COUNTY	1972-73
80.	NORMAN P[ARK] RAMSEY (1922-1993)	BALTIMORE CITY	1973-74
81.	HAL [HENRY] C[ONTEE] B[OWIE] CLAGETT (1916-)	UPPER MARLBORO PRINCE GEORGES COUNTY	1974-75
82.	WILBUR D. PRESTON, JR. (1922-)	BALTIMORE CITY	1975-76
83.	JAMES H. COOK (1918-1993)	TOWSON BALTIMORE COUNTY	1976-77
84.	NORWOOD B[ENTLEY] ORRICK (1908-1996)	BALTIMORE CITY	1977-78

	PRESIDENTS OF THE MARYLAND STATE BAR ASSOCIATION		
85.	VINCENT L. GINGERICH (1917-)	TAKOMA PARK MONTGOMERY COUNTY	1978-79
86.	M[ARTIN] PETER MOSER (1928-)	BALTIMORE CITY	1979-80
87.	CHARLES O[SBORNE] FISHER (1917-)	WESTMINSTER CARROLL COUNTY	1980-81
88.	J. MICHAEL McWILLIAMS (1939-)	BALTIMORE CITY	1981-82
89.	JAMES C[HRIS] CHAPIN (1940-)	ROCKVILLE MONTGOMERY COUNTY	1982-83
90.	JEFFREY B. SMITH (1926-)	BALTIMORE CITY	1983-84
91.	JOHN P[RINTZ] CORDERMAN (1942-)	HAGERSTOWN WASHINGTON COUNTY	1984-85
92.	HERBERT J[OSEPH] BELGRAD (1935-)	BALTIMORE CITY	1985-86
93.	VINCENT E. FERRETTI, JR. (1937-)	ROCKVILLE MONTGOMERY COUNTY	1986-87
94.	CLEAVELAND D. MILLER (1938-)	BALTIMORE CITY	1987-88
95.	ROGER W. TITUS (1941-)	ROCKVILLE MONTGOMERY COUNTY	1988-89
96.	HERBERT S. GARTEN (1928-)	BALTIMORE CITY	1989-90
97.	SEYMOUR B. STERN (1937-)	FREDERICK FREDERICK COUNTY	1990-91
98.	LOUISE MICHAUX GONZALES (1949-)	BALTIMORE CITY	1991-92
99.	ROGER A. PERKINS (1943-)	ANNAPOLIS ANNE ARUNDEL COUNTY	1992-93
100.	EDWARD F[ITZGERALD] SHEA, JR. (1925-1996)	BALTIMORE CITY	1993-94
101.	P. DENNIS BELMAN (1942-)	COLUMBIA HOWARD COUNTY	1994-95
102.	ROBERT T[OMAS] GONZALES (1948-)	BALTIMORE CITY	1995-96

ANNUAL CONVENTIONS OF THE M.S.B.A.		
1st	Blue Mountain House, Pen Mar, Washington County, Maryland	August 28, 1896
2nd	The Atlantic Hotel, Ocean City, Worcester County, Maryland	July 28-29, 1897
3rd	Blue Mountain House, Pen Mar, Washington County, Maryland	July 27-28, 1898
4th	The Atlantic Hotel, Ocean City, Worcester County, Maryland	July 26-27, 1899
5th	Circuit Courtroom, Cumberland, Allegany County, Maryland	July 25-26, 1900
6th	Deer Park Hotel, Deer Park, Allegany County, Maryland	July 31-Aug. 1, 1901
7th	The Atlantic Hotel, Ocean City, Worcester County, Maryland	July 2-3, 1902
8th	The Atlantic Hotel, Ocean City, Worcester County, Maryland	July 7-9, 1903
9th	Old Senate Chamber, State House, Annapolis Anne Arundel County, Maryland	April 27-29, 1904
10th	Circuit Courtroom, Hagerstown, Washington County, Maryland	June 28-30, 1905
11th	The Atlantic Hotel, Ocean City, Worcester County, Maryland	June 11-13, 1906
12th	The Atlantic Hotel, Ocean City, Worcester County, Maryland	July 3-5, 1907
13th	Blue Mountain House, Pen Mar, Washington County, Maryland	July 8-10, 1908
14th	The Hotel Chamberlin, Old Point Comfort, Virginia	July 7-9, 1909
15th	The Homestead, Hot Springs, Virginia (joint meeting with the Virginia State Bar Association)	July 26-28, 1910
16th	Cape May Hotel, Cape May, New Jersey	June 29-July 1, 1911
17th	Cape May Hotel, Cape May, New Jersey	July 1-3, 1912
18th	Cape May Hotel, Cape May, New Jersey	July 1-3, 1913
19th	Cape May Hotel, Cape May, New Jersey	July 1-3, 1914
20th	Cape May Hotel, Cape May, New Jersey	July 7-9, 1915
21st	Deer Park Hotel, Deer Park, Maryland	June 29-30-July 1, 1916

	ANNUAL CONVENTIONS OF THE M.S.B.A.	
22nd	Marlborough-Blenheim Hotel, Atlantic City, New Jersey	June 21-23, 1917
23rd	Hotel Chelsea, Atlantic City, New Jersey	June 27-29, 1918
24th	Hotel Chelsea, Atlantic City, New Jersey	June 26-28, 1919
25th	Hotel Chelsea, Atlantic City, New Jersey	June 24-26, 1920
26th	Cape May Hotel, Cape May, New Jersey	June 30-July 2, 1921
27th	Hotel Traymore, Atlantic City, New Jersey	June 29-July 1, 1922
28th	Hotel Traymore, Atlantic City, New Jersey	June 28-30, 1923
29th	Hotel Chelsea, Atlantic City, New Jersey	June 26-28, 1924
30th	Hotel Chelsea, Atlantic City, New Jersey	June 25-27, 1925
31st	Hotel Chelsea, Atlantic City, New Jersey	June 24-26, 1926
32nd	Hotel Traymore, Atlantic City, New Jersey	June 23-25, 1927
33rd	Hotel Ambassador, Atlantic City, New Jersey	June 28-30, 1928
34th	Hotel Ambassador, Atlantic City, New Jersey	June 27-29, 1929
35th	Hotel Ambassador, Atlantic City, New Jersey	June 26-28, 1930
36th	Hotel Ambassador, Atlantic City, New Jersey	June 25-27, 1931
37th	Hotel Ambassador, Atlantic City, New Jersey	June 30-July 1, 1932
38th	Hotel Ambassador, Atlantic City, New Jersey	Sept. 1-2, 1933
39th	Hotel Ambassador, Atlantic City, New Jersey	June 28-30, 1934
40th	Hotel Ambassador, Atlantic City, New Jersey	June 27-29, 1935
41st	Hotel Ambassador, Atlantic City, New Jersey	July 2-4, 1936
42nd	Hotel Ambassador, Atlantic City, New Jersey	June 24-26, 1937

ANNUAL CONVENTIONS OF THE M.S.B.A.		
43rd	Hotel Ambassador, Atlantic City, New Jersey	June 23-25, 1938
44th	Hotel Ambassador, Atlantic City, New Jersey	June 22-24, 1939
45th	Hotel Ambassador, Atlantic City, New Jersey	June 27-29, 1940
46th	Hotel Ambassador, Atlantic City, New Jersey	June 26-28, 1941
47th	Hotel Traymore, Atlantic City, New Jersey	June 25-27, 1942
48th	The Belvedere Hotel, Baltimore, Maryland	June 25-26, 1943
49th	The Belvedere Hotel, Baltimore, Maryland	June 30- July 1, 1944
50th	The Belvedere Hotel, Baltimore, Maryland	June 29-30, 1945
51st	Hotel Ambassador, Atlantic City, New Jersey	June 27-29, 1946
52nd	Traymore Hotel, Atlantic City, New Jersey	June 19-21, 1947
53rd	Traymore Hotel, Atlantic City, New Jersey	June 24-26, 1948
54th	Traymore Hotel, Atlantic City, New Jersey	June 30-July 2, 1949
55th	Traymore Hotel, Atlantic City, New Jersey	June 29-July 1, 1950
56th	Traymore Hotel, Atlantic City, New Jersey	June 21-23, 1951
57th	Traymore Hotel, Atlantic City, New Jersey	June 19-21, 1952
58th	Traymore Hotel, Atlantic City, New Jersey	June 18-20, 1953
59th	Traymore Hotel, Atlantic City, New Jersey	June 24-26, 1954
60th	Traymore Hotel, Atlantic City, New Jersey	June 23-25, 1955
61st	Traymore Hotel, Atlantic City, New Jersey	June 21-23, 1956
62nd	Traymore Hotel, Atlantic City, New Jersey	June 20-22, 1957
63rd	Traymore Hotel, Atlantic City, New Jersey	June 19-21, 1958

ANNUAL CONVENTIONS OF THE M.S.B.A.		
64th	Traymore Hotel, Atlantic City, New Jersey	June 18-20, 1959
65th	Traymore Hotel, Atlantic City, New Jersey	June 23-25, 1960
66th	M/S Victoria - Cruise to Bermuda	May 23-28, 1961
67th	Traymore Hotel, Atlantic City, New Jersey	June 21-23, 1962
68th	Traymore Hotel, Atlantic City, New Jersey	June 20-22, 1963
69th	Hotel Chalfonte-Haddon Hall, Atlantic City, New Jersey	July 8-11, 1964
70th	Hotel Chalfonte-Haddon Hall, Atlantic City, New Jersey	July 14-17, 1965
71st	Hotel Chalfonte-Haddon Hall, Atlantic City, New Jersey	July 6-9, 1966
72nd	Hotel Chalfonte-Haddon Hall, Atlantic City, New Jersey	July 5-8, 1967
73rd	Hotel Chalfonte-Haddon Hall, Atlantic City, New Jersey	July 10-13, 1968
74th	Hotel Chalfonte-Haddon Hall, Atlantic City, New Jersey	July 9-12, 1969
75th	Hotel Chalfonte-Haddon Hall, Atlantic City, New Jersey	July 8-11, 1970
76th	Ocean City Convention Hall, Ocean City, Worcester County, Maryland	June 16-19, 1971
77th	Hotel Chalfonte-Haddon Hall, Atlantic City, New Jersey	July 5-8, 1972
78th	Ocean City Convention Hall, Ocean City, Worcester County, Maryland	June 13-16, 1973
79th	Ocean City Convention Hall, Ocean City, Worcester County, Maryland	June 12-15, 1974
80th	Ocean City Convention Hall, Ocean City, Worcester County, Maryland	June 11-14, 1975
81st	Ocean City Convention Hall, Ocean City, Worcester County, Maryland	June 9-12, 1976
82nd	Ocean City Convention Hall, Ocean City, Worcester County, Maryland	June 8-11, 1977
83rd	Ocean City Convention Hall, Ocean City, Worcester County, Maryland	June 7-10, 1978
84th	Ocean City Convention Hall, Ocean City, Worcester County, Maryland	June 13-16, 1979

ANNUAL CONVENTIONS OF THE M.S.B.A.		
85th	Ocean City Convention Hall, Ocean City, Worcester County, Maryland	June 11-14, 1980
86th	Ocean City Convention Hall, Ocean City, Worcester County, Maryland	June 10-13, 1981
87th	Hyatt Regency Hotel, Baltimore City, Maryland	June 9-12, 1982
88th	Ocean City Convention Hall, Ocean City, Worcester County, Maryland	June 8-11, 1983
89th	Ocean City Convention Hall, Ocean City, Worcester County, Maryland	June 13-16, 1984
90th	Ocean City Convention Hall, Ocean City, Worcester County, Maryland	June 12-15, 1985
91st	Sheraton Fontainebleau Inn, Ocean City, Worcester County, Maryland	June 11-14, 1986
92nd	Sheraton Fontainebleau Inn, Ocean City, Worcester County, Maryland	June 10-13, 1987
93rd	Sheraton Fontainebleau Inn, Ocean City, Worcester County, Maryland	June 8-11, 1988
94th	Sheraton Fontainebleau Inn, Ocean City, Worcester County, Maryland	June 7-10, 1989
95th	Sheraton Fontainebleau Inn, Ocean City, Worcester County, Maryland	June 6-9, 1990
96th	Sheraton Resort & Conference Center, Ocean City, Worcester County, Maryland	June 5-8, 1991
97th	Sheraton Resort & Conference Center, Ocean City, Worcester County, Maryland	June 10-13, 1992
98th	Sheraton Resort and Conference Center Ocean City, Worcester County, Maryland	June 9-12, 1993
99th	Sheraton Resort and Conference Center Ocean City, Worcester County, Maryland	June 8-11, 1994
100th	Sheraton Fontainebleau Hotel & Conference Center, Ocean City, Worcester County, Maryland	June 7-10, 1995

ANNUAL MID-YEAR MEETINGS OF THE M.S.B.A.		
1st	The Belvedere Hotel, Baltimore, Maryland	January 20, 1940
2nd	The Belvedere Hotel, Baltimore, Maryland	January 11, 1941
3rd	The Belvedere Hotel, Baltimore, Maryland	January 10, 1942
4th	The Belvedere Hotel, Baltimore, Maryland	January 16, 1943
5th	The Belvedere Hotel, Baltimore, Maryland	January 15, 1944
6th	Southern Hotel, Baltimore, Maryland	January 20, 1945
7th	Belvedere Hotel, Baltimore, Maryland	January 26, 1946
8th	Sheraton-Belvedere Hotel, Baltimore, Maryland	February 1, 1947
9th	Sheraton-Belvedere Hotel, Baltimore, Maryland	January 31, 1948
10th	Sheraton-Belvedere Hotel, Baltimore, Maryland	January 29, 1949
11th	Sheraton-Belvedere Hotel, Baltimore, Maryland	January 28, 1950
12th	Sheraton-Belvedere Hotel, Baltimore, Maryland	January 27, 1951
13th	Sheraton-Belvedere Hotel, Baltimore, Maryland	January 26, 1952
14th	Sheraton-Belvedere Hotel, Baltimore, Maryland	January 17, 1953
15th	Sheraton-Belvedere Hotel, Baltimore, Maryland	January 23, 1954
16th	Sheraton-Belvedere Hotel, Baltimore, Maryland	January 29, 1955
17th	Sheraton-Belvedere Hotel, Baltimore, Maryland	January 21, 1956
18th	Sheraton-Belvedere Hotel, Baltimore, Maryland	January 26, 1957
19th	Sheraton-Belvedere Hotel, Baltimore, Maryland	January 25, 1958
20th	Sheraton-Belvedere Hotel, Baltimore, Maryland	December 5-6, 1959
21st	Sheraton-Belvedere Hotel, Baltimore, Maryland	January 23, 1960

ANNUAL MID-YEAR MEETINGS OF THE M.S.B.A.		
22nd	Sheraton-Belvedere Hotel, Baltimore, Maryland	January 21, 1961
23rd	Sheraton-Belvedere Hotel, Baltimore, Maryland	January 19-20, 1962
24th	Sheraton-Belvedere Hotel, Baltimore, Maryland	January 19, 1963
25th	Sheraton-Belvedere Hotel, Baltimore, Maryland	January 17-18, 1964
26th	Sheraton-Belvedere Hotel, Baltimore, Maryland	January 14-16, 1965
27th	Sheraton-Belvedere Hotel, Baltimore, Maryland	January 14-15, 1966
28th	Sheraton-Belvedere Hotel, Baltimore, Maryland	January 12-14, 1967
29th	Sheraton-Belvedere Hotel, Baltimore, Maryland	January 11-13, 1968
30th	Hotel Belvedere, Baltimore, Maryland	January 16-18, 1969
31st	Lord Baltimore Hotel, Baltimore, Maryland	February 5-7, 1970
32nd	Hotel Belvedere, Baltimore, Maryland	January 7-9, 1971
33rd	Hunt Valley Inn, Cockeysville, Maryland	January 6-8, 1972
34th	Lord Baltimore Hotel, Baltimore, Maryland	January 4-6, 1973
35th	Hunt Valley Inn, Cockeysville, Maryland	January 3-5, 1974
36th	Baltimore Hilton Hotel, Baltimore, Maryland	January 9-11, 1975
37th	Baltimore Hilton Hotel, Baltimore, Maryland	January 8-10, 1976
38th	Hunt Valley Inn, Cockeysville, Maryland	January 13-15, 1977
39th	Baltimore Hilton Hotel Baltimore, Maryland	January 12-14, 1978
40th	Hunt Valley Inn, Cockeysville, Maryland	January 10-13, 1979
41st	Hunt Valley Inn, Cockeysville, Maryland	January 9-12, 1980
42nd	Mallards Beach-Hyatt Hotel, Ochos Rios, Jamaica	January 4-11, 1981

ANNUAL MID-YEAR MEETINGS OF THE M.S.B.A.		
43rd	Hyatt Regency Hotel, Baltimore, Maryland	January 14-16, 1982
44th	Baltimore Hilton Hotel, Baltimore, Maryland	January 13-15, 1983
45th	Hyatt Regency Hotel, Baltimore, Maryland	January 5-7, 1984
46th	Hyatt Regency Hotel, Baltimore, Maryland	January 10-12, 1985
47th	Sheraton Inner Harbor Hotel, Baltimore, Maryland	January 9-10, 1986
48th	Hyatt Regency Hotel - Bethesda Bethesda, Maryland	January 8-10, 1987
49th	Hotel Palmas Del Mar, Humacao, Puerto Rico	January 17-21, 1988
50th	Stouffer Harbor Place Hotel Baltimore, Maryland	January 19-21, 1989
51st	Washington Grand Hyatt Hotel, Washington, D.C.	January 18-20, 1990
52nd	Wyndham Heywoods Beach Front Resort, St. Peter, Barbados	January 18-22, 1991
53rd	Omni Inner Harbor Hotel Baltimore, Maryland	November 7-8, 1991
54th	Omni Inner Harbor Hotel Baltimore, Maryland	November 6-7, 1992
55th	Wintergreen Resort, Wintergreen, Virginia	January 13-15, 1994
56th	El San Juan Hotel San Juan, Puerto Rico	January 20-23, 1995
57th	Omni International Hotel Baltimore, Maryland Marriott Casa Magna, Puerto Vallarta, Mexico	February 23, 1996 February 24-March 2, 1996

Vickers, Harrison W., 54-55
Vickers, Harrison W., Jr., 183
Vincent, Richard B., 10-11
Virginia State Bar Association, joint meeting in 1910, 66
"Vision 2000," 82
Volunteer lawyers, 14

Wagaman, Charles and John, 218
Wagaman, Charles D., 22,55,218
Walker, Irving E., 239-240
Wallace, Governor George C., 198
Wallis, Severn Teackle, 102,104,224
Walsh, Eugene, 149
Walsh, Gerald R., 78
Walsh, Bishop James E., 94
Walsh, James E., 55
Walsh, Judge William C., 55,69,94
Walsh, William E., 22,54-55
Walter, Moses R., 55
Warfield, Edwin, 55,58,173
Waring, Everett J., 106,108
Warner, C. Hopewell, 55
Warren, Chief Justice Earl, 76,121
Washington, Booker T., 18
Washington College of Law, American University, 198,235-236
Washington County, xv,17,20,218-224; Courthouse, 222-223
Washington, D.C., 193,232-240
Washington, George, 88-89,96,218,233-234
Washington Hotel, Princess Anne, 213
Washington Suburban Sanitary Commission, 193,200
Waters, Henry J., 22,55-56
Watkins, Clayton K., 188
Watson, I.A., 56
Watts, Judge Robert B., 108,110
Weant, Judge Edward O., Jr., 147
Webb, Burnett, Jackson, Cornbrooks & Wilber, 228
Webb, Frederick W.C., 69,227-228
Webb, John W.T., 225,228
Webster, Daniel 53,220
Webster, J. Edwin, 56
Weinberg, Robert L., 76
Wells, H.G., 18
Wentz, John B., Jr., 56
Western Maryland Railroad, 2,20
Whalen, Michael P., 5
Wharton, Mrs. Elizabeth, trial of, 158
Wheeler, F. Edward, 70
Wheeler, Larry Dodd, 76
Whelan, Thomas A., 56
"White Banks," home of Clarence W. Miles, 206
Whitelock, George, 22-23,25-26,66,115-116
Whitemarsh Church, Talbot County, 216
Wickes, Lewin W., 56
Wicomico County v. Bancroft, 227
Wicomico County, 213,225-228; Courthouse, 225-227
Wilde, Oscar, 18
Williams, Judge Alexander, Jr., 194
Williams, Ferdinand, 64
Williams, Frederick R., 22,26
Williams, George Washington, 72
Williams, George Weems, 119
Williams, Hammond, Moore, Shockley & Harrison, 231

Williams, Jay, 56-57
Williams, John F., 56-57
Williams, Stevenson A., 56-57,176
Williamstadt (Oxford), 215
Willis, Floyd "Ron", III, 5
Wilmer, L. Allison, 22,57,156
Wilmer, Skipwith, 57
Wilner, Chief Judge Alan M., (Court of Special Appeals), 98
Wilson, George W. ("Sunny"), 22,57
Wilson, William S., 57
Winchester, Albert (Buz),III, 10-11,82
Winter, Judge Harrison L., 114
Wirt, John S., 22-24,63,65,150,152
Witzenbacher, William J., 22,57
Wolman, Jeanette Rosner, 209
Woodcock, Amos W.W., 228
Woodcock & Webb, 228
Woods v. Simpson, 187
Woods, Judge Robert, 197
Worcester County, 213,225,228-232; Courthouse, 229,231
Worthington, Judge Glenn H., 57-58
Wright, Judge Daniel G., 58
Wright v. State, 201

Yaocomico tribe, 206
Yellott, Major John I., 132
Young, Eldridge Hood, 67
Young, John S., 22,58
Young, U.S. District Judge Joseph H., 12
Young, William P., Jr., xix,7,218-220,224

Zantzinger, State v., 222
Zetzer, Rose S., 70
Zinman, William, 213